JUN - 9 2009

D0567367

EX LIBRIS

THIS BOOK
BELONGS TO

Also by Thomas Fink
The 85 Ways to Tie a Tie (with Yong Mao)

THE
MAN'S BOOK

THE ESSENTIAL GUIDE
FOR THE MODERN MAN

Thomas Fink

Little, Brown and Company

New York · Boston · London

GLENVIEW PUBLIC LIBRARY
1930 Glenview Road
Glenview, IL 60025

Copyright © 2006, 2007, 2009 by Thomas Fink

All right reserved. Except as permitted under the U.S.
Copyright Act of 1976, no part of this publication may be reproduced,
distributed, or transmitted in any form or by any means, or stored in a database
or retrieval system, without the prior written permission of the publisher.

Little, Brown and Company
Hachette Book Group
237 Park Avenue, New York, NY 10017
Visit our Web site at www.HachetteBookGroup.com

First United States Edition: May 2009
Originally published in Great Britain
by Weidenfeld & Nicolson, 2006

Little, Brown and Company is a division of Hachette Book Group, Inc. The
Little, Brown name and logo are trademarks of Hachette Book Group, Inc.

Baden-Powell quotation used by permission of The Scout Association.

Le Modulor (1945, Le Corbusier) © Fondation Le Corbusier / DACS, 2008

Survival tools reprinted by permission of HarperCollins Publishers Ltd,
© John Wiseman, 1986

"007 in New York" quotation © Ian Fleming, 1962

The techniques and methods presented in this book are the result of the Author's
experience with certain equipment and tools, and proper care should be taken to use
the suitable materials as the Author advises. It is difficult to ensure that all the
instructions given are completely accurate, and the possibility of error can never be
eliminated fully. This book and the material contained herein have not been examined
for safety engineering, consumer or workplace safety, or similar or dissimilar laws and
regulations. The Author and the Publisher are not responsible for any injury and or
damage to persons or property which is incurred as a consequence, directly or
indirectly, of the use and application of any of the contents in this book.

ISBN 978-0-316-03364-0
LCCN 2008942334

10 9 8 7 6 5 4 3 2 1

RRD-IN

Printed in the United States of America

GLENVIEW PUBLIC LIBRARY
1930 Glenview Road
Glenview, IL 60025

CONTENTS

AUTHOR'S NOTE

The Man's Book is the authoritative handbook for men's customs, habits, and pursuits – a compendium for modern-day manliness. Organized in a man-logical way, it records unspoken customs, catalogs essential information, and guides you through the sometimes complex rituals of a man's life. It is also up to date: it notes the latest trends and anticipates what lies ahead.

At a time when the sexes are muddled and masculinity is marginalized, *The Man's Book* unabashedly celebrates being male. Guys, dads, fellows, and lads, rejoice: *The Man's Book* will bring you back to where you belong.

THE
MAN'S BOOK

HEALTH

The standard symbol for man is an arrow emanating from a circle in a northeast direction, believed to represent a shield and spear. It is also the symbol for the planet Mars, named after the Roman war god of the same name. It is the symbol for the male connector, the alchemic symbol for the element iron, and the Volvo automobile logo. Its Unicode representation is U+2642 and its Alt code is Alt+11.

Ian Fleming • You only live twice: / Once when you are born / And once when you look death in the face. (*You Only Live Twice*, 1964)

Samuel Johnson • It is so *very* difficult (said he, always) for a sick man not to be a scoundrel. (Mrs. Piozzi, *Anecdotes*)

Arnold Schwarzenegger • If you want to be a champion you cannot have any kind of an outside negative force coming in and affect you.

Let's say before a contest, if I get emotionally involved with a girl – that can have a negative effect on my mind and therefore destroy my workout. So I have to cut my emotions off and be kind of cold, in a way… That's what you do with the rest of the things. If somebody steals my car outside of my door right now I don't care… I trained myself for that. To be totally cold and not have things go into my mind. (*Pumping Iron*, 1977)

AC/DC • I always fill my ballroom / The event is never small / The social pages say I've got / The biggest balls of all. (*Dirty Deeds Done Dirt Cheap*, 1976)

Benjamin Franklin • He's a fool that makes his doctor his heir. • Keep your mouth wet, feet dry. • Beware of the young doctor and the old barber. • A good wife and health is a man's best wealth. • There's more old drunkards than old doctors. (*Poor Richard's Almanack*, 1732–1757)

❦1 IDEAL MAN

1.1 VITRUVIAN MAN

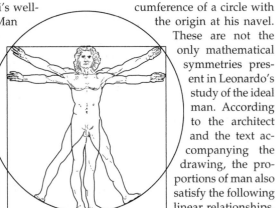

Leonardo da Vinci's well-known Vitruvian Man is based on the ancient ideal proportions of man written down by the Roman architect Vitruvius. Man's outstretched span is equal to his height, marking out a square, and his spread-eagled body marks the circumference of a circle with the origin at his navel. These are not the only mathematical symmetries present in Leonardo's study of the ideal man. According to the architect and the text accompanying the drawing, the proportions of man also satisfy the following linear relationships.

1.2 PROPORTIONS OF MAN

1 height	= 4 nipples up	= 8 upper arms	= 30 ears
= 1 arm span	= 5 forearms	= 10 hands	= 30 foreheads
= 2 halves	= 7 feet	= 10 faces	= 30 mouths
= 4 widths	= 8 heads	= 24 palms	= 96 fingers

where half = beginning of genitals to top of head · width = width at shoulders · nipples up = center of nipples to top of head · forearm = elbow to tip of hand · head = bottom of chin to top of head · upper arm = elbow to armpit · hand = length of hand · face = bottom of chin to hairline · palm = width of palm · ear = length of ear · forehead = eyebrows to hairline · mouth = bottom of chin to bottom of nose · finger = width of finger

1.3 MODULOR

The Swiss architect and designer Le Corbusier (Charles-Edouard Jeanneret) developed the Modulor, "a measure based on mathematics and the human scale: it is constituted of a double series of numbers, the red series and the blue." The blue series is twice the red, and any two consecutive lengths in the same series differ by a factor of the Golden ratio (Colophon, p 228). Le Corbusier's proportions for man and his surroundings are shown opposite. The numbers in the diagram are the height of the horizontal bar.

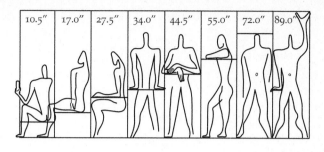

	−5	−4	−3	−2	−1	0	1	2	3	4
Red series (inches)	2.5	4.0	6.5	10.5	17.0	27.5	44.5	72.0	116	188
Blue series (inches)	5.0	8.0	13.0	21.0	34.0	55.0	89.0	144	233	377

1.4 BODY MASS INDEX

The ideal relationship between height and weight can be quantified by the body mass index (BMI). The BMI is the number obtained by taking your weight in kilograms divided by your height in meters squared, or 703 times your weight in pounds divided by your height in inches squared. For example, a 5 ft 10 in (1.78 m) man weighing 160 lb (73 kg) has a BMI of 23. For men, 23 to 25 is ideal (highlighted below), although there is some room for fluctuation. An endomorphic (broadset) build might be just above this range; an ectomorphic (slim) build, just below. James Bond, who is known to have a lean figure, has a BMI of 22.4. Below is a table of values for different heights and weights. There may be slight discrepancies due to rounding.

Height							*Weight (lb)*											*Height*
(ft in)	140	145	150	155	160	165	170	175	180	185	190	195	200	205	210	215	220	*(cm)*
5′5″	23	24	25	26	27	27	28	29	30	31	32	32	33	34	35	36	37	165
5′6″	23	23	24	25	26	27	27	28	29	30	31	31	32	33	34	35	35	168
5′7″	22	23	23	24	25	26	27	27	28	29	30	31	31	32	33	34	35	170
5′8″	21	22	23	24	24	25	26	27	27	28	29	30	30	31	32	33	33	173
5′9″	21	21	22	23	24	24	25	26	27	27	28	29	30	30	31	32	33	175
5′10″	20	21	22	22	23	24	24	25	26	27	27	28	29	29	30	31	32	178
5′11″	20	20	21	22	22	23	24	24	25	26	26	27	28	29	29	30	31	180
6′0″	19	20	20	21	22	22	23	24	24	25	26	26	27	28	28	29	30	183
6′1″	18	19	20	20	21	22	22	23	24	24	25	26	26	27	28	29	29	185
6′2″	18	19	19	20	21	21	22	22	23	24	24	25	26	26	27	28	28	188
6′3″	17	18	19	19	20	21	21	22	22	23	24	24	25	26	26	27	28	190
6′4″	17	18	18	19	19	20	21	21	22	23	23	24	24	25	26	26	27	193
	64	66	68	70	73	75	77	79	82	84	86	88	91	93	95	98	100	

Weight (kg)

❦2 BEARDS

The beard is one of the most striking visual differences between man and woman. It "is the badge of a man," wrote St. Clement of Alexandria. "Whatever smoothness or softness there was in him God took from him when he fashioned the delicate Eve from his side…" Today, we have become so accustomed to men shaving that we forget that the most immediate way of differentiating the sexes was that men had hairy faces and women didn't.

2.1 BEARD LENGTH

On average, facial hair grows as long as it is wide every three hours. It grows about 0.4 inches a month, or 0.013 inches a day. A more natural unit for beard length can be borrowed from typography: the point, where 72.3 points = 1 inch. Beards grow 1 point per day. Different lengths of facial hair have different names, as set out below. Notice that the number of days of growth, which is the same as the length in points, doubles at every level.

Name	Days' growth = length in points	Notes
Shadow	<1	change of shade; whiskers not noticeable
Umbra	1–2	worn with impunity: "I've been very busy"
Stubble	3–4	ambiguous: "Did he forget to shave?"
Designer stubble	5–8	stubble with intent; no longer negligence
Bristle	9–16	most awkward stage of growing a beard
Beard	17+	will continue to grow at 5 inches a year

2.2 BEARD TRIMMING

Trimming a beard not only reduces its length but also makes it thicker: the surface of an untrimmed beard is sparse, because not all hairs grow at the same rate. Most men shave the hair below the neckline, even in the case of full beards. The only facial hair allowed in the British armed forces is the moustache, except in the Royal Navy, which permits a "full set," that is, a moustache and beard combined (short boxed beard, opposite). At one point, the Catholic Church allowed priests to have facial hair only on the condition that they did not trim it – this being a sign of vanity. The fashion for facial topiary during the 1990s now seems studied, and today the most accepted form of facial hair is a full set not longer than ¾ inch = 54 points = 54 days.

There are two myths about beards which can be dispelled. The first is that shorter hair grows faster. This is not possible, since the hair follicle cannot tell how long the hair has been cut: there is no communication along the hair shaft, which is dead. But the follicle does know how old the hair is, and after a fixed period the hair is expelled and a new hair emerges, which is why hair does not grow beyond a fixed length. The second myth is that shaved hair grows back thicker. This is only partly true, in that the first growth from a follicle is fine and tapered, with further growth of normal thickness. Cutting off the tip makes the new end thicker, but cutting it again has no effect.

2.3 BEARD TYPES

Most, if not all, of the different styles of beards have been popular at some point in the past. One of the best classifications was printed in about 1900 for the Yale University November Beard Club. Note the illustrative names.

| Hollywoodian | Mutton Chops | A la Souvarov | French Fork |

| Handlebar and Chin Puff | Van Dyke | Friendly Mutton Chops | Balbo |

| Short Boxed Beard | Goatee | Chin Curtain | Hulihee |

| Petit Goatee | Franz Josef | Anchor | Napoleon III Imperial |

❧3 SHAVING

A typical man will shave his beard approximately 12,000 times during his lifetime, which is the equivalent of being a full-time barber for six months. For most men, shaving is their most practiced craft outside of their profession, so it is worth considering how this masculine ritual is best executed.

3.1 RAZOR

Wet shaving · Shaving razors fall into two categories: traditional straight or safety razors, which must be regularly sharpened on a leather strop or stone; and razors that are never sharpened but instead thrown out when dull. Disposable razors have advanced considerably since Gillette first introduced the disposable blade in 1903. Despite the superior aesthetic and ceremony of a straight razor, today disposable razors are invariably the superior choice.

Dry (electric) shaving · Shaving with an electric razor is analogous to wearing wrinkle-free polyester shirts – an inferior product driven by a philosophy of comfort and pragmatism. Because the lubricant in a wet shave causes the whiskers to swell, it is unlikely that dry shaving will ever compete with the closeness of a razor. Use an electric razor if you must – for example, if you have particularly sensitive skin. But don't tell anyone about it.

3.2 LUBRICANT

Shaving with a razor is sometimes called wet shaving, because it requires the use of a lubricating cream to reduce the friction between the razor and the skin. There are two kinds of common creams: foams and gels, which can be applied to the skin directly from the source; and creams and soaps, which must first be whisked into a foam with hot water and a shaving brush.

Foams and gels · A comparatively recent innovation, these are the most popular and convenient type of lubricant. A small shot from the can is spread over the already wet face with the hand. There is not much difference between a foam and a gel: both produce a thick white lather on application.

Creams and soaps · Cream comes in a tub and is whisked into a foam in the palm of the hand or directly onto the face with a wet shaving brush. Shaving soap, on the other hand, has the consistency of hand soap when dry, but lathers into a dense foam with a brush and a shaving pot (a small bowl in which it is mixed). For those who have sensitive skin, it is wise to use a cream mixed with an equal part of skin lotion, which is lathered as usual.

3.3 SHAVING BRUSHES

Brushes are used to whisk creams and soaps into a lather. They can be made from several kinds of bristle, but the best bristle comes from badgers. Badger hair is flexible, stores heat, and retains water. But not all badger bristles are equal; the softest, finest-tipped hairs are found around the badger's neck, and only in winter. A brush of these materials makes anything lather.

Name	Source	Texture and color	Animal rights activist response
Boar	various	coarse, white or dark	tepid
Dark badger	underbelly	coarse, nearly black	threatening stares
Pure badger	tail	medium, gray	hate mail
Best badger	back	fine, light-dark-light	slash car tires
Super badger	neck	very fine, silver-tipped	tar & feather owner

3.4 INSTRUCTIONS FOR WET SHAVING

Wet shaving comprises three steps: preparing the whiskers with lather, shaving the whiskers with a razor, and rinsing and assessing the skin.

Lather up · The most important ingredient for shaving with a razor is water. Not only should the face be wet, but the skin and whiskers should have absorbed water, which takes time. The best time to shave is right after a shower or bath; otherwise, rinse your face generously with warm water a few minutes before shaving. Then, using your hand or a brush, apply a foam or a gel, or whisked cream or soap, onto your face for at least 15 seconds.

Shave · Using a sharp razor, apply short strokes along the direction of growth. Don't press down – a light contact will do if the blade is sharp. "The rhythm of a morning shave is a slow blues – a quiet, solitary, contemplative experience," explain B. Sloan and S. Guarnaccia in *A Stiff Drink and a Close Shave*. There is a natural order of which parts to shave when. Begin with the least dense areas and finish with the densest: first the sides, then cheeks, neck, upper lip, and lower lip, finishing with the chin. Shaving against the grain gives the best results; shaving with it causes the least irritation. As a compromise, the best barbers finish by shaving across the grain.

Rinse and assess · Rinse your face with cold water to remove the cream and close the pores. Press small cuts with wet paper, then dry paper, or apply an alum stick. A skin cream at this stage would not go amiss (though no eyebrow plucking). If using a shaving brush, rinse it in water, shake out any excess, and stand it up or, preferably, hang it upside down on a holder to dry.

❦4 PUBLIC BATHROOMS

There is an unstated code of behavior in men's public bathrooms that, while more instinctive than prescriptive, remains surprisingly universal.

4.1 RULES OF CONDUCT

No pairing · Unlike women, men visit the lavatory entirely for practical reasons, and it is suspect to immediately follow a friend to the bathroom.

No talking · Terse conversation in the bathroom can take place before and after, but not during, use of the urinals.

No looking · Eyes should be aimed straight ahead or down in concentration; glances towards your neighbor are very suggestive.

No touching · Hands should be in front of you. A bump of the elbows can be deflated by a sober apology, but without turning the head.

4.2 OPTIMAL STRATEGY

When faced with an array of urinals to choose from, which one should you take? The basic idea is that the distance between users should be maximized, at the same time minimizing a newcomer's chance of getting too close. The latter makes the endmost urinals highly desirable. Never go between two men if it can be avoided. Below are sample situations for six urinals and the best strategy for each, where ○ means vacant and ⋔ means occupied. (Assume that any man following you chooses a vacant urinal at random.) Once you have got the idea, move on to the urinal test opposite.

1 2 3 4 5 6	*Best strategy*
○ ○ ○ ○ ○ ○	Urinals 1 and 6 are correct, and every man knows this.
⋔ ○ ○ ○ ○ ○	6 is correct, but 5 can be picked to avoid showing paranoia.
⋔ ○ ○ ○ ○ ⋔	3 and 4 maximize the distance from others.
⋔ ○ ○ ⋔ ○ ⋔	Urinal 2 offers a slight advantage over 3.
○ ⋔ ⋔ ○ ○ ⋔	Urinal 1 is the surprise correct answer.
⋔ ○ ⋔ ○ ⋔ ⋔	An unpleasant scenario, but 2 is the lesser of two evils.

4.3 LOO MAN

The symbol for the man's public bathroom is a stylized profile of a man standing with arms down. Unlike the Mars symbol for man (p 3), it is a pictogram: its meaning can be deduced from its shape. The male bathroom symbol differs from the female one (⋔) in having broader shoulders and straight legs as opposed to a flared dress.

4.4 URINAL TEST

Below is a test of where to stand along a line-up of seven urinals. It includes all possible configurations with two or more vacancies, excluding mirror images. What is the optimal choice for each? The answers are listed on p 13.

	1	2	3	4	5	6	7
1	○	○	○	○	○	○	○
2	●	○	○	○	○	○	○
3	○	○	○	○	●	○	○
4	○	●	○	○	○	○	○
5	○	○	○	●	○	○	○
6	○	○	○	○	○	●	●
7	○	●	○	●	○	○	○
8	○	●	○	○	○	○	●
9	○	○	○	●	●	○	○
10	○	○	●	○	○	○	●
11	●	○	○	●	○	○	○
12	○	○	●	○	○	●	○
13	●	○	○	○	○	○	●
14	●	○	●	○	○	○	○
15	○	○	○	○	●	●	○
16	○	●	○	○	○	●	○
17	○	○	●	○	●	○	○
18	●	●	●	○	○	○	○
19	●	○	○	○	○	●	●
20	●	○	○	○	●	○	●
21	○	○	●	●	○	○	○
22	○	○	○	●	●	●	○
23	●	●	○	○	○	●	○

	1	2	3	4	5	6	7
24	○	○	●	●	○	●	○
25	○	●	○	●	○	○	●
26	○	●	○	●	○	●	○
27	●	●	○	○	○	○	○
28	○	○	●	○	●	●	○
29	○	●	○	○	●	○	●
30	○	●	●	○	○	○	●
31	●	○	○	●	○	○	●
32	●	○	●	●	○	○	○
33	○	○	●	○	○	●	●
34	○	○	●	○	●	○	●
35	○	●	○	○	●	●	○
36	○	○	●	●	○	○	●
37	○	○	○	●	●	●	●
38	○	○	●	●	●	●	○
39	●	○	●	○	○	●	●
40	●	●	○	○	○	●	●
41	○	●	●	●	○	○	●
42	○	●	○	●	○	○	●
43	●	●	●	○	○	●	○
44	●	●	●	○	○	○	●
45	○	●	○	●	●	○	●
46	●	○	○	●	○	●	●

	1	2	3	4	5	6	7
47	○	●	●	○	●	●	○
48	○	●	●	○	○	●	●
49	○	●	●	○	●	○	●
50	●	●	●	○	●	○	○
51	○	○	●	●	○	●	●
52	●	○	●	●	●	○	○
53	●	○	●	○	●	○	●
54	●	●	○	●	○	●	○
55	○	●	○	●	●	●	○
56	●	●	●	●	●	○	○
57	○	●	●	●	○	●	●
58	●	○	○	●	●	●	●
59	●	●	○	●	○	●	●
60	○	●	○	●	●	●	●
61	●	○	●	○	●	●	●
62	○	●	●	●	●	●	○
63	○	●	●	●	●	○	●
64	●	●	●	○	○	●	●
65	●	○	●	●	○	●	●
66	●	●	●	○	●	●	○
67	●	○	●	●	●	○	●

4.5 AN EQUATION FOR THE BEST URINAL

Let N be the total number of urinals, labeled from left to right by $k = 1, 2,...,$ N, of which $q + 1$ are vacant. Assume on average one new man approaches a random vacant urinal (without applying any strategy) during the typical period of occupation. As he may come in at any point after you, the average intersection of his and your occupation time is $\frac{1}{2}$. Further assume that the interaction between men is repulsive with an inverse square law. Then the optimal unoccupied urinal k_{opt} is the one that minimizes $E(k)$ below:

$$E(k) = 1/(2q) \sum_{i \neq k} 1/(k-i)^2 + (2q-1)/(2q) \sum_{i\ occupied} 1/(k-i)^2.$$

❦5 FAMILY JEWELS

5.1 HIGH BALL

Zoe: How's the nuts? / Bloom: Off side. Curiously they are on the right. Heavier I suppose. One in a million my tailor, Mesias, says. (James Joyce, *Ulysses*)

The Ancient Greeks were well aware that a man's testicles were not symmetrical, but that one – usually the left – descended lower than the other. This anatomical subtlety is borne out in their sculpture. Of 187 statues considered by the psychologist I. C. McManus, 51% show the left testicle to be lower and 22% the right, the remainder being of equal descent ("Right-left and the scrotum in Greek sculpture," *Laterality*, **9**, 189 (2004)). This correlates with modern-day observations. Chang et al. (*Journal of Anatomy*, **94**, 543 (1960)) found the left testicle to be lower in 62% of subjects and the right in 27%, the rest being indistinguishable. The reason for this bias is not known, but Bloom's explanation above can be dismissed. It is widely accepted that, surprisingly, the right testicle tends to be both heavier and larger. (For the cylindrical drinking vessel, highball, see Glasses, p 104.)

5.2 DRESSING

Dressing is the persistent self-positioning of a man's jewels to the same side of his trousers. A man is said to "dress to the left" or "dress to the right" if he predominantly falls to the left or right trouser leg. The best time to tell which side you're on is while sitting down. When making a suit (p 65), some tailors assemble the crotch of the trousers asymmetrically to account for this bias. There are a number of theories to account for dressing, none of which has been substantiated: the direction of dress corresponds with left-/right-handedness; it is the side of the lower testicle (see High ball, above); the trousers are twisted around the waist, with the fly off center.

5.3 VARICOCELE

Generally harmless and often overlooked, a varicocele is the enlargement of the blood vessels that drain blood from one of the testicles. As with varicose veins common in women, a varicocele is caused by the malfunction of the one-way valves in the vessels. When the valves can no longer counteract the force of gravity, blood pools in the lower veins. The condition affects around 15% of men, the bulk of cases involving the left testicle, and feels like a soft testicular lump. There are usually no symptoms, although the varicocele may seem to disappear when a man lies down and the blood drains away from it.

5.4 CIRCUMCISION

The ancient Egyptians practiced circumcision, and the Book of Jeremiah (9:26) adds the Jews, Edomites, Ammonites, and Moabites to this tradition. On the other hand, the ancient Greeks thought circumcision unbecoming, and associated it with satyrs, the promiscuous man-goat race that wandered the forest. The early Christian Church frowned on the practice, and by medieval times it was prohibited: "[The Holy Roman Church] strictly orders all who glory in the name of Christian not to practice circumcision either before or after baptism, since…it cannot possibly be observed without loss of eternal salvation," declared Pope Eugenius IV in his 1442 papal bull. The curious popularity of circumcision among the English-speaking peoples largely originated in the late 19th century in the United States, where the removal of the foreskin was said to be associated with all sorts of remedial and preventive medicine. Although circumcision is now believed to confer no significant medical benefits, the majority of males in the United States, the Philippines, and South Korea are circumcised for non-religious reasons.

5.5 BLUE BALLS

Although sometimes dismissed as an old wives' – or rather husbands' – tale, blue balls is well recognized, if not fully understood or documented. It is a painful ache in the scrotum, caused by prolonged sexual arousal, and affects many adolescent and mature men, though infrequently. While the pathophysiology is not understood, J. M. Chalett and L. T. Nerenberg conjecture that, in tandem with persistent pelvic venous dilation, "testicular venous drainage is slowed, pressure builds and causes pain" ("Blue Balls," *Pediatrics*, **106**, 843 (2000)). The discomfort ceases on sexual release or subsides on its own after one or two hours. Circumstantial evidence suggests that the name may derive from a blue tint in the scrotum caused by reduced circulation – de-oxygenated blood being darker than oxygenated.

5.6 ANSWERS TO THE URINAL TEST (ON P 11)

#		#		#		#		#		#		#		#		#	
1.	1, 7	9.	1	17.	1, 7	25.	1	33.	1	41.	1	49.	1	57.	1	65.	2
2.	7	10.	1	18.	7	26.	1, 7	34.	1	42.	6	50.	7	58.	2	66.	7
3.	1	11.	7	19.	3	27.	7	35.	1	43.	7	51.	1	59.	3, 5	67.	2, 6
4.	7	12.	1	20.	3	28.	1	36.	1	44.	5	52.	7	60.	1		
5.	1, 7	13.	4	21.	1, 7	29.	1	37.	1	45.	1	53.	2, 6	61.	2		
6.	1	14.	7	22.	1	30.	5	38.	1	46.	2	54.	7	62.	1, 7		
7.	7	15.	1	23.	4	31.	2, 6	39.	4	47.	1, 7	55.	1	63.	1		
8.	5	16.	4	24.	1	32.	7	40.	4	48.	1	56.	7	64.	5		

❦6 HANGOVERS

A hangover, in medicine called veisalgia, refers to the nausea, headache, and weakness that follows excessive alcohol consumption and lasts from several hours to more than a day. Although the pathology of hangovers is poorly understood, it is believed to be a combination of dehydration, the side effects of the breakdown of ethanol, and congeners, chemical impurities that are by-products of fermentation. Here is a guide to prevention and cures.

6.1 HANGOVER PREVENTION

Order of drinks

It is widely accepted that the order in which different types of alcohol are consumed partly determines how bad you feel afterwards. In Evelyn Waugh's *Brideshead Revisited*, after Sebastian throws up on Charles's floor, Sebastian's friend apologizes on his behalf: "The wines were too various," he says. "It was neither the quality nor the quantity that was at fault. It was the mixture. Grasp that and you have the root of the matter. To understand all is to forgive all." The alcoholic commutation rhymes below advise which drinks to drink before others. While some of them are at odds, it is widely held that grain followed by grape is preferable to the alternative, and champagne should not follow anything – it is best had as a first drink. A single species of drink throughout the night is preferable to mixing among them.

Beer before wine, you're fine;	Whiskey before beer, never fear;
Wine before beer, oh dear.	Beer before whisky, kind of risky.
Liquor before beer, in the clear;	*Bier auf Wein, das lasse sein;*
Beer before liquor, never sicker.	*Wein auf Bier, das rat ich Dir.*

Eat and drink water

The simplest way to mitigate a hangover is to have a full meal before you start drinking and a large glass of water after you stop. A full stomach reduces the rate at which alcohol enters the system, giving the liver a head start in breaking it down. Ethanol acts as a diuretic, which means it makes you urinate more. Drinking extra water will alleviate the associated dehydration.

Avoid congeners

Ethanol is not the only cause of hangovers. Congeners, which are responsible for much of the flavor of wine and liqueurs, also play a role. In general, the darker the drink, the more congeners it contains, which makes red wine, port, and dark rum worse than their paler cousins. For a clear head the next day, drink neat grain spirit, such as whiskey or vodka, all evening.

6.2 HANGOVER CURES

There is no shortage of remedies that are supposed to alleviate or cure a hangover, most of which are meant to amuse as much as perform. But the scientific evidence for hangover cures is scarce. In a study of the leading treatments published in the *British Medical Journal*, the authors report:*

> Our findings show that no compelling evidence exists to suggest that any complementary or conventional intervention is effective for treating or preventing the alcohol hangover.

On the other hand, cures that address the core symptoms of hangovers, such as dehydration and headache, can help. Here are some favorite remedies:

Coke and ibuprofen

One of the best remedies is a can of Coke and two ibuprofen. The drink is at least as essential as the pills. Why Coke is so much more effective than other beverages is a mystery; the high sugar content explains part of it, but not all.

Hair of the dog

This is an abbreviation of the phrase "hair of the dog that bit you": treating a hangover with another drink. According to *Brewer's Dictionary of Phrase and Fable*, the term alludes to "the old notion that the burned hair of a dog is an antidote to its bite," an application of "like cures like." The best known is a Bloody Mary: vodka, tomato juice, lemon juice, Worcestershire sauce, Tabasco, salt, and pepper. Note the difference from alcoholism: the hair of the dog is meant to make you *tipsy* while you recover from being *drunk*.

Prairie oyster

This classic pick-me-up is enough to frighten most men into sobriety: 1 raw egg, 1 teaspoon tomato juice, 1 teaspoon Worcestershire sauce, a dash of Tabasco, salt, and pepper. Some include only the egg yolk. Down in one.

Sick

Every man has been there – on his hands and knees with his head over the toilet at three in the morning. Vomiting from excessive alcohol is always unpleasant. But if it happens early enough to rid the stomach of its toxic contents it does diminish the intensity of any hangover the following day.

*M. H. Pittler, J. C. Verster and E. Ernst, "Interventions for preventing or treating alcohol hangover," *BMJ*, **331**, 1515 (2005). The agents tested were propranolol, tropisetron, tolfenamic acid, fructose or glucose, borage, artichoke, prickly pear, and a yeast-based preparation.

❦7 HAIR LOSS

Given that two thirds of men will suffer from hair loss at some point in their lives, it is puzzling to find the subject so full of misinformation, pseudoscience, and charlatanism. In part this is explained by a limited understanding of what causes – and prevents – the spontaneous thinning of hair. The rest is due to opportunistic marketing of alternative and quack medicines to gullible and often desperate men. Differentiating fact from fiction and finding reliable, transparent information on the subject remains difficult.

7.1 HEALTHY HAIR GROWTH

Healthy hair on the scalp has a two-stage life cycle: a growth period of two to six years, during which hair grows about ⅓ mm per day or 10–30 inches in total; followed by a dormant period of two to four months when the hair does not grow. After this the hair falls out, and a new hair emerges from the same hair follicle. (Hair on other parts of the body has a shorter life cycle and therefore does not grow as lengthy.) Different hairs are in different phases in this cycle at any one time, so that on a given day only about 50–150 hairs fall out, which is less than 0.1% of the total number of hairs on the scalp.

7.2 MALE PATTERN BALDNESS

The dominant form of hair loss in men is called androgenetic alopecia, more commonly known as male pattern baldness. It generally follows a fixed pattern of progression: the corners of the hairline recede first, giving rise to an "M"-shaped hairline. This is followed by a thinning of the hairline generally and also the crown (the top of the head). Eventually the exposed areas of the hairline and crown join, leaving hair at the back and sides only, which itself may continue to thin. This is the course to total baldness; in most men, hair loss will cease at some intermediate point. The type and degree of hair loss can be classified using the Hamilton-Norwood (HN) scale, opposite, first devised by James Hamilton and later revised by O'Tar Norwood in 1975. The scale ranges from HN 1 (a full head of hair; not shown) to HN 7; higher numbers correspond to more severe cases.

In male pattern baldness, hair loss is not caused by the sudden loss of hair but rather by the increasingly diminished growth of individual hairs over time. In the early stages, the number of hairs remains constant, and what appears as hair loss is in fact a reduction in the thickness and rate of growth of new hairs. Each generation of new hair grows back finer, shorter, and often lighter-colored than before. As the condition progresses, hair appears wispy, then like peach fuzz, and eventually cannot be seen at all.

7.3 HAMILTON-NORWOOD SCALE

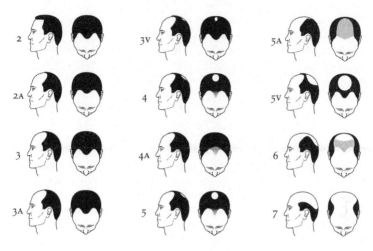

7.4 MYTHS

There are several commonly held myths about hair loss. One is that the incidence of hair loss in a man is solely determined by the maternal grandfather. Although it is heritable, there is at present no way to accurately predict who will lose his hair or when he will lose it. A recent study has found that men whose fathers exhibit hair loss are 2–2.5 times as likely to suffer from hair loss as those whose fathers have a full head of hair. Another myth is that wearing hats, caps, or bandannas promotes hair loss, for which there is no support. It is often claimed that stress or significant mental exercise can initiate or hasten hair loss, but the evidence for this too is scant.

7.5 TREATMENTS

While it is possible to revive dormant follicles which produce fine, wispy hair, all hair-loss drugs are more successful at preventing the decay of healthy hair follicles. So the earlier that hair loss is treated, the greater is the amount of hair that is likely to be maintained. For the time being, baldness is more preventable than reversible.

The primary contributing factor in male pattern baldness is believed to be dihydrotestosterone (DHT), which like testosterone is one of the male sex hormones. Increased levels of DHT are known to inhibit hair growth, although how this occurs remains poorly understood. Higher testosterone levels are not in themselves correlated with increased likelihood of hair loss.

In what might appear to be a stroke of fortune for drug companies, hair-loss treatments do not cure hair loss once and for all; rather, the medicine has to be taken indefinitely. If the treatment is terminated, the rate of hair loss will return to its pre-treatment levels. Bear in mind, however, that the way baldness is treated is changing rapidly, and today's maintenance will likely prove to be a stop-gap until the arrival of superior, possibly permanent treatments.

7.6 PROPECIA

Finasteride, marketed as Propecia, is, along with Minoxidil, the only US Food and Drug Administration-approved hair-loss drug. This does not imply that other treatments are not effective; gaining FDA approval is expensive and requires additionally that a drug's side-effects be understood and minimal. Propecia is currently accepted as the most effective treatment for hair loss, with 30–75% of users reporting constant or increased hair levels. It works by inhibiting the production of DHT, and is administered in the form of a pill taken daily, a significant advantage over topical Minoxidil.

7.7 MINOXIDIL

Minoxidil, marketed as Rogaine in America and Regaine in most other countries, has been shown to slow or stop hair loss and promote regrowth in 25–40% of patients. Now that generic versions are available, it can be bought at a fraction of the brand-name price. It was originally developed as a high-blood-pressure treatment, with increased hair growth an unintended side-effect. Despite its success in clinical trials, how it fights hair loss is not well understood. It is applied as a solution or cream directly to the afflicted area once or twice a day. Unlike Homer Simpson's immediate results with Dimoxinil (Simpson and Delilah, episode 7F02, 1990), both Propecia and Rogaine require three to six months' use before clear results appear.

7.8 BOLD

Despite the relative advances in dealing with baldness, I admire the man who resolutely refuses to resort to medicine to halt hair loss. And even a strict regimen of treatments cannot reverse stubborn genetics. As with most aspects of men's appearance, an air of indifference is essential to wearing thin hair well. At some point, manipulating sparse hair to hide the head must come to an end. Yul Brynner shaved his head completely and made baldness chic. Zinedine Zidane knew when to make the cut, as did Andre Agassi, both of whom keep their hair close-cropped. John Malkovich and Sean Connery kept their hair mid-length but never wore a comb-over.

SPORTS AND GAMES

Samuel Johnson · I take the true definition of exercise to be labour without weariness. (Boswell, *Life of Johnson,* 1791)

Izaak Walton · As inward love breeds outward talk, / The hound some praise, and some the hawk; / Some, better pleased with private sport, / Use tennis; some a mistress court; / But these delights I neither wish / Nor envy, while I freely fish. (The Angler's Song, *The Compleat Angler,* 1653)

Olympic oath · In the name of all the competitors I promise that we shall take part in these Olympic Games, respecting and abiding by the rules which govern them, committing ourselves to a sport without doping and without drugs, in the true spirit of sportsmanship, for the glory of sport and the honor of our teams. (Last modified at Sydney, 2000)

Vince Lombardi · Show me a good loser, and I'll show you a loser.

Ernest Hemingway · There are only three sports: bullfighting, motor racing and mountaineering; all the rest are merely games. (Attributed to Hemingway but likely derived from *Blood Sport* by Ken Purdy, 1957)

Arnold Schwarzenegger · Pain divides a champion from someone who is not a champion. That's what most people lack, having the guts to go on and just say they'll go through the pain no matter what happens. I have no fear of fainting. I do squats until I fall over and pass out. So what? It's not going to kill me. I wake up five minutes later and I'm OK. A lot of other athletes are afraid of this. So they don't pass out. They don't go on.

Yogi Berra · So I'm ugly. So what? I never saw anyone hit with his face. (Attributed to Berra by Bert Sugar in *The Book of Sports Quotes,* 1979)

Ron Atkinson · Well, either side could win it, or it could be a draw.

❦8 EXERCISES IN A GYM

The most effective method of lifting weights – and by this is meant high-resistance anaerobic exercise for size and strength – is to use free weights instead of machines where possible. Of course, some exercises are difficult or impossible to perform without machines – leg curls, for instance. But free weights or the body's own weight should be used for most exercises. Part of the reason is that machines invariably lock the motion into a fixed path. This means that (i) the auxiliary muscles that keep the movement on course are neglected and (ii) the weaker side no longer needs to work harder to catch up with the stronger. The result is a body without tie-ins between muscle groups and lacking symmetry. As a practical advantage, because free weights are standardized, they can be loaded the same way in any gym.

8.1 ROUTINE

Weight training is usually organized by a fixed routine, repeated each week:

Session	Visit to the gym	2–6 times per week
Exercise	Focus on specific muscles	6–12 per session
Set	Period of continuous exertion	3–5 per exercise
Rep	Repetition of the same movement	7–12 per set

Sessions may incorporate a fixed set of exercises, or cycle through different major muscle groups: legs and abdominals one session, arms and shoulders the next, for example. The number and intensity of repetitions is determined by the weight-training goal: do higher numbers of repetitions to increase strength; do lower numbers, with heavier weights, to increase bulk.

8.2 SINGLE-REPETITION MAXIMUM

The single-repetition maximum is the highest weight you can push, pull, or lift. It can be calculated for any exercise from your performance at a lower weight – and with a lower risk of injury – as follows. Let r be the maximum number of repetitions that can be done at some weight w. Then $C(r) \times w$ is your single-repetition maximum, where $C(r)$ is given in the table below:

Reps r	2	3	4	5	6	7	8	9	10
$C(r)$	1.062	1.109	1.152	1.191	1.227	1.259	1.287	1.311	1.332

For example, if you can bench-press 135 lb just 8 times, then your maximum for a single repetition is 1.287 × 135 lb = 173.7 lb – a 28.7% increase.

8.3 FREE WEIGHT SIZES

Conventional weightlifting bars have a solid 1-inch-diameter central segment and 2-inch-diameter ends for loading appropriately fitted metal plates. There are two standards for the weight sizes. One is the international competition standard: 20, 10, 5, 2½, and 1¼-kg plates, along with a 20-kg bar. More common in American gyms is the following Imperial standard:

Plate sizes (lb): 45 25 10 5 2½   Bar (lb): 45

8.4 OPTIMAL LOADING OF PLATES

Below is the optimal way of loading American plates to make any given total weight. It gives the fewest number of plates per side; if two different ways have the same number of plates, it gives the one with the bigger plates, if only because bigger plates look more impressive. For example, to make a total of 175 pounds, load one 45-lb and two 10-lb plates on each side.

Total (lb)	45	25	10	5	2½
50					1
55				1	
60				1	1
65			1		
70			1		1
75			1	1	
80			1	1	1
85			2		
90			2		1
95		1			
100		1			1
105		1		1	
110		1		1	1
115		1	1		
120		1	1		1
125		1	1	1	
130		1	1	1	1
135	1				
140	1				1
145	1			1	
150	1			1	1
155	1	1			
160	1	1			1

Total	45	25	10	5	2½
165	1		1	1	
170	1		1	1	1
175	1		2		
180	1		2		1
185	1	1			
190	1	1			1
195	1	1		1	
200	1	1		1	1
205	1	1	1		
210	1	1	1		1
215	1	1	1	1	
220	1	1	1	1	1
225	2				
230	2				1
235	2			1	
240	2			1	1
245	2		1		
250	2		1		1
255	2		1	1	
260	2		1	1	1
265	2		2		
270	2		2		1
275	2	1			
280	2	1			1

Total	45	25	10	5	2½
285	2	1		1	
290	2	1		1	1
295	2	1	1		
300	2	1	1		1
305	2	1	1	1	
310	2	1	1	1	1
315	3				
320	3				1
325	3			1	
330	3			1	1
335	3		1		
340	3		1		1
345	3		1	1	
350	3		1	1	1
355	3		2		
360	3		2		1
365	3	1			
370	3	1			1
375	3	1		1	
380	3	1		1	1
385	3	1	1		
390	3	1	1		1
395	3	1	1	1	
400	3	1	1	1	1

8.5 WEIGHTLIFTING HINTS

Correct form

Most successful weightlifters agree that doing an exercise correctly at a lighter weight is more beneficial than doing it poorly at a heavier weight. Correct forms means: (i) completing the entire intended motion of the exercise; (ii) keeping still any part of the body not associated with the exercise; and (iii) using a controlled, jerk-free motion every step of the way.

Spotting

Spotting is the oversight and, if need be, assistance of a person lifting weights. A spotter's principal job is offering help in completing a repetition if the lifter cannot complete it himself. In addition, a spotter may verbally motivate the lifter in pushing himself. Key to spotting well is the realization that spotting relies significantly on the placebo effect: tricking the lifter's mind into thinking he can finish a repetition by placing the spotter's hands under the bar and offering little or no assistance. It is thoroughly acceptable to ask a stranger in the gym to spot you, though it is best not to ask him for much more than a few spots – find someone else or a regular lifting partner. Conversely, it is bad form to turn down someone who asks for a spot.

Proportion

A serious bodybuilder is as concerned with symmetry – a harmonious balance of the relative size of his muscles – as he is in size itself. But most men spend more time on the exercises they are better at than on the ones they are worse at. As a means of attaining proportion, the opposite strategy should be employed: focus more on your weak points, less on your strong. For example, if your quadriceps are your least developed, then you need to train them more intensely, even if it means sacrificing an even larger chest.

8.6 EXERCISES BY PRINCIPAL MUSCLE WORKED

Below are 30 classic lifting exercises, comprehensively covering all muscle groups. A moderate routine might be 3–4 sets per exercise, 8 exercises per session, and 3 sessions per week; for intensive training, 10 exercises per session and 6 sessions per week. The 10 most essential exercises are marked ★.

Biceps

★ Standing barbell curls .... A bent barbell works best. Keep elbows fixed.
 Seated dumbbell curls .... Rest elbow in hand, one arm at a time.
 Dumbbell curls on incline bench. Curl as usual but with body lying at 45°.
 Pull-ups .... With palms facing in and a close grip (see p 25).

Triceps

★ Triceps extensions . . . . Use bent grip from overhead cable. Elbows fixed.
French press . . . . Lock elbows straight up, lower barbell to back of neck.
Parallel bar dips. . . . Bend your elbows back, not out to the sides (p 25).

Forearms

★ Wrist curls . . . . . With forearms flat on bench, move wrists to lift barbell.
Reverse wrist curls. . . . . Like wrist curls but with palms-down grip.

Chest

★ Bench press. . . . . Wider grip for pectorals, closer grip for triceps.
Incline press . . Same as bench but with body at 45°. Works upper pecs.
Bent-arm flies . . Lying on bench, lift dumbbells from sides to over chest.
Machine flies . . Sitting at machine, bring arms together from 180° apart.

Shoulders

★ Military press (a.k.a. shoulder press) . . Standing, lift barbell above head.
Dumbbell lateral raises . While standing, raise dumbbells to horizontal.
Upright rows. . . . . . While standing, lift barbell with close grip to chest.
Bent-over cable laterals. . . . . Requires two floor-level pulleys.

Calves

Standing calf raises. . . . . Keep knees locked. Beware of back strains.
★ Seated calf raises. . . . . Use heavy loads. Do not rock back and forth.
Calf extensions on leg press . . Keep knees locked and just move ankles.

Thighs

Leg press . . . . .Contract until legs are 70° or 80° at the knee.
★ Squats . . . . Foundation exercise for working the quadriceps.
★ Leg curls . . . . . . Done lying on stomach. Isolates the back of the thighs.
Leg extensions. . . . . . . Don't kick your legs out but extend them slowly.

Abdominals

★ Sit-ups . . . . Done on a decline bench gives more resistance.
Crunches . . . . Either lying on your back or with a vertical bench.
Bent-knee leg raises . . . . Lying on back, lift and contract legs.

Back (including lats)

★ Wide-grip chins. . . . With palms facing out. Also try behind neck (p 25).
Bent-over rows. . . Stand with back parallel to floor, lift barbell to waist.
Seated rows . . . . Done with cable and T-bar with close grip.

❦9 EXERCISES AT HOME

James Bond (p 178), often away from home for days at a time, exercises in his room in the mornings to rouse himself from self-pity or a hangover. Here is a typical routine, described in Ian Fleming's *From Russia with Love:*

> Bond went down on his hands and did twenty slow press-ups, lingering over each one so that his muscles had no rest. When his arms could stand the pain no longer, he rolled over on his back and, with his hands at his sides, did the straight leg-lift until his stomach muscles screamed. He got to his feet and, after touching his toes twenty times, went over to arm and chest exercises combined with deep breathing until he was dizzy.

Despite the modern obsession with exercising in a gym, it is possible to do a serious workout at home with no equipment apart from two sturdy chairs and a bar or broomstick. The number of repetitions tends to be higher because the weight is less, but rest assured: these are serious exercises.

9.1 SUMMARY OF EXERCISES

Exercise	*Muscles worked, in order*	*Repetitions per set*
Push-ups	pectorals, triceps	15–50
Pull-ups	biceps, lats	5–15
Chair dips	triceps, deltoid	10–25
Reverse bench (rows)	back, biceps	10–30
Triceps extensions	triceps, back, lats	10–30
Bent-knee sit-ups	abdominals	20–50
Squats	thighs	10–25
Standing calf raises	calves	15–40

9.2 PUSH-UPS

This is the most versatile weights-free exercise of all. Lie face down on the floor with your palms outstretched in front of you. With your weight on your toes and hands and your back straight, push yourself up until your arms are fully extended. Then lower yourself down until your chest or head just touches the ground, and repeat. With the hands directly under the shoulders, the triceps are emphasized; a wider hand placement works the pectoral muscles. The difficulty can be increased by raising the feet off the ground: for example, on the front of a chair or, higher still, the back of a chair. As the body approaches vertical (a handstand), this exercise approaches a military press with the body's own weight – very difficult.

9.3 PULL-UPS

This is one of the most effective of all exercises, and the most difficult of those without weights. "This is probably the only exercise you can do without gym equipment to build impressive biceps," writes Arnold Schwarzenegger in *The Education of a Bodybuilder* (p 194). To do it, you need a raised, fixed bar to grab hold of. One option is to place a bar inside a door jamb; another is to use a tree branch. Hanging from the bar by your hands, lift yourself until your collarbone meets the bar. There are two kinds of pull-ups: hands facing in, with a closer grip, and hands facing out, with a wider grip. Hands-in mainly works the biceps, then lats; hands-out works the lats, then biceps. If you can do three sets of 12 in five minutes, rejoice.

9.4 CHAIR DIPS

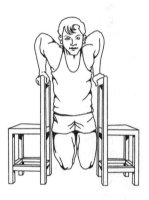

Chair dips are excellent for working the triceps and also the deltoid (the main muscle of the shoulder). Find two chairs with sturdy, straight backs, and place them back-to-back, just farther apart than the width of your shoulders. Standing between them, put your hands on the top of the chair backs and, keeping your legs bent, rest your entire weight on the chairs. Lower yourself as much as possible by bending your arms, then extend your arms to lift your weight. Keep your head and back straight. This exercise will be difficult at first, but you will soon improve. Aim for sets of 20.

9.5 REVERSE BENCH (ROWS)

This exercise is good for the back, similar in its effect to seated rows. Put two chairs back-to-back, four feet apart, and place a bar or broomstick across the backs of both. Lie on your back with your chest under the bar and hold it overhand with a wide grip, pulling yourself slowly to the top; your legs should be straight with your feet acting as a pivot point. The resistance can be increased by putting your feet on a chair, thereby starting from a decline position. Make sure your back does not touch the floor between repetitions.

9.6 TRICEPS EXTENSIONS

This is another focus on the triceps, but also works the back and lats. Put two chairs front-to-front, three or four feet apart. Place your heels on the seat of one, and your hands, behind your back, on the corners of the seat of the other. The idea is to use your arms to lower and
raise your body with the feet stationary and acting as the pivot point. Lower yourself as far as you can and then fully extend your arms, all the while keeping your legs as straight as possible. Work towards sets of 30; if these become easy, put a couple of heavy books on your lap for added resistance.

9.7 BENT-KNEE SIT-UPS

Sit-ups are one of the best exercises for the upper abdominals. Keep your knees bent and fix your feet under, say, a sofa. Put your hands at your sides, or against the sides of your neck to make them more difficult. "It is not necessary to lie back fully – only about three-quarters of the way – but the movement should be very smooth and rhythmical. With abdominals all you need is contraction. It's actually one of the few sets of muscles we don't give a full movement," explains Schwarzenegger. If you can do 50 in one set, hold a couple of heavy books against your chest for added resistance.

9.8 SQUATS AND STANDING CALF RAISES

The legs are one of the hardest muscle groups to work without free weights or machines because the body is not heavy enough – the legs already support the body's own weight all day long. One effective option is to lift the combined weight of yourself and another person. Holding a friend on your back, perform squats as usual: bend the legs to about 90 degrees and rise. Similarly, with the added weight of a friend, the calves can be worked: put a thick book on the floor and place the front half of one foot on it. Using a solid table or chair to balance, work one calf at a time (not shown)

❦10 FITNESS

10.1 US MARINE CORPS FITNESS TEST

Physical fitness generally refers to a combination of muscular endurance and aerobic endurance. The Marine Corps measures fitness on the basis of three individual exercises: pull-ups, crunches (sit-ups), and running.

Exercise	Time limit or duration	Min	Max
Pull-ups	Maximum while hanging on the bar	3	20
Crunches	Maximum in two minutes	50	100
Running	Three miles	28:00	18:00

The score for each exercise is determined as follows: 5 points for every pull-up; 1 point for every crunch (effectively defined to be a sit-up); and 100 points for running three miles minus 1 point for every 10 seconds slower than 18 minutes. To pass the test, it is necessary to achieve the minimum performance for each exercise (shown for men aged 17–26, the most stringent age bracket). Performing beyond the maximum does not earn more points. A perfect score is 300: 100 points in each exercise.

The easiest way to improve your combined score is by training to do more pull-ups: doing an extra pull-up is equivalent to shaving 50 seconds off your three-mile run time, or 17 seconds off the time for each mile.

10.2 US ARMY FITNESS TEST

The Army fitness test is similar to the Marine Corps test, but less stringent in its scoring. It measures the maximum number of push-ups and sit-ups you can do in two minutes and your time for a two-mile run. Points are awarded (for men aged 22–26, the most stringent age bracket) as shown below; there is no simple formula like above. It is necessary to earn at least 50 points in each exercise to pass Basic Combat Training and 60 points in each to pass Advanced Individual Training. Performing beyond the maximum does not earn more points. A perfect score is 300: 100 points in each.

Exercise / Score	100	90	80	70	60	50
Push-ups	75	66	58	49	40	31
Sit-ups	80	73	65	58	50	43
Two-mile run	13:00	13:54	14:48	15:42	16:36	17:30

In both the Marine Corps and Army tests, perfect scorers are eligible to claim their unofficial extended (300+) scores, which are used to rank them.

❦11 DRINKING GAMES

While drinking games are an aid to quaffing quickly, the object of most games is to *avoid* getting drunk, at least relative to other players. Here is a collection of popular and ingenious games. Penalties are either buying a round of drinks or taking a drink, the latter of which can take three forms:

A drink · Reduce the contents of your glass by at least two fingers' width.
A glass · Imbibe a standard serving; the size depends on the drink (p 104).
Emptying a glass · Finish the contents of your glass. This means that the glass must not be more than ¼ inch full after it has been emptied.

Quarters

The goal of this popular game is to throw a quarter into a specified glass by bouncing it off the surface of a hard table. Everyone sits around a table with an empty shot glass in the center; an old-fashioned drinking glass can be used instead for easier play. A player tries to bounce a quarter into the glass. If the attempt fails, the coin is passed clockwise; if the attempt succeeds, the thrower chooses who must drink, usually a small glass of beer, and throws again. If the quarter bounces off the edge of the glass but does not fall in, the player gets another throw. If this happens three times in a row, however, he must drink a glass of beer and play continues to his left. Accurate bouncing requires a certain knack which, once learned, comes readily.

Thumbmaster

This game can be played within other games. One person is chosen to be Master of Thumbs. Every time he places his thumb on the edge of the table, everyone else must too. The last person to do so must empty his glass, and he becomes the new Master. To discourage cheats, anyone who has his thumb on the table when the Master does not must also finish his glass.

Pennies in a pitcher

This simple game allows considerable psychological and strategic play. Everyone sits in a circle, and a pitcher of beer is passed around clockwise. Each time a person receives the pitcher, he must drink from it directly or pour some of it into his glass and drink that before passing. The person to the right of the one who empties the contents of the pitcher must buy the next round. The strategy has two regimes: if the pitcher is near full, it is advantageous to drink only a small amount, and pass; whereas if it is near empty, it is best to finish it. Alternatively, the game can be turned into a betting game. Each time someone drinks from the pitcher, he must add a fixed amount of money to a pot. Whoever finishes the pitcher collects the money.

Beer pong

To play this popular game you need a hard, rectangular table, a table tennis ball, and 12 or 20 identical cups. On each end of the table six or 10 cups filled with beer are arranged in a triangular formation, with the base of the triangle flush against the table edge and centered along it. The amount of beer per cup can vary, but a can per three cups is common. Two teams, of two players each, play against each other as follows. A player attempts to throw the ball, which may bounce first, into any of the cups on the opposite side. One of three strategies is used: an arc shot, a fastball, or a bounce shot. If the player succeeds, a member of the opposite team must drink the contents of the glass that the ball landed in. The ball is then given to the other member of the same team, who throws as before; play then passes to the opposing team. The first team to eliminate all of the other team's cups wins, and the losing team must drink the contents of the winners' remaining glasses.

Here are some variations, sometimes called "house rules." (i) If both players make their shots, they each get another turn. (ii) Each team is allowed a fixed number of re-racks: rearranging the cups which they are aiming for so they are closer together. (iii) If a ball bounces, the opposing team may try to deflect it away from the cups by striking it.

Arc shot

Fastball

Bounce shot

Boat race and flip cup

Boat race, named after the annual Oxford and Cambridge rowing competition, is a beer-drinking relay race in which two or more equal-sized teams compete. Sitting along a table, each team member has before him a glass of beer. Players are not allowed to touch their glasses before their turn. At a fixed time, the first members of each team start to empty their glasses. When someone finishes his glass, he places it back on the table and the player ahead of him begins to drink. The first team to finish wins.

Flip cup is a variation on boat race in which each player must flip his cup upside down after he finishes drinking. The cups are usually plastic and disposable. To flip, the empty cup is placed upright on the edge of the table such that part of the base protrudes. The object is to flip the cup with an upward motion from one hand such that it lands upside down. A player can take as many chances as he needs. Play passes when he succeeds.

President

Also known as "asshole," this is a drinking version of the Asian card game *dai hin min*. There are many variations of president; the standard rules are given here. President requires four or more people and a deck of cards. The cards are dealt such that everyone has the same number of cards, and the object of the game – played as a series of rounds – is to get rid of all your cards first. The following social offices are appointed after each round:

> *President* · First in the previous round (first to get rid of all his cards).
> *Vice president* · Second in the previous round.
> *Commoner* · Everyone apart from the top two and bottom two players.
> *Vice asshole* · Second to last in the previous round.
> *Asshole* · Last in the previous round (last to get rid of all his cards).

In the first round, everyone starts off as a commoner. Cards are ranked from low to high as 3, 4, 5, 6, 7, 8, 9, 10, J, Q, K, A, 2; suits are irrelevant throughout the game. The first player plays one or more cards of equal rank. The next player must play the same number of cards of identical rank which are higher than the card(s) just played. If a person cannot play, he must drink instead. If a person makes a mistake before the next player plays, he must drink. If, however, his mistake goes unnoticed, everyone but he must drink. Certain social rules are usually in force, for example: in a new round play begins with the president; the asshole must refill any empty glasses; the president gets the best chair at the table; the vice asshole must deal and collect the cards; the president gives his lowest two cards to the asshole.

Never have I ever

Each person announces in turn something that he has never done: for example, "I've never used an electric razor" or "I've never been dumped by a girlfriend." Everyone who *has* used an electric razor or been dumped stands and drinks from his glass. It is advantageous to announce one's rarer omissions, thereby maximizing the number of others who have to drink.

Drop the dime

Secure a piece of cigarette rolling paper (Rizla King Size works well) over a wide-mouthed glass with tape or a rubber band, and place a dime on top of it in the center. Moving clockwise, each person in turn touches a lit cigarette to the paper, burning away a small piece of it. Whoever causes the dime to fall through the paper must drink a glass. As play continues, an intricate web supporting the coin will emerge.

Six shooter

This simple game, also known as "six pack," is fast paced and cannot be kept up for long. It is played with a die and six shot or beer glasses, numbered 1 to 6. To start, all six glasses are filled halfway. A player rolls the die, and if the corresponding glass is not empty, he must drink its contents and roll again. If it is empty, he fills it with as much spirit or beer as he wishes, and play continues to his left. The last one standing, or willing to play, wins.

The name game

In this simple game of word association (also known as "drink while you think") everyone sits around a table with a glass of beer. Someone begins with a well-known name. The person to his left must immediately begin drinking until he thinks of a well-known name in which the first name begins with the same letter as the previous last name. If a player finishes his glass, he does not answer but refills it and play continues to his left. For example, the game might go as follows: Ian Fleming

Fred Astaire

Arnold Schwarzenegger

Sean Connery.

Shot-glass chess

The king of games is played with 32 shot glasses as per standard chess rules. Each time a piece is lost, the loser of it must drink what it contains. The loser of the game must drink the winner's remaining pieces; the winner must drink the loser's. This means that, unlike in normal chess, it is not enough to win (achieve checkmate) – you want to win after first capturing most of your opponent's pieces, thereby reducing what you must drink afterwards.

Shot glass sets are commercially available with six shapes of glasses, corresponding to the six different chess pieces. Alternatively, if there are two different kinds of shot glasses at hand, a set of 16 for each player, the identity of a piece can be set by the drink it contains. Below is a possible assignment, which gives each piece a different color. The total alcohol per side is equivalent to 8.4 cans of beer (5% ABV), so don't take losing lightly.

Piece	Drink	Color	ABV	ml ethanol
King	bourbon or Scotch	gold	40	17.8
Queen	vodka or gin	clear (silver)	40	17.8
Rook	Benedictine	brown	40	17.8
Bishop	Chartreuse	green	55	24.4
Knight	red wine	burgundy	12	5.3
Pawn	beer	sparkling gold	5	2.2

❦12 DARTS

While regional variations of the game of darts were played in England during the 19th century, the game as we know it was created in 1896 when Brian Gamlin arranged the 20 numbers around the board as shown below.

12.1 RULES

In the standard game of darts, players start with a score of 301, 501, 701, or 1001. One player throws three darts, adds up the scores, and subtracts this from his total; play then moves to the next player. The first person to get to exactly zero wins. Scoring is as follows. All wedges are face value, apart from the double and triple regions, which are two and three times face value. The bull is 50 and the outer bull ("the 25") is 25. No points are awarded for darts landing outside the double ring or bouncing off the wire. The last dart thrown must land in the double ring or bull and bring the score to exactly zero; this is called doubling out or checking out. How long a game lasts depends on the skill of the players. In principle, 501 can be reached with nine darts: seven triple-20s, triple-19, and double-12 is one way of many.

Checking out is one of the most strategic parts of the game. The maximum score with which the game can be won with three darts is 170: two triple-20s and a bull. It can be won with all scores below this except 159, 162, 163, 165, 166, 168, and 169. Sometimes it is more important when checking out to hit an even or odd wedge than one with a specific value. Even-rich regions of the board are 18-4, 6-10, 16-8; odd-rich regions are 17-3-19-7.

12.2 SET-UP

The center of the bull should be 5 feet 8 inches off the ground. The oche, a raised ridge beyond which a player cannot step but can lean, is parallel to the face of the board and is 7 feet 9¼ inches from a plumb line dropped from it.

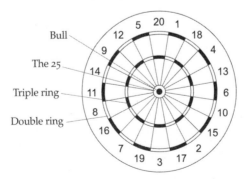

12.3 BEST PLACES TO AIM

The distribution of the numbers 1–20 around the board is far from random. They are strategically placed such that the advantage of high numbers is offset by low-number neighbors; this penalizes inaccurate throwing. One way of measuring the difficulty of an ordering is to add up the differences between consecutive numbers around the board. By this reckoning, the most difficult ordering of the numbers yields a total of differences of 200. Gamlin's ordering is near perfect: the differences add up to 198.

While the very best players can always hit a given wedge, the aim of beginners and amateurs is less predictable. Therefore they should seek the most points-rich regions on the board. The location of these regions depends on just how bad a player's aim is. The table below shows the average face value for darts thrown with increasingly large spreads. The bold numbers are the face values of the wedges. A spread of zero means that you can hit a given wedge; a spread of one means that, if you aim for the wire between two numbers, you will hit one of them; a spread of two means that you can hit a wedge or one of its two nearest neighbors; and so on.

What are the best parts of the board to aim at? Overall, the left side is more generous than the right, with 19-7-16 and 11-14-9 especially valuable regions. Consult the table below for more detailed hot and cool regions.*

12.4 AVERAGE SCORE FOR A SINGLE DART

Spread				Right half of board					
0	**20**	**1**	**18**	**4**	**13**	**6**	**10**	**15**	**2**	**17**
1	10.5	9.5	11.0	8.5	9.5	8.0	12.5	8.5	9.5	10.0
2	11.5	10.0	10.2	9.8	9.0	8.8	10.2	10.5	9.0	9.8
3	10.8	10.1	10.0	9.4	8.9	9.5	10.4	9.8	9.4	10.1
4	10.9	10.4	10.1	9.7	9.1	9.2	9.9	10.1	9.6	9.8

Spread				Left half of board					
0	**3**	**19**	**7**	**16**	**8**	**11**	**14**	**9**	**12**	**5**
1	11.0	13.0	11.5	12.0	9.5	12.5	11.5	10.5	8.5	12.5
2	10.5	12.0	12.2	11.8	10.8	11.0	12.0	11.0	9.5	10.5
3	11.2	12.1	12.0	11.2	10.9	11.5	11.5	10.2	10.0	11.0
4	10.7	11.7	12.1	11.6	11.1	11.2	11.5	10.9	10.1	10.5

*The expected point scores here are not uniform but weighted averages, biased towards the number or wire aimed for. For spread 1, the weights are ½ and ½; for spread 2, ¼, ¾, and ¼; for spread 3, ⅛, ⅜, ⅜, and ⅛. In general, if the spread is s, the denominator is 2^s and the numerators are the binomial coefficients that sum to 2^s.

❦13 POKER

The rules for poker are not complicated, but the game allows for consider-able strategic and psychological play. Texas Hold'em poker is by far the most popular version of the game, both in private tournaments and Amer-ican casinos. It is the main event at the World Series of Poker in Las Vegas.

13.1 TEXAS HOLD'EM RULES

The game is played with a standard 52-card deck, and aces counting high, by two or more players. Eventually two private (called hole) cards and five public (called community) cards will have been dealt, and the object of the game is to form the highest five-card hand using any combination of one's two hole cards and the five community cards.

The dealer (whether he actually deals or not) is marked by a disc. Before any cards are dealt, the person to the left of the dealer contributes to the pot the small blind (usually half the minimum bet) and the person to the left of him contributes to the pot the big blind (usually the minimum bet). Each person is dealt two hole cards, face down. The first round of betting begins with the player to the left of the two blinds, and rotates clockwise until it returns to the dealer. At his turn a player may do any one of the following:

Call · make a bet equal to the most recent bet in the round;
Raise · bet more than the most recent bet in the round; or
Fold · quit the game, forfeiting any chips he may have bet.

After the first round of betting, players have four options: in addition to call, raise, and fold, a player can now "check," which means to remain in the game but bet no money, so long as no one before him in the round has made a bet. Three more betting rounds follow, each after more rounds of community cards are dealt. (After the first round, betting begins with the player to the dealer's left.) These three card dealings are known as the:

Flop · first three community cards, dealt before the second round of bet-ting;
Turn · fourth community card, dealt before the third round of betting;
River · fifth community card, dealt before the fourth round of betting.

If during any round of betting all but one player have folded, the remain-ing player wins the pot but need not show his hole cards. If after the fourth and final round of betting two or more players remain, they enter a show-down. Here the players turn their two hole cards face up, and the player with the highest hand formed by any combination of his two hole and the five community cards wins the pot. If two players have the same hand, then the player with the highest hole card not forming part of his hand (the kicker) wins. If there are no kickers (both players' hole cards are part of their winning hands) or the kickers are the same, the pot is divided equally. The next round begins with the dealer disc passed clockwise by one player.

13.2 ORDER OF HANDS

Given a 52-card deck, there are 2,598,960 distinct five-card hands possible. The order of hands, which are never broken by suit, and their frequencies are:

Hand	Definition	Example	No.	Prob. (%)
Royal flush	10–A, same suit	10◇ J◇ Q◇ K◇ A◇	4	0.00015
Straight flush	seq. of five, same suit	4♠ 5♠ 6♠ 7♠ 8♠	40	0.0015
Four of a kind	four of same rank	8♠ 8♡ 8♣ 8◇	624	0.024
Full house	pair + three of a kind	5♣ 5◇ 9♡ 9♠ 9◇	3,744	0.14
Flush	five of same suit	3♠ 6♠ 7♠ J♠ A♠	5,108	0.20
Straight	sequence of five	7♡ 8◇ 9♠ 10◇ J♡	10,200	0.39
Three of a kind	three of same rank	9♠ 9♡ 9♣	54,912	2.1
Two pair	pair + pair	2♣ 2◇ 8♡ 8◇	123,552	4.7
One pair	two of same rank	10♠ 10◇	1,098,240	42
No pair	none of the above		1,302,540	50

13.3 ORDER OF PRE-FLOP HANDS

Before the flop, each player has the option of folding on the basis of his first two (pre-flop) cards, thereby avoiding any losses if his cards are poor. There are 1,326 distinct possible pre-flop hands, but these can be reduced to 169 by bearing in mind that in poker suits have no relative value. In *Hold'em Poker for Advanced Players*, David Sklansky and Mason Malmuth arranged the 73 best pre-flop hands into eight groups, where group 1 contains the most valuable hands, group 2 the next most valuable hands, and so on; hands are not ordered within a group. "T" means 10; "s" means same suit.

Group 1	AA	KK	QQ	JJ	AKS					
Group 2	TT	AQS	AJS	KQS	AK					
Group 3	99	JTS	QJS	KJS	ATS	AQ				
Group 4	T9S	KQ	88	QTS	98S	J9S	AJ	KTS		
Group 5	77	87S	Q9S	T8S	KJ	QJ	JT	76S	97S	AXS	65S
Group 6	66	AT	55	86S	KT	QT	54S	K9S	J8S	75S
Group 7	44	J9	64S	T9	53S	33	98	43S	22	KXS	T7S	Q8S
Group 8	87	A9	Q9	76	42S	32S	96S	85S	J8	J7S	65	54

35

♣14 BLACKJACK

Blackjack is the most popular betting card game. It is played with one or more packs, and each player and a dealer are dealt two cards: both face down for the players; one down, one showing for the dealer. Each player bets against only the dealer. The object is to get closer to 21 than the dealer without going over, called going bust, where cards 2 through 10 are worth face value; the jack, queen, and king are worth 10; and the ace is worth 11 or, would that cause a bust, 1. After the cards are dealt, each player has four options, which he can repeat until he stands, doubles down, or busts.

Hit · receive an additional card;
Stand · receive no additional cards;
Double down · double the bet, receive one additional card, then stand;
Split · if the player's two cards are a pair, he can double his wager, split
    them into two hands, and play them independently.

The dealer's play is strictly formulaic: he must hit on 16 or less and stand otherwise. If both the player and the dealer bust, the dealer wins; if they tie, no money is exchanged. If the player's first two cards total 21 (blackjack), the dealer pays 3:2, unless he has the same, and no money is exchanged.

14.1 BASIC STRATEGY

Below are the best options for a player's hand given the dealer's showing card. It assumes the following: dealer stands on 17; infinite number of packs; double on any two cards; double after split allowed; dealer peaks.

Player's hand	2	3	4	5	6	7	8	9	10	A
5–8	·	·	·	·	·	·	·	·	·	·
9	·	D	D	D	D	·	·	·	·	·
10	D	D	D	D	D	D	D	D	·	·
11	D	D	D	D	D	D	D	D	D	·
12	·	·	s	s	s	·	·	·	·	·
13–16	s	s	s	s	s	·	·	·	·	·
17	s	s	s	s	s	s	s	s	s	s
A,2 A,3	·	·	·	D	D	·	·	·	·	·
A,4 A,5	·	·	D	D	D	·	·	·	·	·
A,6	·	D	D	D	D	·	·	·	·	·
A,7	s	D	D	D	D	s	s	·	·	·

Player's hand	2	3	4	5	6	7	8	9	10	A
A,8 A,9	s	s	s	s	s	s	s	s	s	s
2,2 3,3	P	P	P	P	P	P	·	·	·	·
4,4	·	·	·	P	P	·	·	·	·	·
5,5	D	D	D	D	D	D	D	D	·	·
6,6	P	P	P	P	P	·	·	·	·	·
7,7	P	P	P	P	P	P	·	·	·	·
8,8	P	P	P	P	P	P	P	P	P	P
9,9	P	P	P	P	P	s	P	P	s	s
T,T	s	s	s	s	s	s	s	s	s	s
A,A	P	P	P	P	P	P	P	P	P	P

KEY   T = 10, J, Q, K   · = hit   s = stand   D = double down   P = split

WOMEN

Homer Simpson • Son, a woman is a lot like a refrigerator. They're about six feet tall, 300 pounds. They make ice. (*The Simpsons*, New Kid on the Block, episode 9F06, 1992)

Samuel Johnson • Marriage, Sir, is much more necessary to a man than to a woman; for he is much less able to supply himself with domestick comforts… I had often wondered why young women should marry, as they have so much more freedom, and so much more attention paid to them while unmarried. (Boswell, *Life of Johnson*, 1791)

Naff dear Johns • I've been thinking about us… • We're not going anywhere… • You'll always be very special to me. • I hope we can always be friends. • I'm leaving you, Simon. I want to discover who I really am. (*The Complete Naff Guide*, 1983)

Lord Chesterfield • There are but two objects in marriage, love or money.

If you marry for love, you will certainly have some very happy days, and probably many uneasy ones; if you marry for money, you will have no happy days and probably no uneasy ones. (*Lord Chesterfield's Letters*, 1776)

Hardy Amies • I never see any elegantly dressed young women. They don't try hard enough.

Benjamin Franklin • Happy's the wooing that's not long a doing. • Love well, whip well. • Keep your eyes open wide before marriage, half shut afterwards. • Pretty & witty will wound if they hit ye. • Good wives and good plantations are made by good husbands. • He that takes a wife, takes care. • An undutiful daughter, will prove an unmanageable wife. • If Jack's in love, he's no judge of Jill's beauty. • Let thy maid-servant be faithful, strong and homely. • There are no ugly loves, nor handsome prisons. (*Poor Richard's Almanack*, 1732–1757)

❦15 BEAUTY

A woman's beauty is notoriously difficult to define, dependent as it is on non-physical attributes such as style and demeanor. Jacqueline Kennedy and Princess Diana, not classically beautiful, were two of the most photographed women of the 20th century. Even a strict physical interpretation of beauty must concede that it waxes and wanes with a woman's effort.

15.1 QUANTIFYING BEAUTY

Without attempting to define beauty, we can nevertheless quantify it. Our starting point is Helen of Troy, the offspring of the Greek god Zeus and Leda, wife of the king of Sparta. Helen, whose abduction sparked the Trojan War, was thought to be the most beautiful woman in the world around the 12th century BC. In Christopher Marlowe's *The Tragical History of Doctor Faustus*, Mephistopheles calls up a vision of Helen, and Faustus reponds:

> Was this the face that launched a thousand ships
> And burned the topless towers of Ilium?

From this we can deduce two things: the extent of Helen's beauty, and its effect. The population of the earth in the 12th century BC is estimated to be at most 100 million, making her the most beautiful of 50 million women. If Helen's beauty launched a thousand ships, we may infer that the most beautiful of 50,000 women would launch a single ship. The military vessels of the time were simple galleys powered by 25 oarsmen on each side. Accordingly, the pick of a thousand women would bring a single oarsman to risk his life in war. Let such a beauty be the colloquial "perfect 10" on a scale of 0 to 10. We call a single point on this scale a Helena (Ha).

The beauty of a thousand women is not, of course, uniformly distributed; there are invariably more 8s than 9s, more 7s than 8s, and so on. Like the Richter scale for measuring earthquakes, beauty is logarithmic, but with a base of 2 rather than 32. This means that, for beauty to increase by one Helena, the woman must be the most beautiful of twice as many women. Thus if a woman is the most striking of 2 women, her beauty is 1 Helena; of 4 women, 2 Helenas; of 8 women, 3 Helenas; and, in general, of 2^N women, N Helenas. While 10 Helenas would cause a man to risk his life, a woman's beauty does occasionally exceed 10. The beauty of Helen herself is $\log_2$ (50,000,000) = 25.6 (50 million is $2 \times 2 \times \ldots \times 2$, between 25 and 26 times). Thus we define one Helen (H) to be 25.6 Helenas (Ha).

Of any large population of women, ½ of the women have beauty 0 Ha, ¼ have 1 Ha, ⅛ have 2 Ha, and so on. This contrasts with the more common but less systematic beauty scale in which 0 is plain, 5 average, and 10 stunning. Alas, Helenas can be used to measure only beauty, not homeliness.

15.2 SOME WOMEN'S BEAUTY

Woman	Number	Ha	H
Best of a dozen	12	3.6	0.14
Most beautiful of a martyr's 72 virgins	72	6.2	0.24
Would cause a man to risk his life	1,000	10.0	0.39
Best beauty seen in a lifetime	10^5	16.6	0.65
Helen of Troy	5×10^7	25.6	1.00
Miss World	3.2×10^9	31.6	1.23
Most beautiful woman who ever lived	2×10^{10}	34.2	1.34

15.3 FLATTERY

It is one thing to believe a woman to be beautiful, another to proclaim it. Flattery is best offered to women of intermediate beauty, not extreme.

> Women who are either indisputably beautiful, or indisputably ugly, are best flattered, upon the score of their understandings; but those who are in a state of mediocrity, are best flattered upon their beauty, or at least their graces; for every woman who is not absolutely ugly thinks herself handsome; but not hearing often that she is so, is the more grateful and the more obliged to the few who tell her so; whereas a decided and conscious beauty looks upon every tribute paid to her beauty only as her due; but wants to shine, and to be considered on the side of her understanding; and a woman who is ugly enough to know that she is so, knows that she has nothing left for it but her understanding, which is consequently and probably...her weak side.
> *Letters to His Son*, Philip Stanhope, 4th Earl of Chesterfield

Paradoxically, beauty seems to safeguard modesty. The more a woman is admired by men, the less likely she is to indulge in casual passion; whereas a woman whose beauty is contested, finding herself unable to compete with the beautiful head-on, compensates by offering easy access. Beauty has its price, of course. As a kept animal, used to daily provision without toil, loses its instinct to find food on it own, a beautiful woman, accustomed to men's attention, can forget how to earn it through kindness. Perhaps this explains Shakespeare's inversion of Marlowe in the *History of Troilus and Cressida*:

> Is she worth keeping? Why, she is a pearl
> Whose price hath launch'd above a thousand ships.

☙16 CHIVALRY

Chivalry – meaning disinterested courage, honor, and courteousness, according to the *Oxford English Dictionary* – is rather out of fashion, being a potential source of conflict between modern feminism and accepted custom. It is fundamentally predicated on an asymmetry between the sexes.

16.1 PRECEDENCE

All else being equal, women take precedence over men, and this is the basis of a number of customs. Men are introduced to women, as in "Daisy Buchanan, may I introduce Jay Gatsby," or, more simply, "Marge, this is Homer." It is the woman rather than the man who initiates, and thereby determines, the form of recognition – a kiss, a handshake, or a glance – on greeting and departing. Women are in general served food before men, and their glasses are filled first (unless the table is large, in which case wine is served around the table clockwise). It is correct for men to rise when a woman arrives or departs, although the coming and going of a man does not justify this. A man lights a woman's cigarette (see p 143), carries her heavy bags, and offers his seat if she is forced to stand, though the last can be dispensed with in busy settings, such as a bus or subway.

The protocol for walking with a woman can be easily formulated. In general, a man walks to the right of a woman, unless the couple is walking beside a road, in which case the man puts himself between the woman and the road. If the couple passes another man, the man keeps to the side of the woman and allows the man to walk into the street, but if they pass a woman the man walks into the street himself.

The protocol for opening doors can also be formulated. It is motivated first by considerations of labor, then of precedent. Thus if the door opens towards a man, he opens it and allows the woman to walk through first. But if the door opens away from him, he walks through and the woman follows. If others are coming from the opposite side, in the first case the man holds the door open and the others take precedence, but in the second the woman, then the man, precede. In the case of revolving doors, both on account of labor and of them opening away, the man is the first to go through.

16.2 PROVISION

One of the most innate chivalric tendencies is the provision – though not necessarily the preparation – of food. This can be seen in the actual procurement of fish and fowl, of course, but is also symbolized by the carving of meat at the dinner table (see p 162 for instructions).

Today provision often takes the form of paying for dinner and drinks. Whatever the arguments might be for going Dutch, a woman who insists on splitting the bill is either romantically uninterested or tedious. In early courtship it is correct to pay even when a woman offers once or twice, though if three times a man must concede. The foxiest females seem most willing to let men cover the costs. French women never offer to pay for dinner – or lunch, for that matter – and are certainly no less desirable than *les américaines*. In the case that a woman thinks it her due, a casual suggestion to split the bill is often more likely to secure a second date.

A constant outlay on women can cause near-bankruptcy, and for men who find themselves pinching pennies it is advisable to *pay only for women you fancy*. A thoughtful woman will recognize any financial disparity and contribute accordingly after the first few outings.

Wine remains a male preserve, despite the increasing number of female oenologists. At a restaurant the man chooses the wine; though he may ask the woman for input, he is under no obligation to do so. He fills the woman's glass when low and each time he fills his own, even if only symbolically. A sensitive woman – and indeed a man if he is a guest – will slowly nurse a half-full glass rather than refuse when she has had her fill.

16.3 PROTECTION

The custom of returning a woman home after an evening out remains correct in principle, but varies in practice according to the circumstances. It is correct to walk or drive a woman to her door if she does not live far away, but if she does it is impractical to make a long detour, as well as alarming from the woman's point of view. Better to send her home in a taxi. The man is not required to pay, unless he insists on her taking a taxi as opposed to, say, a bus. When entertaining a group, a man's first priority is to his guests, and it is his guests who should look after the safe return of any women.

When is a man welcome inside a woman's house after returning her? "If a woman does not want a man to come in, then gentle but clear suggestions...should be put into the conversation," explains John Morgan in *Debrett's New Guide to Etiquette and Modern Manners*. "If a man is asked in, he must not assume that he has the green light for sex, although a woman who does this shouldn't be surprised if he does."

An insult to a man's girlfriend or wife in his presence is always a gross offense. The Code Duello, the most widely accepted set of prescriptions on dueling and honor, states: "Any insult to a lady under a gentleman's care or protection [is] to be considered as, by one degree, a greater offense than if given to the gentleman personally, and to be regulated accordingly." Offenses are, in increasing order of severity, an insult, a lie, and a blow.

🐦17 FIRST DATE

The first thing to keep in mind in early courtship is that men chase and women are chased. A man finds this both pleasurable and instinctive; he is:

> Like the hunter who chases the hare
> Through heat and cold, o'er hill and dale,
> Yet, once he has bagged it, he thinks nothing of it;
> Only while it flees away does he pound after it.
> > Ariosto, *Orlando Furioso*, X, vii, translated by M. A. Screech

Men chase what they desire. Intelligent women recognize this, and invert it: a man who does not chase does not desire. The best-selling book *The Rules* by Ellen Fein and Sherrie Schneider lists "time-tested secrets for capturing the heart of Mr. Right," shown below. The central message is that playing hard to get provides a litmus test for a man's interest. The chase-chased courtship asymmetry is not male chauvinism – it is an essential ritual in forming stable matches.

The second thing is that men fall in love more quickly than women. Where a woman takes her time and considers what is real, a man runs with first impressions and invents the rest according to his fantasy. This invention is both intoxicating and intimidating; ultimately it makes men fear women. In Lermontov's *A Hero of Our Time*, the practiced seducer Pechorin tells us: "Women ought to wish that all men knew them as well as I because I have loved them a hundred times better since I have ceased to be afraid of them and have comprehended their little weaknesses." Hence the importance in early conquest of approaching women with insouciance, as one might a potential male friend. This requires acting, but the game is short-lived – it need only last until love (or its absence) has replaced infatuation.

17.1 THE RULES FOR WOMEN

Don't talk to a man first (and don't ask him to dance). • Don't stare at men or talk too much. • Don't meet him halfway or go Dutch on a date. • Don't call him and rarely return his phone calls. • Always end phone calls first. • Don't accept a Saturday night date after Wednesday. • Always end the date first. • Stop dating him if he doesn't buy you a romantic gift for your birthday or Valentine's Day. • Don't see him more than once or twice a week. • No more than casual kissing on the first date. • Don't tell him what to do. • Let him take the lead. • Don't expect a man to change or try to change him. • Don't open up too fast. • Don't live with a man (or leave your things in his apartment). • Don't date a married man. • Be easy to live with.

17.2 LOGISTICS

Except perhaps on Sadie Hawkins Day (p 212), on a first date a man invites a woman by suggesting a fixed plan, without negotiation as to where to meet or what to do. It is not a time to be original in your choice of venue. A first date should merely be a setting for easy and unimpeded conversation, hence the custom of having it in a public place. Dinner is ideal: it is conducive to talking; it affords the chance to drink alcohol; and there is no set time to finish by. If you do not have plans for afterwards, such as music or the theater or the cinema, it is wise to begin with separate drinks beforehand, which brings a sense of motion to the evening.

While it remains correct to collect a woman by car, in some cities and university settings it is often more practical to meet her at a pre-arranged location. In this case it is essential to arrive ten minutes early. By the time the girl arrives, you should be seated and have in hand a drink and a slim novel (Pushkin or Turgenev is ideal). In any event do not talk to others or use your cell phone; you may appear interested in things, not other people.

You should have a reservation at a restaurant and know how to get there, which may require reconnaissance beforehand. (If you find yourself stuck with nowhere in mind, choose one on the spot using the algorithm below.) A schoolboy error is the over-ambitious choice of restaurant. Apart from being expensive, it is intimidating for the woman, who tends to think that allowing you to pay a large bill obligates her affection, and usually has the reverse effect. On whether and when to pay the bill, see Provision, p 40.

The end of the date is as important as the beginning. The essential thing – and remember we are talking about the *first* date – is to show no interest in her physically. Your restraint should grow in proportion to her beauty. A pretty girl considers a man's affection her due (p 38). When her desirableness is rebuffed, a man becomes more, not less, fascinating to her. Which makes securing a second date straightforward by comparison.

17.3 CHOOSING THE BEST RESTAURANT

Consider the familiar experience of walking down a street looking for somewhere to eat. One would like, on the one hand, to sample many restaurants before making a choice, and on the other, to avoid passing a good candidate in the hope of something better. What strategy maximizes the probability of choosing the best restaurant? If there are numerous restaurants on the street, the optimal policy is to walk past the first $37\% = 1/e$, then pick the next one better than all of those. (Here e is the base of the natural logarithm, 2.718.) This is a universal strategy, and can be equally applied to accepting an offer or buying a house or, in the case of women, accepting a marriage proposal.

🌵18 MARRIAGE

18.1 WEDDING ANNIVERSARIES

The first widely accepted list of wedding anniversary gifts was published by Emily Post in her best-selling book, *Etiquette,* in 1922. It listed eight anniversaries: 1, 5, 10, 15, 20, 25, 50, and 75. "[The gifts] need not, however, be of value; in fact the paper, wooden, and tin wedding presents are seldom anything but jokes. Crystal is the earliest that is likely to be taken seriously by the gift-bearers. Silver is always serious, and the golden wedding a quite sacred event." In later editions Post increased the list to the years 1–15 and multiples of 5 up to 60. Today these are the only years for which broad consensus exists. Some freedom in choosing what to give can be had by giving two or three alternative objects whose sum is the requisite anniversary. Thus cotton and bronze might be given for a 10th anniversary instead of tin.

1	paper	7	wool	13	lace	35	coral
2	cotton	8	bronze	14	ivory	40	ruby
3	leather	9	pottery	15	crystal	45	sapphire
4	linen	10	tin	20	china	50	gold
5	wood	11	steel	25	silver	55	emerald
6	iron	12	silk	30	pearl	60	diamond

18.2 ENGAGEMENT RINGS

An engagement ring is normally given to a woman on or soon after proposing. While there is much talk today about letting the woman choose the design, I admire the man who without warning proposes with ring in hand. There are various rules of thumb as to how much an engagement ring should cost, ranging from two weeks' to two months' salary. About one months' salary is typical.

Often an engagement ring is adorned with one of the five cardinal gemstones: amethyst, diamond, emerald, ruby, and sapphire (amethyst is no longer considered valuable following the discovery of large deposits in Brazil and elsewhere). During the 19th century a popular form of engagement ring made use of different gemstones to form an acrostic, a sequence of words whose initial letters form a message. The most popular spelled RE-GARDS, making use of the five cardinal stones and garnet: ruby, emerald, garnet, amethyst, ruby, diamond, sapphire. Another spells LOVE: lapis lazuli, opal, vermarine, emerald – though the color coordination and inclusion of vermarine makes such a combination suspect. Much better is EROS: emerald, ruby, opal, sapphire. See p 188 for a table of birthstones.

18.3 WHOM TO MARRY

Consanguinity has always constrained who can marry whom. According to *The Book of Common Prayer*, by tradition a man should not marry his:

mother	wife's mother	mother's father's wife
daughter	wife's daughter	wife's father's mother
sister	father's wife	wife's mother's
father's mother	son's wife	mother
mother's mother	father's sister	wife's son's daughter
son's daughter	mother's sister	wife's daughter's
daughter's daughter	brother's daughter	daughter
father's daughter	sister's daughter	son's son's wife
mother's daughter	father's father's wife	daughter's son's wife

Laws prohibiting some of the more arcane combinations above have been relaxed. Despite popular belief, first-cousin marriage is legal in most countries and widespread in many. Laws prohibiting first-cousin marriage usually predate modern genetic theory, although one half of American states has yet to repeal them. Texas recently banned first cousins from marrying.

18.4 WHEN TO MARRY

The most common rule of thumb for the ideal age of your bride at marriage is ½ your age + 7. For women readers, it's (your age − 7) × 2. Thus for a man of 30, a bride of 22 is most suitable; for a man of 40, a bride of 27. The formula adjusts for women's comparatively advanced emotional strength and matches the fertile period of a woman (14–45) to that of a man (14–76). Proponents suggest it also reduces the risk of later infidelity on the side of men: "I like my whiskey old and my women young," in the words of Errol Flynn. (For a list of single malts and aged bourbons, see pp 119 and 122).

Man's age at marriage (a):	16	24	32	40	48	56	64	72
Woman's age at marriage ($\frac{1}{2}a + 7$):	15	19	23	27	31	35	39	43

An alternative guide to marriage ages, and one which gives less disparate numbers, matches the Fibonacci numbers (1 + 2 = 3, 2 + 3 = 5, 3 + 5 = 8...) and the Lucas numbers (1 + 3 = 4, 3 + 4 = 7, 4 + 7 = 11...). These two sequences mark the notable stages of a man's and woman's life, respectively.

Man's age at marriage (F_n):	21	34	55	89
Woman's age at marriage (L_{n-1}):	18	29	47	76

❦19 BEST MAN

The best man is the chief attendant and aide-de-camp to the groom and he officiates at the wedding on the groom's behalf. Apart from the wedding couple, he plays the most significant role in the ceremony. It is always an honor to be asked to be best man, and not without its rewards: being the preeminent bachelor, he has the attention of all the single women present.

19.1 CHOOSING A BEST MAN

While the best man is invariably a close friend or relative of the groom, there are a few other things to consider when choosing one. Ideally the best man should be a bachelor. It is customary that he hold the same religion as that in which the wedding will be celebrated, although this is not essential, even among devout grooms. Finally, it is worth considering how good a public speaker he is, as the best man's speech is the most memorable part of his performance. So it sometimes happens that one's best man is not one's best friend. It is also perfectly acceptable for the groom to ask a close relative, usually a brother, to be best man, which avoids any hurt feelings associated with choosing one close friend over another.

The best man must lead and organize the groomsmen, being chief among them. They are the groom's regiment, comprising up to a dozen young male friends and relatives of the groom and bride. Apart from seating guests and handing out programs during the ceremony, during the reception they should make introductions and look after any lone or lonely female guests.

19.2 BEST MAN'S DUTIES

While the best man's duties are significant, they are very clearly prescribed:

1 Organize and lead the bachelor party (described opposite).
2 Ensure the groom wakes up on time and is perfectly dressed.
3 Make sure he has packed his luggage for going away.
4 Have lunch with the groom and drive him to the wedding on time.
5 Organize buttonhole flowers to be available at the front of the church.
6 Wait with the groom at the front of the church until the bride arrives.
7 Stand beside the groom to his right near the altar after she arrives.
8 Having safely looked after the wedding rings, offer them when needed.
9 Look after any church, choir, or photography administration on the day.
10 Prepare and give the best man's speech (described opposite).
11 Announce the speeches and the cutting of the cake at the reception.
12 Send off the new couple when they leave the reception.

19.3 BACHELOR PARTY

The bachelor party is a kind of rite of passage from single to married life. Like Mardi Gras celebrations on the day before Lent begins, the bachelor party is a symbolic final indulgence in boyish camaraderie and independence. It can range from a dinner out to a multi-day affair involving travel across state or even national borders. It usually takes place one to three weeks before the wedding. Women, of course, are not allowed, and outdoor activities, alcohol, and fraternal excess tend to play a significant role.

In consultation with the groom, the best man should plan the party and invite the guests, which usually include the groomsmen from the groom's side, among others. On the day, he must protect the groom from excessive humiliation, drunkenness, and harm. Every man pays his own way, apart from the groom, whose expenses are covered by the rest of the party.

19.4 BEST MAN'S SPEECH

Traditionally there are three men's speeches at a wedding: the father of the bride, who introduces the bride; the groom, who offers thanks to the parents of the bride and the guests; and the best man, who introduces the groom.

The best man's speech should be a well-rehearsed, five to 10 minute character sketch of the groom. It may be risqué but not lewd, mischievous but not embarrassing. Any questionable divulgences should be checked with the groom himself. Keep in mind that half of the wedding party will be from the bride's clan and will know little about the groom, so it is a good idea to provide some basic biographical background. If humor is not your strength, it is perfectly acceptable to give a serious speech, but it should be leavened with a few light-hearted anecdotes. Sometimes the most effective humor is implicit, as in the following well-known speech:

> Ladies and gentlemen, I'm sorry to drag you from your desserts. There are just one or two little things I feel I should say, as best man. This is only the second time I've been a best man. I hope I did OK that time. The couple in question are at least still talking to me. Unfortunately, they're not actually talking to each other. The divorce came through a couple of months ago. But I'm assured it had absolutely nothing to do with me... Anyway, enough of that. My job today is to talk about Angus. There are no skeletons in his cupboard. Or so I thought. I'll come on to that in a minute. I would just like to say this. I am, as ever, in bewildered awe of anyone who makes this kind of commitment that Angus and Laura have made today. I know I couldn't do it and I think it's wonderful they can. So, back to Angus and those sheep.
> "Charles" (Hugh Grant), *Four Weddings and a Funeral*

❦20 SAYING GOODBYE

In English there is a broad range of customary closings, particularly for men, who do not end the bulk of their correspondence with *Love* or a string of x's. Some closings are more appropriate on paper; others are best suited to email or text messages. Which variations mean what, and which parts are made explicit, is a subject of some subtlety, conveying as much about the sender as about his relationship with the recipient. Here is a guide.

20.1 XOX

The emoticons x and o are mostly used by women at the end of text messages and emails. An x and an o, of course, denote a kiss and a hug, but what do these kisses and hugs convey? Affection grows with their number, but only up to a point; after, say, four, the intended intimacy *decreases*. Many women consider one x a minimum civilized closing, but there is no set convention, and it is only the relative increase of x's and o's that is significant.

x = friendship   xox = eros?   xoxox = friendship

20.2 POSTAL ACRONYMS

Although the recent surge of interest in abbreviations and acronyms was motivated by text messaging, it is not unprecedented. During the Second World War, servicemen adopted a number of sentimental acronyms in their censored letters home to spouses. Unlike FUBAR and SNAFU, these were usually in the form of place names. One theory holds that they were originally written out in full as a means of communicating where the men were stationed, which they were not allowed to disclose. Only later was their usage reversed, with the acronyms written to indicate the full expressions.

BOLTOP . . . . Better on lips than on paper
BURMA . . . . Be undressed ready my angel
CHINA . . . . Come home I need affection
HOLLAND . . . . Hope our love lasts and never dies
ITALY . . . . I trust and love you
MALAYA . . . . My ardent lips await your arrival
MEXICO CITY . . . . May every x I can offer carry itself to you
NORWICH . . . . [K]nickers off ready when I come home
SIAM . . . . Sexual intercourse at midnight
SWALK . . . . Sealed with a loving kiss
WALES . . . . With a love eternal sweetheart

20.3 DICTIONARY OF CLOSINGS

In essence, the closing of letters, email, and text messages indicates how *I* relate to *you*, with the basic formulae being *I* [verb] *your* [noun phrase]; or *I* [verb] *yours* [modifier]. The verb is usually *am* or *remain*; the noun phrase might be *humble subject* or *friend* or *affectionate brother*; the modifier can be an adverb, like *sincerely*, or an adverbial clause, usually *with...*, as in *with best wishes*. Today these formulae are usually not written out in full but implied, and we are left with such familiar artifacts as *Yours sincerely* or *With best wishes*. (Note that only the first word is capitalized.)

Closings range from common (coarse) to smart (civilized) as follows:

Common   C → c → ~ → s → S   Smart

Adieu	s	Literally, "to God" (see you in Heaven). Used when the next meeting is distant or uncertain.
All good wishes	s	Curiously warmer than *Best wishes*, perhaps because it is less common.
All my love	s	For romantic or familial contexts. Simple but effectual.
All the best	c	Hackneyed, although *All best* is not. The latter is frequently used by those in the literary business.
Best	c	Short for *With best wishes* or *With best regards*. OK for short emails; clumsy when written on paper.
Best regards	~	One of the most common closings. More familiar than *Best wishes*, but unoriginal.
Best wishes	~	*With best wishes* is more intimate.
Cheerio	~	"A parting exclamation of encouragement," according to the *Oxford English Dictionary*. Now it is outdated *Famous Five* speech.
Cheers	c	In writing, mostly used by the French and Americans, thinking it is colloquial among the British. In Britain it is mainly spoken as a mild expression of thanks. Sometimes extended to *Cheers, mate* (C), also used in speech.
Ciao	~	From the Italian *schiavo* (servant), it now means hello or goodbye. In English it first appeared in Hemingway's *A Farewell to Arms*.
Farewell	s	In correspondence it suggests finality.
Fond regards	S	*Fond* once suggested doting, but now means affectionate, loving. It can imply mild romantic interest.
I have the...	S	*...honor to remain, Madam, Your Majesty's most humble and obedient servant*. When addressing a monarch.

I remain, Sir…	s	…*your obedient servant*. Once widely used, now rare.
Kind regards	s	Often cool. But *Kindest regards* (S) is meant to be warm.
Lots of love	c	From women. Less intimate than *Love*, it is an example of a phrop – a phrase which means the opposite of what it says. Sometimes abbreviated by LOL.
Love	s	Apart from romantic contexts, indiscriminate use can have camp associations.
Luv	C	Tries to deflate the meaning by a parody of spelling.
Regards	~	Literally affection and good wishes. Cool if unqualified.
See you later	c	This and its derivatives (*See you soon*) are part of the letter proper, not closings. *See you later, alligator* (~), on the other hand, is a closing, and invites the response *In a while, crocodile*.
Take care	C	From women or metrosexuals; less grating when spoken rather than written.
TTYL, TTFN	C, S	Initialisms for *Talk to you later* (text-message speak) and *Ta ta for now* (twee). TTFN was popularized in the 1940s and was later adopted by the animated Tigger.
Warm regards	s	Hearty. Used both with friends and acquaintances.
Yours	c	*I am* or *I remain* is implied. Informal, if somewhat cool.
Yours affectionately	s	Sometimes used between family members or friends. Attributed to the writer John Gay (1685–1732).
Yours aye	s	*Aye* means always, ever. Used in the British military and by Scots between close acquaints.
Yours cordially	C	Meant to be between *Yours sincerely* and *Yours affectionately*, but self-conscious and pretentious.
Yours ever	S	Between friends. The variation *As ever*, short for *Yours as ever*, suggests frequent correspondence.
Yours faithfully	s	The correct closing when a letter begins *Dear Sir*.
Yours in Christ	s	Apart from use by clerics, can be awkward. *Yours in Jesus* (c) suggests a Protestant sender.
Yours in haste	s	A handy construction for short notes. Note the change of adverbial clause from the usual *with…* to *in…*
Yours respectfully	s	To Catholic clergy. In letters to the pope, brother bishops close with *Yours devotedly in Christ*.
Yours sincerely	~	*Sincerely* means honestly, without pretense. The correct closing when a letter begins *Dear Mr. Simpson*. Frequently written *Sincerely yours*.
Yours truly	c	Faintly earnest version of *Yours sincerely*.
–	~	No closing. Many people sign emails with only their name, and text messages with only their initial.

DRESS

Lord Chesterfield · Take great care always to be dressed like the reasonable people of your own age, in the place where you are, whose dress is never spoken of one way or another, as either too negligent or too much studied. (*Lord Chesterfield's Letters*, 1776)

P. G. Wodehouse · [Jeeves lugged my purple socks] out of the drawer as if he were a vegetarian fishing a caterpillar out of the salad. (*Death at the Excelsior*, 1914)

Hardy Amies · A man should look as if he had bought his clothes with intelligence, put them on with care, and then forgotten all about them. (*ABC of Men's Fashion*, 1964)

Umberto Angeloni · The most challenging part to dressing well is knowing how to be elegant while being casual.

George Meredith · Cynicism is intellectual dandyism.

F. Scott Fitzgerald · Can't repeat the past? Why, of course you can! (*The Great Gatsby*, 1925)

August von Kotzebue · Everything a man of fashion puts on his body must be broken in, nothing should appear new. (1804)

Beau Brummell · If John Bull turns round to look after you, you are not well dressed, but either too stiff, too tight, or too fashionable.

Alfred, Lord Tennyson · What profits now to understand / The merits of a spotless shirt – / A dapper boot – a little hand – / If half the little soul is dirt? (*Punch*, 1846)

August Luchet · Last briefly and change often, appear rather than be – that is what suffices. (*L'Art Industriel à l'Exposition Universelle de 1867*)

Paris Hilton · The only rule is don't be boring and dress cute wherever you go.

❦21 SHOES

There is a well-known saying that the best way to tell whether a man is well dressed is to look down. Hardy Amies, recent dressmaker to Queen Elizabeth II, concurs: "It is totally impossible to be well dressed in cheap shoes. To buy the best you can afford, to go for what you really can't afford, is not extravagance. But to fail to look after shoes is profligacy." Looking after shoes requires a modest amount of effort: regular polishing (p 54) and the use of shoe trees are key. The shoes' life will be much extended if you can avoid wearing the same pair two days in a row.

A short word on which shoes should be worn with what. The rule is simple: black shoes with black, blue, and gray trousers; brown shoes (including penny loafers) with anything but black trousers. All other colored shoes are of questionable taste, apart from tennis shoes and white canvas. Disregard the dictum that brown shoes should not be worn with a blue suit. Many of the best-dressed men, especially Italians, have always worn brown brogues or suede toecaps with their navy suits. Of more concern is the wearing of black shoes with casual clothes, such as jeans, chinos, and cords. Apart from black loafers, this won't do. Wear brown shoes instead.

21.1 SHOE SIZE

Shoe size is one of the least standardized of all measurements, largely because, for a given size, the length of the foot and the length of the last are not the same. The last is the shape that a shoe is made around, and it is slightly bigger than the foot so that there is room to move. The most common units of shoe size are the barleycorn (⅓ inch) and the Paris point (⅔ cm). In the US, shoe size is equal to the length of the last in barleycorns minus the constant 24.75. The same applies to the UK, except that the constant is 25.25. In Europe, shoe size is the length of the last in Paris points. Thus the equivalence between US and UK sizes and EU sizes is only approximate.

last (inches)	US size	UK size	EU size	last (cm)	last (inches)	US size	UK size	EU size	last (cm)
10.25	6	5½	39	26.0	11.58	10	9½	44	29.3
10.42	6½	6	40	26.7	11.75	10½	10	45	30.0
10.58	7	6½	40	26.7	11.92	11	10½	45	30.0
10.75	7½	7	41	27.3	12.08	11½	11	46	30.7
10.92	8	7½	42	28.0	12.25	12	11½	47	31.3
11.08	8½	8	42	28.0	12.42	12½	12	47	31.3
11.25	9	8½	43	28.7	12.58	13	12½	48	32.0
11.42	9½	9	44	29.3	12.75	13½	13	49	32.7

21.2 SHOELACES

There are many different ways of lacing a shoe, and the number of ways grows quickly with the number of eyelets. According to a mathematical study by B. Polster ("What is the best way to lace your shoes?," *Nature,* **420,** 476 (2002)), for two pairs of eyelets, there are three ways of lacing; for four pairs, 1,080 ways; for the six pairs shown below, 43,200 ways.

Below are some of the more interesting shoe-lacing methods. According to Polster, the crisscross and shoe shop lacings are the strongest possible, and the bow tie is the shortest – useful when the laces are too short. The bow tie and straight European lacings show only crosses and horizontal lines, respectively, whereas the Roman lacing shows an alternating series of lines and crosses (l's and x's, hence the name). All three are particularly suitable for dress shoes. The lattice, double back, and double cross lacings exhibit a woven pattern and, apart from being decorative, are useful for taking up long laces. For more lacing possibilities, see www.fieggen.com/shoelace.

As for the actual tying of shoes, the reef bow (Knots, p 88) is the standard method, although many men mistakenly use the granny bow instead.

21.3 EIGHT WAYS TO LACE YOUR SHOES

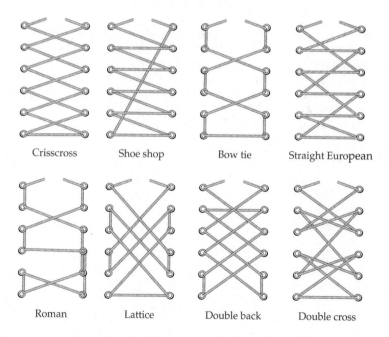

| Crisscross | Shoe shop | Bow tie | Straight European |

| Roman | Lattice | Double back | Double cross |

❦22 POLISHING SHOES

There are three domestic arts a man should know: how to iron a shirt (p 59); how to carve a roast (p 162); and how to polish shoes. All other chores can in principle be delegated, but these will prove necessary at some point in a man's life. Polishing shoes, which involves a certain craftsmanship, is the most satisfying of them all, and for many men is as much a source of relaxation as of industry. Here is a guide to the theory and practice of polishing.

22.1 PATINA

You cannot have well-polished shoes without understanding the concept of patina. The word often refers to the surface coloring and texture of a piece of furniture that comes from polish and day-to-day use over a long time. In shoes patina is the complex patchwork of colors, tones, creases, and imperfections that results from a combination of frequent polishing and wear over a long period. An attractive patina is the ultimate goal of looking after shoes. Well-made shoes may fit better and last longer, but without a handsome patina they will not look remarkable.

Brown shoes – and this includes all shades of tan and cordovan – should be polished in a color just lighter than the shoe itself; the leather will naturally darken with age. The trick is to polish lightly but often, emphasizing those areas which receive the most wear: the toe and creases along the side. The toe is sometimes given polish a shade darker than the rest of the shoe.

With black shoes, it is not patina but gloss that should be emphasized. Having no color of their own, black shoes should reflect light and therefore be highly polished. Black toecap shoes are sometimes polished to a moderate shine, with the toecaps themselves polished to a spit shine (p 56).

22.2 BRUSHES

Two types of brushes are necessary to polish shoes. The first is used to apply the polish; the second is used to bring it to a shine once it has dried.

On-brush · This typically has a handle with a small patch of horsehair bristles at the end of it. You will need two: one for applying dark polish and one for light. Some men prefer to use an old cloth instead of a brush. A cloth applies polish more evenly and is disposable, whereas a brush is quicker and reaches into crevices but must be cleaned after use with soap and water.

Off-brush · This is used to give luster to the dried polish and should be a separate, larger brush made of horsehair. In a pinch a cloth could be used.

22.3 POLISHES

Wax polish · This is the most commonly used type of polish. Until the 20th century, the recipe for shoe polish was not standardized, with as many homemade concoctions as proprietary brands. In 1906 Australians Ramsay and McKellan introduced their black boot polish, called Kiwi. The first successful polish for brown shoes – dark tan – followed in 1908. Kiwi is now the most popular brand of polish, commonly available in 12 varieties:

black	cordovan	mahogany	white
blue	dark tan	mid tan	parade gloss black
brown	light tan	neutral	parade gloss brown

However, only a handful of colors are necessary: black, brown, various shades of tan (light, mid, and dark), and cordovan, a burgundy-brown color for penny loafers. Dark tan, also called military tan, is a reddish-brown color, similar to mahogany. Neutral is sometimes used on light-colored leathers.

Cream · Unlike shoe polish, shoe cream does not contain wax and cannot be brought to a shine, instead leaving an opaque, dull finish. It is particularly detrimental to maintaining a patina and should be avoided at all times.

Leather conditioner · This is a mild conditioner which keeps leather soft, imparting no color or gloss. It can be used on all types of smooth leather.

Saddle soap · Used to clean and nourish natural-colored leather, this mild dressing contains neat's-foot oil, an oil made from the boiled feet of cattle.

22.4 STANDARD SHINE

Smooth leather shoes should be polished with a wax-based polish. The standard method of polishing shoes is concisely described on the back of the Kiwi tin: "Apply polish with a cloth or brush. Let dry for one to two minutes, then brush to a bright shine. For heightened gloss, apply another light coat, sprinkle with water and buff with a soft cloth." Depending on how much polish was applied, it may take longer than a couple of minutes for the polish to dry, but generally not more than ten. The gloss can be enhanced by a final buff with a nylon stocking.

How often should shoes be polished? Roughly once every week of wear, which means every seven times the shoes are worn. Bear in mind that frequent polishing means faster polishing, because the leather will have dried out less and have fewer nicks and therefore take less polish.

22.5 SPIT SHINE

A more laborious method of polishing shoes, known as a spit shine or bulling, is used to obtain the mirror-like finish especially prized on black shoes. Bulling is the repeated application of thin layers of polish to create an extremely smooth, glossy surface. Bulling is popular in the military, where it has been honed to a science. It is labor intensive: the first time will take about two hours per shoe; subsequent bulls are faster. So it is best to pour yourself a drink or invite a friend to join you while you polish.

To understand how bulling works, it helps to understand what it means for something to shine. Dried shoe polish reflects a fixed amount of light whether it is polished or not; what varies is whether the light is reflected in all directions (diffuse reflection) or in one direction (specular reflection). The smoother a surface is, the more it exhibits specular reflection. So to make shoes shiny, you need to make them as smooth as possible, by filling in the grain of the leather and the nicks and scratches that come with wear.

The most efficient way to bull is to begin with normal applications of polish, and to reduce the amount slowly until you are adding only a smudge at a time. The idea is analogous to sanding wood, moving from coarse sandpaper to fine, except in polishing the indentations are filled, rather than the bumps removed. Start by giving your shoes a few ordinary shines in succession. Then fill the top half of the polish tin with water and wrap a cloth around your middle three fingers, secured with a rubber band if desired. Dip the cloth into the water so that it is damp but not wet. Take a substantial amount of polish, and rub it vig-orously but lightly into the entire shoe until it is no longer cloudy. Repeat the process, each time with a slightly smaller amount of polish, focusing on smaller patches of the shoe, until the leather begins to resemble a black mirror.

22.6 SUEDE

Suede is leather turned inside out, with the flesh side brushed or rubbed to show a nap. Suede is always brushed, never polished. Brushing and natural wear erode the material, revealing new layers of suede; this will continue until the leather itself is worn through. Without regular brushing, the surface will lose its nap and become smooth.

Suede is cleaned with a suede brush. It is usually made of plastic bristles, and is much firmer than the off-brush used in shining shoes. Alternatively, a scrubbing tool with rubber layers is sometimes used. A sort of pumice-filled eraser is used for cleaning trouble spots, such as the toe.

❦23 SHIRTS

The original function of the shirt was to protect the expensive and difficult-to-clean suit from the body. Hence the popularity of cotton – easily laundered and pleasant against the skin. Silk remains an indulgence, wool a mortification. Today a shirt is as likely to be worn without a suit as with one and to be short-sleeved as long. Different customs apply in each case.

23.1 SHORT-SLEEVED SHIRTS

T-shirts are the simplest style of shirts. Crew collars are preferable to V-necks, and tank tops should be strictly avoided. Some young men wear white T-shirts underneath dress shirts as a sign of status. The polo shirt, first popularized by Lacoste in the 1930s, is traditionally made of a relatively coarse, piqué cloth. It can be worn tucked in or out, but the collar should never be turned up, or "popped." Popularized in the early 1980s by *The Official Preppy Handbook*, today the popped collar looks effete. Of course, wearing any short-sleeved shirt with a suit is an act of sartorial terrorism, even if Ian Fleming always wore them thus (he found cuffs uncomfortable).

23.2 LONG-SLEEVED SHIRTS

With a suit
Worn with a suit, a shirt should contrast with the suit's dark cloth and therefore be light-colored – white, light blue, or pink, for example. Checks and stripes on a light background are popular. There should be no breast pocket, and embroidered initials, if present, should never be seen. Of particular importance are the collar and cuffs which, when worn under a jacket, become the shirt's most prominent parts. Cuffs should always "show," extending ¾ inch beyond the jacket sleeve. Double cuffs, also known as French cuffs, are worn with cuff links (Jewelry, p 81). They are more formal than button cuffs, but a confident man might wear them casually with a pair of jeans.

Without a suit
No suit usually means no tie, in which case the top placket buttons are invariably undone, exposing the top of the chest. One open button is safe; two suggests insouciance; three smacks of an Italian playboy. Rolling up your sleeves is acceptable with both button and double-cuffed shirts alike. There is a recent trend towards shirts fitted through the torso – not as tight as those worn in the 1970s, but enough to emphasize the male form. Nothing wrong with that. More casual fabrics, stronger colors, and bold checks and tartans are all on display alongside the more civilized colors of dress shirts.

23.3 NUMBER OF SHIRTS

Here is a rule of thumb for what to pack when traveling. The minimum number of shirts and trousers to bring on a trip (in addition to the clothes on your back) is the square root and cube root, respectively, of the number of days:

$$\text{shirts} = \sqrt{\text{days}} \quad \text{and} \quad \text{trousers} = \sqrt[3]{\text{days}}.$$

This means that, for 1, 2, 3, 4,..., 365 days, you should pack 1, 1, 2, 2,..., 19 shirts and 1, 1, 1, 2,..., 7 pairs of trousers. Combining the two rules, the relationship between the number of shirts and trousers in your possession is:

$$\text{shirts}^2 = \text{trousers}^3.$$

For example, a man with 3 pairs of trousers should have approximately 5 shirts; with 6 pairs of trousers, 15 shirts; with 9 pairs of trousers, 27 shirts.

23.4 ESSENTIAL SHIRTS

According to the first rule above, a man needs a minimum of 19 shirts over a period of 365 days. Here is a list of the most essential 19 dress shirts:

Ordinary	W	broadcloth	a plain white shirt is the most essential
	W	twill	a heavier, ribbed diagonal weave
	B	broadcloth	the most formal of blue shirts
	B	end-on-end	woven from blue and white threads
	B or P	twill	best if weft & warp are blue & white or pink & white
	BW	stripe	pin, pencil, or butcher stripes
	BW	fine check	one of the most versatile of shirts
	BW	coarse check	gingham or windowpane checks
	PW	fine check	gone are the days when pink meant wink
Formal	W	marcella	with turn-down collar, for dinner jacket
	W	marcella	with detachable wing collar, for tail coat
	BW	fine check	with white turn-down collar, for morning suit
	W	silk	plain off-white, like James Bond's
Informal	W	oxford	a long-lasting, heavy, informal weave
	B or P	oxford	best worn with jeans or khakis
	B	chambray	a coarse, uneven weave for the country
	W	linen	an essential shirt for summer and the tropics
	B	linen	worn with cotton trousers or a linen suit
	any	check	muted checks on white ground, for tweeds

KEY   W = white   B = light blue   P = pink   BW = B and W   PW = P and W

23.5 IRONING A SHIRT

Ironing well is less about doing it correctly – many methods give the same result – than about doing it quickly and sufficiently. The first thing to remember is that different fibers burn at different temperatures. The standard recommended ironing temperatures, listed on most irons, are as follows:

230 °F	110 °C	acetate, acrylic, modacrylic, nylon, spandex
302 °F	150 °C	polyester, rayon, silk, triacetate, wool
392 °F	200 °C	cotton, linen

Directions

With practice, a shirt can be ironed in five minutes. If the iron doesn't steam, a spray bottle can be used to keep the shirt damp, but this takes longer. Note that dark fabrics should be ironed on the wrong side to avoid a shine.

Collar (25 sec.) · Keep the collar flat – there is no need to iron in a crease where it turns down. Iron the underside first, then the outside. Move from the collar tips to the center to prevent creasing at the edges.

Cuffs (45 sec.) · Iron the non-showing side first, then the showing side, being sure to iron from the edges inwards. Double or French cuffs should be ironed flat – again there is no need to iron in a crease.

Yoke (25 sec.) · This part of the shirt covers the shoulders, and is the trickiest part to get to. Use the narrow end of the ironing board.

Sleeves (90 sec.) · Start from the shoulder and finish near the cuff, ironing in the gauntlet pleats leading into it. Most sleeves are creased, but there is no consensus as to whether they should be. (Creases are avoided with the aid of a specialized narrow board inserted into the sleeve.)

Back (45 sec.) · This large but uninterrupted piece of cloth is one of the fastest to iron. Since the bottom half will be tucked in, it need not be done.

Front (70 sec.) · Again, disregard the bottom half. Ironing around the buttons need not be perfect since, done up, the inside placket will not show.

Hasty directions

If time is short and a sweater or jacket is to be worn, the time can be reduced to two minutes by ironing the collar, cuffs, and front only.

A stiff shirt is worn with white tie (p 70) and, by some, a tuxedo (p 68). The stiffness comes from starch, which is usually applied by a dry-cleaner. In a pinch it can be done at home by repeated applications of spray starch, after each of which the shirt is ironed on the wrong side to avoid yellowing. Only the front, collar, and cuffs are starched. DIY starching of detachable collars is hopeless and they should always be done professionally.

❦24 JEANS

Although the origin of denim work clothes is disputed, it was during the second half of the 19th century that they became widespread. The invention of jeans arguably came with the introduction of copper reinforcing rivets by Jacob Davis and Levi Strauss in 1873. It was not until the 1950s, however, that jeans were in any sense fashionable and worn outside their manual-labor context. Wearing jeans was a minor act of rebellion, a supposed association with the proletariat.

Jeans today are so ingrained in popular culture that it is difficult to view their symbolism objectively. The old motivation – association with Everyman – remains partially true. Today part of their attraction is that jeans attenuate the formality of the overall costume, thereby allowing you to dress smartly with impunity. Andy Warhol was not the first man to combine jeans with a suit jacket and tie, but he made the juxtaposition popular. Today a blazer with a worn pair of jeans does not draw attention. It suggests spontaneity – not for the first time we see the desire for studied indifference.

24.1 DEFINITION

Along with the other quintessentially male garment, the suit, jeans are the most common element of Western men's dress. Everyone knows about jeans, but few understand them. A fair definition is close-fitting, blue denim trousers, which we consider in detail.

Close-fitting · Despite the short-lived popularity of bagginess in the 1990s, jeans are fundamentally close-fitting. A slim fit is inherent in their design: jeans do not have pleats below the waistband; they grip the hips rather than suspend from the natural waist; the generous vertical pockets found on suit trousers are replaced with horizontal ones; jeans conform rather than drape, and for this reason need not be ironed. The narrow cut emphasizes a man's breadth of chest and muscularity. "The tightness of fit, the showing of a good leg, fitted in with the Edwardian look of the modern dandy and the humbler Teddy Boy. The shape of course affected that of all trousers which were belted low over the hips," writes Hardy Amies.

Blue · The vast majority of jeans are blue jeans. Black and white jeans resurface once a decade or so, but in such small numbers as to be negligible. It is perhaps not coincidental that blue is the dominant color of the suit. In jeans the blue is made from indigo, a natural dye derived from plants in the genus *Indigofera*, or a synthetic equivalent. The exposed thread (weft) is dyed blue and the perpendicular, covered thread (warp) is left white, a telltale sign of which is the diagonal stripe pattern on the reverse. It is a common misconception that the fading of jeans results from the dark weft being worn through, exposing the white warp, which happens only with extreme wear.

Fading is in fact the result of the poor adhesive properties of indigo dye. Tiny fragments of indigo are embedded in, rather than bonded to, the cotton fibers. Friction results in the loss of dye fragments, hence the particular fading properties of denim with washing and wearing.

Denim • The cloth itself is a kind of heavy cotton twill with a pronounced diagonal rib. Denim is a contraction of *serge de Nîmes*: Nîmes is a southern French city; and serge is a kind of weave with diagonal ribs, now used more to describe wool cloths (James Bond liked his suits made from blue serge, p 179). The cloth is known to shrink, usually about 3% over the first couple of years, which is about an inch for a 34-inch inseam. Denim shrinks further when dried at high temperature, although this is reversible by washing. For this reason jeans should be hung up to dry rather than dried in a dryer.

24.2 STYLE

Unlike with most clothes, with jeans the appearance of age through fading and wear is not only accepted but encouraged. This is not new: Jules Barbey d'Aurevilly, writing in 1844, describes English swells who distressed the surface of their newly made clothes with glass-paper: "They were at the end of their impertinence, they just couldn't go any further… They had their clothes distressed before they put them on, all over the cloth…" Today this worn look is more often ready-made, with jeans sold in various states of decline. Just how much wear is acceptable varies from year to year. The recent look of extreme distress, frayed edges and faded seat and legs, has been replaced by more moderately worn cloth in uniform shades. The most flattering cut of jeans is straight-leg, with boot cut (though not flares) an acceptable and sometimes practical alternative. In either case, it is essential that jeans are worn slightly longer than your usual trousers.

24.3 BRANDS

The oldest jeans companies, Levi's, Lee, and Wrangler, continue to be the most successful, though only Levi's are much seen in urban settings. Their straight-leg, undecorated jeans are perhaps the only branded article of clothing that is truly egalitarian. The most dramatic shift in how denim is worn has, of course, been the meteoric rise in popularity of high-end jeans like Diesel, True Religion, and 7 For All Mankind. Designers are giving unprecedented attention to fit and details, while firmly maintaining the proletarian, utilitarian look. Importantly, the brand itself takes second place to cut, cloth, and detailing, which discourages analogies with the designer-jeans fad 25 years earlier. The situation is more reminiscent of traditional men's tailoring, which relies on sober detailing and above all else fit; it too puts limited stock in labels. Will bespoke jeans be widely available soon?

❦ 25 SUITS

As fashion goes, men's dress is not complicated. Like architecture and typography, it is a mixture of a lot of system and a little trend. It contains a hi-
erarchy of formality, each level evolving at a pace in inverse proportion to
its sobriety. Casual clothes – those seen on the streets of New York, London,
Berlin, and Tokyo – evolve most quickly, with currents visibly shifting from
year to year. The turnover for jackets is longer – velvet jackets are now mainstream, and more two-button jackets are being made. Suits change more
slowly yet, and on the time scale of a decade motion only in the details is
detectable: shoulders, vents, buttoning. Least volatile of all are formal
clothes, like the tuxedo and morning suit. They *do* evolve, but very slowly.

25.1 DESCRIPTION

The suit is foremost a masculine garment, both in its simplicity of decoration and emphasis of the male form. Its matching fabric in muted colors forms the backdrop against which the color and finery of women's
clothes are displayed. The V shape rising from the tapered trousers to the
jacket's broad, padded shoulders sets man distinctly apart from woman.

Jacket

The suit jacket comes in two varieties: single-breasted and double-breasted.
Single-breasted jackets have notched lapels (opposite) and usually two,
three, or four buttons. Three buttons is classic, four showbiz, and two making a comeback after being out of favor. Only the middle, middle two, and
top buttons, respectively, are done up, these being level with the natural waist
and the jackets' narrowest points. Double-breasted jackets have peaked
lapels and the jacket fronts overlap (opposite), with only the top working
buttons done up. The number of vents is largely a matter of taste, although
single-breasted jackets tend to have none or one; double, none or two.

Trousers

There is less scope for variation in trousers. Cuffs, also called turn-ups,
while perfectly acceptable are presently not *la mode*. If present, they are 1½
inches deep. Belts, appropriate with separate jacket and trousers, interrupt
the matching fabric of the suit; in their place, side fasteners or suspenders
are preferable. Vertical front pockets and one back pocket are correct.

Vest

Vests, when worn, are made of the same fabric as the suit, except with morning coats (p 66). Like the single-breasted jacket, a vest (or waistcoat) should
have notched lapels. By tradition, the lowest vest button is not fastened.

25.2 ANATOMY OF A GOOD SUIT

This image, after a painting by the *Esquire* fashion illustrator known as "L. Fellows," shows fine examples of both double- and single-breasted jackets. Note in both cases the fit: well-fitting shoulders, high armholes, narrow sleeves, jackets slightly tapered at the waist, well-cut trousers. The younger man's jacket shows his shirt cuffs. Notice also the simplicity of the shirts, ties, and accessories. One man wears an American regimental tie (English stripes run the other way), the other a houndstooth tie. Both are tied in four-in-hand knots. See how the handkerchief is casually arranged.

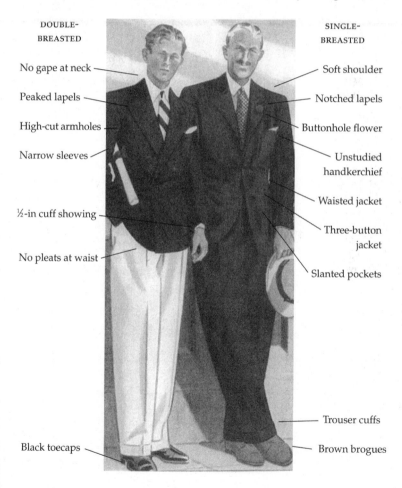

DOUBLE-BREASTED

No gape at neck

Peaked lapels

High-cut armholes

Narrow sleeves

½-in cuff showing

No pleats at waist

Black toecaps

SINGLE-BREASTED

Soft shoulder

Notched lapels

Buttonhole flower

Unstudied handkerchief

Waisted jacket

Three-button jacket

Slanted pockets

Trouser cuffs

Brown brogues

25.3 BUYING A SUIT

What to look for

A suit is built up out of minor variations on inherited wisdom. Small deviations speak loudly. "Never in your dress altogether desert that taste which is general," advises Edward Bulwer-Lytton in *Pelham*. "The world considers eccentricity in great things genius, in small things folly." Your first couple of suits should be dark blue or dark gray. Black suits, apart from formal clothes, clothes for the clergy, and clothes for funerals (and even here navy is perfectly correct), look cheap. First learn to wear with ease a plain navy suit, white shirt, and solid navy tie, which is not as easy as it sounds. Once you have developed an eye for the basics, you can turn to other cloths – chalk stripes, checks, Prince of Wales, tweeds, corduroy, even velvet.

Price does not guarantee that a suit will look good, and indeed the most expensive suits, selected without a practiced eye, are often unattractive and ill-fitting. A number of details signify a well-made suit: pocket flaps; sewn rather than fused canvas lining; a button as opposed to zip fly; side adjusters instead of belt loops; working cuff buttons; matching lining inside the pocket flaps and jacket; a thread behind the lapel buttonhole to hold stems.

Fit

The single most important aspect of a good suit is fit. Always begin with the shoulders. Here the suit should be close-fitting, with little space for the cloth to indent against the arms. The collar must not gape at the back. The armholes should be high and the sleeves narrow. The jacket should be just long enough to cover the seat entirely. It should be slightly waisted: tapered at the waist to give a faint hourglass shape. A close-fitting garment around the legs has always been important in defining the masculine form, first in the form of hose, then breeches, then trousers. Accordingly, trousers should be narrow through the seat and thigh and have one or no front pleats, not two.

Secondhand clothes

The good news for men is that hand-me-down and secondhand jackets, suits, and evening clothes are as desirable now as when they were made. They are often finer and better-looking than clothes bought ready-made today, partly because many of the garments were bespoke (opposite) and hand-stitched, partly because in previous years more attention was given to fit. It is well worth tracking down shops that specialize in good secondhand clothes for men. Frequently stocked are retro items such as high-fastening pinstripe suits, forties and fifties print ties, and authentic velvet jackets from the seventies. A simple alteration can solve many problems, but it is wise to have the clothes altered by an alterations tailor rather than on the premises.

25.4 HAVING A SUIT MADE

Two kinds of tailoring

While most men's suits are ready-made, having a suit made brings with it the possibility of improved fit and the choice of cloth, lining, vents, pockets, and button placement. There are two kinds of tailoring: made-to-measure and bespoke. A made-to-measure suit costs one and a half times the price of a ready-made suit. The suit is made to a fixed pattern but adapted to your basic measurements: chest, waist, arms, legs, and back. These details are sent away for the cloth to be cut by machine and made into a suit. When the finished product is returned, only minor further changes can be made, like waist size or trouser length. A bespoke suit, on the other hand, is stagewise assembled on site over the course of a number of fittings (and costs twice as much as made-to-measure). Attention to detail is paramount, and much effort will be made to ensure a perfect fit. Few men are constructed in the image of Ideal Man (p 4), and the tailor will ruthlessly spot and adjust for any human defects, such as one arm being longer than the other; one shoulder being higher; a beer belly; or a hunched posture.

Some advice

Bear in mind that a tailor is only as demanding as his client, so it is important to be a stickler for details. When having clothes made, you learn by mistakes, and your first suit will not be your favorite. It is wise to begin with an inexpensive tailor and advance from there. Two telltale signs that a suit has been tailored is the absence of a brand label inside the jacket and the choice of lining, which is customarily bolder than that found on ready-made suits. Burgundy is the most traditional color. Also smart are crimson, salmon pink, and orange, with blue suits; and bottle green, navy, and ivory, with gray suits. Light and royal blue linings tend to conflict with blue shirts.

25.5 HISTORY

It is worth remembering that the worldwide uniformity of men's dress, taken for granted today, did not come into being of its own accord. The Western civilized world – and much of the Eastern – has adopted English national dress. In 1649, King Charles I was executed and with him went doublet and hose. The history of the suit – in its earliest form a knee-length coat, waistcoat, and breeches – begins with the English Restoration under King Charles II. Unlike in France, where the aristocracy was concentrated at court, the English nobility was scattered about the countryside. Sport played a decisive role in shaping English fashion, and by the late 18th century the frock coat was cut away for horse riding. A hundred years later the tails were removed altogether and the suit in its modern form appeared.

❦26 CLOTHES FOR WEDDINGS

Here we must turn to our sartorial next of kin, the English, for authority. Despite the American habit of wearing tuxedos (described on p 68) to daytime weddings, the correct dress is a morning suit or, barring that, a suit. Black and white tie are correctly worn in the evening only, usually taken to start at six o'clock. Even in America this is observed at traditional weddings: John F. Kennedy wore a morning suit when he got married, as did Arnold Schwarzenegger.

A morning suit is the most formal of daytime clothes, mostly worn at weddings but also at formal garden parties. The only alternative is an ordinary suit. We have discussed the suit on p 62; here we focus on morning dress and its furnishings. But if you do wear a suit to a wedding, make sure it is of the plainest variety, which means dark blue or dark gray. Wear a shirt with double cuffs and, if you can, a detachable stiff turn-down collar.

26.1 JACKET AND TROUSERS

The morning coat has tails, of course, but it is not shaped like a tailcoat. It is closer to a frock coat with the corners cut away, with continuous curves from lapels to tail; hence a morning coat is sometimes called a cutaway. Morning coats come in two colors: gray, worn with matching gray trousers; or black, usually in a herringbone weave, worn with black-and-gray-striped or, less often, black-and-white houndstooth trousers. A black coat is the smarter of the two, reminding us of the Regency coat and breeches from which it descends. These did not match either, the coat being dark and the trousers light. Unlike a tailcoat, the lapels do not have silk facings. The trousers should be worn with suspenders and have plain hems (no cuffs).

26.2 SHIRT AND VEST

A white shirt, dove-gray vest, and black-and-white tie are correct, if uninspired. Much more handsome is the incorporation of color, which also helps dispel the rented look. Solid, checked, and striped shirts are suitable in any light color, although light blue is a wise starting point. The collar, however, should be white, preferably stiff. A stiff turn-down collar is attached by studs, and weaving a necktie through it is not easy. A colored shirt calls for a colored vest, in buff (a light brownish yellow) or cream or pale blue or even pink, preferably made of linen. The vest should have lapels, but whether it is single- or double-breasted is purely a matter of taste; since the wedding of Charles, Prince of Wales, and Camilla Parker Bowles, double-breasted has been somewhat more fashionable. Both the shirt and the vest are closed with the usual buttons rather than studs.

26.3 TIE OR CRAVAT

A colored shirt or vest means that you can choose your tie more liberally, in navy or burgundy, for example, rather than in black and white. It should be in heavy silk and, if not plain, woven rather than printed. The tie can be fixed to the shirt with a tie tack (p 82). It is acceptable to wear a cravat (p 77) instead of a necktie, tied in an overhand knot and pinned in place with a stick pin. Nevertheless a tie is the less studied and smarter of the two. It forms a link between the morning coat and the modern suit, without which a morning suit risks looking like costume dress. A man should feel as much at ease in formal clothes as in any others, but he needs reference points.

26.4 TOP HAT

Though not essential, a top hat is often worn or carried. In *The Englishman's Suit* (Books, p 195), Hardy Amies advises how to wear one confidently:

> Wear the hat high on your head like a crown and not low down on your ears like a candle-snuffer. If you are hiring a "topper," see that you tilt it well over your nose and never to the back of your head. It should look too small rather than too big… Squat crowns [make] you look, if you are not careful, like a doorman at a provincial hotel in Holland. The smartest top hat is indubitably that made of black silk. It is, of course, difficult to maintain with its surface unruffled. It is, I think, correct to wear it all the year round, whereas a grey topper looks silly in winter.

26.5 ET CETERA

Shoes should be well-polished black toecaps. As with white tie (p 70), a pocket watch can be worn. If ever there was a time to wear a buttonhole, this is it. But make sure it is a single flower, and not a miniature floral arrangement sometimes seen in American *boutonnières*.

Disregard the dictum that the principal male members of the wedding party should dress alike, probably inspired by the for-hire companies which rent to them. Indeed the opposite is true: exercising the limited freedoms in morning dress is one of the principal pleasures in wearing it. At the smartest weddings, there is a broad mix of pastel shirts and vests, and no two ties are identical.

If buying a new morning suit is prohibitively expensive, fine old ones can be bought second-hand for little more than the cost of renting. The trick is finding a store that sells them. But if you do rent, go for the simplest design, try to get a buff vest, and wear your own colored shirt and tie.

❦27 TUXEDO

Men's formal clothes invariably have their roots in sporting and military costume, first accepted as day wear and eventually as clothes for the evening. The tuxedo does not, as is often thought, derive from the evening tailcoat but from a short Victorian lounge jacket popular in the late 1800s. The short jacket was later worn as informal evening wear and in the 1920s made a fashionable alternative to the tailcoat by the Prince of Wales.

Today a tuxedo is worn in the evening when the occasion calls for clothes more formal than a suit. A tuxedo is also known as black tie, a dinner jacket, or "dress for dinner" – the last only found on invitations, usually British.

27.1 JACKET

Tuxedo jackets come in three varieties: single-breasted, with peaked lapels; single-breasted, with a round shawl collar; and double-breasted, which is always peaked. Unlike a black suit, a tuxedo never has notched lapels, which is an immediate sign of a cheaply made garment. The silk facings of the lapels and collar are one of two types: satin – a smooth, glossy weave; or grosgrain – a matte silk weave with pronounced ribs. Both are permissible on all three jacket styles, although the shawl collar tends to show satin facings and the double-breasted tends to show grosgrain. Tuxedos are black, of course, but also sometimes midnight blue, which under artificial light appears blacker than black; true black by comparison can have a greenish tinge. A white tuxedo should not be worn, not in the summer, not by the sea.

27.2 TROUSERS

Trousers are cut in the same material as the jacket with a silk braid running down the outside leg. They should be slim-fitting, straight-legged, and have one or no pleats running from the waistband. Being formal, the trousers should not have cuffs, and the hem should be slightly longer in the back than the front, reaching the heel of the shoe. Suspenders are normally worn; in their absence, there should be side fasteners. Belts, which are relatively informal, are off limits, and thus the trousers should not have belt loops.

27.3 CUMMERBUND OR VEST

Formal clothes require that the place where the trousers and the shirt meet be covered. A double-breasted jacket, of course, looks after this itself. In the case of a single-breasted jacket, it is the job of a cummerbund or vest. A cummerbund, originally an Indian sash (*kamar-band*), is a pleated silk band worn around the waist. The pleats by convention face up, supposedly to catch crumbs or to hold theater tickets; both explanations are likely apocryphal. A vest is equally correct, if slightly more formal, and ideally comes with a deep opening which displays a large expanse of shirt. The cummerbund or vest should be plain and black; colored or patterned varieties are questionable at the high school prom, a solecism elsewhere.

27.4 SHIRTS

Tuxedos are worn with a white marcella (piqué) shirt or, in a pinch, plain white broadcloth. Pleated shirts, while sometimes worn, have an aged look; ruffles suggest a costume party. The unstarched shirt collar should turn down, although there remains an interest in the once popular and correct stiff wing collars. Shirt studs and cuff links are worn, usually in black, silver, and gold. The cuff links should have faces on both sides, not one.

27.5 BOW TIE

The bow tie comes today in three shapes (p 76). Its weave should reflect the silk facings of the jacket: satin if the lapels are satin and barathea (a textured basket weave) if the lapels are grosgrain. The bow should be tied by hand, not bought ready-made; for the clumsy there are ties that attach in the back which can be first tied around the leg in full view. As Hardy Amies notes in *The Englishman's Suit*, it must be undecorated and black:

> I now have to be severe with the young. You simply cannot wear a scarlet satin tie; it is overwhelmingly "naff." Nor may you wear any colored or any patterned tie. European invitations say firmly "black tie." Color blindness is not excused. And oldies must throw away that velvet butterfly tie. You can revive a passing fashion of 100 years; not one of ten.

27.6 ET CETERA

Shoes are of course black, with patent black lace-ups or well-polished black toecaps correct; black brogues, less so. Slip-ons (whether they bear a penny or a tassel or a snaffle) are in bad taste. Socks should be long enough to cover the calf, and may be black or colored. Pocket handkerchiefs are essential and should be silk; a colored one is ideal, but if you wear a white one, it should be off-white rather than bright white. Never wear a white silk scarf.

Few things are more ruined by poor fit than evening clothes. Secondhand (which is to say, old) tuxedos seem to fit best, probably because they were hand-made by skilled tailors. But beware of trousers made in the early- to mid-19th century, which tend to be wide and baggy – a sartorial crime.

❦28 WHITE TIE

Not often seen today, white tie is the most formal evening garment a man can wear. It is also known as a tailcoat or evening dress. The tailcoat descended from the double-breasted riding coat such that the two halves could never be fastened. Hence the two rows of buttons still seen today.

28.1 JACKET AND TROUSERS

Like the double-breasted dinner jacket, the tailcoat has peaked lapels, usually in grosgrain, a ribbed silk. The coat fronts should just cover the waistband of the trousers and the tails should reach the back of the knee. White-tie trousers differ from black-tie trousers in two respects. First, they are cut to be worn a couple of inches higher on the waist. This is because the white vest must cover the trousers' waistband without extending below the coat fronts worn over it. Second, by tradition, the trousers have two, not one, silk braid stripes running down the outside seam of each leg.

28.2 SHIRT, VEST, AND BOW TIE

The shirt is made of marcella or, less commonly, plain broadcloth and is starched stiff at the front and cuffs. A cleverly designed shirt has a loop which attaches to the fly of the trousers to keep the shirt from billowing. A stiff wing collar is essential, and this means it must be detachable – it is very hard to make an attached collar stiff. The collar should be at least 1¾ inches high, despite the preponderance of shorter specimens. Like the shirt, the vest is cut from white marcella and is worn stiff. It has a deep opening and closes only at the base, with studs. It may have a back, usually in satin, or attach behind with only an adjustable band. Cuff links and studs for the shirt and vest are traditionally gold or mother-of-pearl, with precious stones also seen. The marcella bow is tied like any other bow tie.

28.3 ET CETERA

Shoes are undecorated patent leather, either lace-ups or (less commonly) court pumps with a ribbed satin bow. Socks are now black and pocket handkerchiefs white or cream, although some color can be displayed by a man who knows the rules. It is not ostentatious to wear a pocket watch, the fob (chain) being attached to a purpose-made hole in the vest. The wristwatch is removed if a pocket watch is worn, and arguably even if one isn't. Decorations are worn if they are indicated on the invitation, as in "Evening dress – decorations." They are usually worn at occasions of state.

❦29 UNDERWEAR

There are three types of men's underwear. Briefs, also known as Y-fronts because of the inverted Y-shaped opening at the front, cover the groin and have elastic edges around the thighs; they are usually white. Boxer shorts, sometimes called boxers or shorts, are loose fitting and extend partially down the thigh. They are usually made of material similar to that used to make men's dress shirts. Boxer briefs, a more recent innovation, are a hybrid of the two – briefs with short snug legs attached. The history of all three is not long, as Hardy Amies explains in *The Englishman's Suit*:

> It is important to remember that all undergarments were used to protect the suit from contact with the body, not just the loins. Suits were objects of value and by the poor considered heirlooms to be handed down to the next generation. They were not washable and, of course, there was no dry-cleaning. So there were no "briefs" or shorts until well into the [20th] century. By the 1920s the modern lounge suit required the abandonment of "long johns" – certainly in the summer. Also of one piece underwear known as "combinations."

29.1 BOXERS VERSUS BRIEFS

A perennial men's question is whether boxers or briefs are best. From a fashion point of view, the biggest difference between them is that briefs are more revealing. Is this more attractive? Bear in mind that men's dress, unlike women's, has never sought to attract by exposing the flesh: shorts are not sexier than trousers. The interest in briefs seems, in part, to derive from a false analogy with women's underwear, where less is usually more.

The most common argument in favor of briefs is that they offer "support." However, it is not clear that this is what Nature intended. It is well known that men's testicles are designed to function at a lower temperature than the rest of the body. Do briefs interfere with temperature regulation by keeping the testicles in proximity with the groin? A scientific investigation into the question was conducted by R. Munkelwitz and B. R. Gilbert ("Are boxer shorts really better? A critical analysis of the role of underwear type in male subfertility," *The Journal of Urology*, **160**, 1337 (1998)). The authors find:

> Mean scrotal temperature plus or minus standard deviation was 33.8 +/− 0.8 °C and 33.6 +/− 1.1 °C in the boxer and brief group, respectively [body temperature is 37.0 °C]. There were no significant temperature differences between the groups. Differential temperatures comparing core to scrotal temperature and semen parameters also were not significantly different... It is unlikely that underwear type has a significant effect on male fertility.

❦30 TIES

Like most elements of Western men's dress, the knotted neckcloth has its origins in England, where the cravat replaced the ruff collar in the mid-17th century. The earliest record of the tie in its modern form is in the 1850s, where it was worn by young men as sporting attire. The style became fashionable at once, eclipsing the bow tie in popularity by the early 20th century.

Two essential ties

We will not talk about the color or pattern of ties here, apart from saying that two ties are essential in any man's wardrobe: a solid navy tie in woven silk; and a solid black tie in woven or knitted silk. An undecorated navy tie never goes amiss, whether it is worn with a pair of jeans, a blazer, or a morning suit. Plain black ties, despite their relatively recent exclusive association with funerals, have long been a favorite of James Bond and Italian men.

Tie size

The ideal width of a tie is 3–3½ inches, which is in natural proportion with the typical man's suit. While most ties available today are wider than this, the best tie makers, such as Hermès and many of the shops along London's Jermyn Street, have consistently produced ties of the ideal width. Once tied, the length should be such that the tip of the wide blade ends anywhere within 1 inch above or below the waistband. If the thin blade descends below the wide blade, there are a number of ways to fix it. One is to choose a bigger knot (p 74); another is to tuck the thin blade into the shirt between the second and third buttons down; a third is described in Label, opposite.

Tie handkerchief

If you can't make up your mind as to whether to wear a tie, you can keep the option open and put the tie in the breast pocket of your jacket, where it doubles as a handkerchief. This looks best with solid-colored ties, with the tie folded in half three times over, to one eighth of its original length.

Dimple

"When the fabric of the tie permits (if it is silk twill or a supple Jacquard silk, for example), a beautiful effect can be obtained by using the index finger to press a slight convex cavity into the tie just below the knot. The French call this little hollow a *cuillère*, which means spoon or scoop," explains François Chaille in *The Book of Ties*. This hollow is called a dimple in English, and it is best suited to wide and medium-width ties. But while one dimple is smart, two is very much an affectation.

Label

On the back of the wide blade a small horizontal band can be found, usually a label with the name of the maker or, on better-made ties, a band of the same material as the tie itself. While most men slip the thin blade through this band to secure it, it is arguably smarter to leave it free to flow. If the thin blade is too long after the tie is tied, one way of shortening it is to slip the excess through the label and pass the thin blade through it, as shown.

Storage

Tie experts are divided over the best way to store a tie. Some say that a tie should be rolled up in a coil when not in use, starting from the thin end. Others suggest simply hanging it from the middle over a hanger or bar. In either case a tie should never be left knotted when not in use, which tends to leave heavy creases in it. It is possible, of course, to tie a tie once and never untie it, but this comes at the expense of wearing the same knot, tied with the same execution, whatever the occasion, collar style, or mood.

Cleaning

It is often said that ties should never be dry-cleaned, but this is not quite true. It is not the cleaning but the inevitable pressing afterwards which most harms a tie, and the latter can be avoided if a cleaner is warned beforehand. Nonetheless a tie should not be cleaned unless it shows visible marks or stains. The death of a much-loved tie invariably results from the fraying of the wide blade's bottom edges, which usually happens long before any other part of the tie wears out. The solution is to have the tie shortened by half an inch, which many alterations tailors will do if asked. It is a somewhat delicate operation but, if done with care, it can double a tie's life.

No tie

Much has been said about the demise of the tie, and throughout the last hundred years its death has been repeatedly prophesied. It should be borne in mind, however, that knotted neckcloths have been standard attire for 350 years, and if the tie does vanish something knotted around the neck will almost certainly replace it. If you do decide to wear a suit without a tie, however, here are a few pointers. Always wear a dress shirt (a shirt with buttons all the way down the front); a suit with a T-shirt always looks faintly ridiculous. Keep the top one or two buttons of your shirt unbuttoned. If you take off your tie and jacket, think about rolling up your sleeves as well.

❦31 TIE KNOTS

In *The 85 Ways to Tie a Tie* (Books, p 195), Thomas Fink and Yong Mao proved that there are 85 different knots which can be tied with a conventional necktie. Of these, the 15 knots listed here are of particular interest. Instructions for the four most popular are included below. For further tie knot theory and instructions, see the author's homepage (Colophon, p 229).

Oriental	Nicky	Half-Windsor	Cavendish	Grantchester
Four-in-hand	Pratt	St. Andrew	Christensen	Hanover
Kelvin	Victoria	Plattsburgh	Windsor	Balthus

31.1 FOUR-IN-HAND

Number: 2   *Size*: 4 moves   *Sequence*: Li Ro Li Co T

The four-in-hand is today the most frequently worn tie knot of all. It was introduced simultaneously with the modern necktie in the 1850s. Tied in an ordinary silk tie, it is a small knot with a characteristic elongated, asymmetric shape. In thicker ties, the four-in-hand can look deceptively large (see the Windsor knot, right). "Four-in-hand" refers not only to the knot described here, but also to the modern necktie itself. There are a number of possible explanations of the name: drivers of the four-in-hand carriage tied their scarves with the knot; the reigns of the carriage were tied in the same way; it was worn by members of the now-defunct Four-in-Hand Club.

31.2 NICKY

Number: 4   *Size*: 5 moves   *Sequence*: Lo Ci Ro Li Co T

The Nicky is between the four-in-hand and half-Windsor in size and has a compact, symmetric shape. It is a natural choice for those seeking a symmetric knot of modest volume. Unlike the three other knots described here, the Nicky begins with the tie inside-out around the neck. The odd number of moves, however, ensures that the wide blade always emerges outside-out.

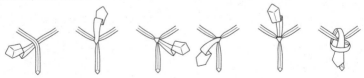

31.3 HALF-WINDSOR

Number: 7   *Size*: 6 moves   *Sequence*: Li Ro Ci Lo Ri Co T
This symmetrical knot is medium-sized and shaped like an equilateral triangle. Its origin remains mysterious. Although its name suggests that it was derived from the Windsor, there is little evidence for this. The half-Windsor is not half the size of the Windsor, but three-quarters (six moves versus eight), and the two sequences of moves seem unrelated. Like the Nicky, it is a versatile knot, and can be worn with collars of most sizes and spreads.

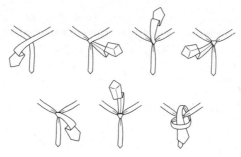

31.4 WINDSOR

Number: 31   *Size*: 8 moves   *Sequence*: Li Co Ri Lo Ci Ro Li Co T
The Windsor is a large, bulbous, triangular knot, sometimes erroneously referred to as a double-Windsor. In Ian Fleming's novels, James Bond (p 178) thinks the Windsor knot is "the mark of a cad." Today it is the knot of choice of (once) communist leaders and dictators: Hugo Chávez, Vladimir Putin, and the Chinese leaders Jiang Zemin and Hu Jintao are all fans (but so is Arnold Schwarzenegger). Despite the knot's name, it was not invented by Edward VIII, later the Duke of Windsor, as is commonly held. In *A Family Album*, the duke plainly explains that it was his specially made thick ties, rather than a complicated knot, that produced the effect.

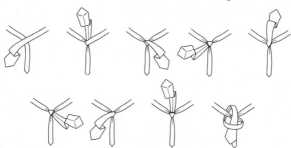

♥32 BOW TIES, ETC.

32.1 BOW TIE

Despite its longer lineage than the necktie, today the bow tie is worn almost exclusively with formal clothes. Some men persist in wearing a bow tie with a jacket or suit, but at a cost: against the backdrop of modern men's dress, bow ties appear studied or eccentric. They do not give the impression of authority. A man's dress is made remarkable only by its absence of defect. Conspicuous inconspicuousness is the rule, and the bow tie does nothing if not draw attention. "If you insist on wearing a bow tie to business – and bow tie wearers are a stubborn lot – I suggest you wear it with the proper accessories," writes John Molloy in *Dress for Success*. "A red nose and a beanie cap with a propeller."

Bow ties worn with a tuxedo or tailcoat are made of black silk or white cotton, respectively, and can be found in three shapes: the butterfly, the batswing, and the one-hander (left to right). All are tied the same way.

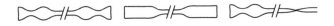

32.2 TYING A BOW TIE

Unlike with a necktie, both ends of a bow tie can be manipulated to form a knot, making bow tie knots potentially much more complicated than tie knots. The only known knot which can be tied with conventional bow ties is the usual reef bow, below. The granny bow (p 88) causes the tied bow to

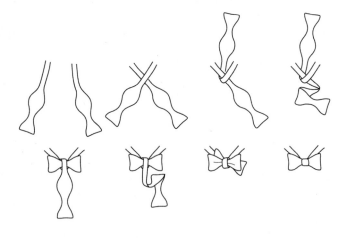

sit vertically rather than horizontally. Alternative knots may exist but have yet to be discovered. The author welcomes candidates for new knots – or a proof of their impossibility. Of course, bow ties should be self-tied rather than ready-tied. "[The bow tie] and the stiff wing collar are the direct descendants of Beau Brummell's starched cravats. He had trouble tying these. How could the rising middle classes cope?...I cannot blame men for buying 'made-up' ties, sin though it is to wear one," writes Hardy Amies.

The tied bow has four layers of cloth emanating from each side of the knot: three form the bow, shown top-down below; one goes around the neck, not shown. Pulling on the three different bow layers produces different effects, essential to optimizing all but the most expertly tied knots.

A Pulling here increases one side while decreasing the other half as much.
B Pulling here increases one side while tightening the knot.
C Pulling here increases one side while decreasing the other twice as much.

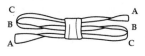

32.3 CRAVAT

The modern cravat is a long, rectangular neckcloth, pleated in the center to form a neckband. It is made of silk, usually in a print of polka dot, paisley, or foulard. Despite being a direct descendant of the plain white linen neckcloths of Beau Brummell, it is rarely found in plain colors. Continental Europeans often wear a cravat loose around the neck, casually tucked under an open-collared shirt; this practice has not caught on in America, where cravats are limited to weddings with a morning suit (p 66). A cravat is tied just like a four-in-hand tie knot, but without the final step through the loop.

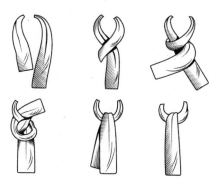

❦33 ACCESSORIES

33.1 HANDKERCHIEFS

Contrary to popular belief, the purpose of the handkerchief is not aesthetics but utility. It has for centuries been a practical accessory: to catch a sneeze, open a bottle, or dry up tears. During the First World War, the handkerchief was kept tucked into the jacket sleeve because the uniform pockets buttoned down. It has since returned to the breast pocket, and whether it is on display or not, that is where it belongs. "The most important [rule] is that it must look as though you use it; and you must. To have a handkerchief showing in the breast pocket and another one for use is to provide the most 'naff' gesture a man can make," writes Hardy Amies in *The Englishman's Suit*. The second rule is that it must not look like a piece of origami; tricorns, shells, and bird bases should be avoided. If a handkerchief is to be arranged it must be done so with studied indifference, like Prince Charles's, or simply folded, like his father's.

Apart from being square and having rolled edges, a handkerchief can be made from just about anything: silk, linen, even cotton – the backs of old shirts are a thrifty source for making your own. It should not match the tie but rather in its luster oppose it: linen or cotton for satin ties, silk for matte or wool ties. "Of course it's extravagant to blow your nose in a silk handkerchief, but we are talking about style and not economics," writes Amies. "There are now quite beautiful colored cotton handkerchiefs…of the bandanna type… Very good to add a touch of the country squire."

33.2 BUTTONHOLES

Like most details of the men's suit, the buttonhole on the left lapel is not fanciful. Originally it was a true hole for a button – an artifact of the high-fastening lapels of the 18th century. Buttoning descended but the button holes did not. Putting the buttonhole to unintended use is not new: in the early 18th century the ends of the lace cravats popular at the time were pulled through it, a style known as the Steinkerk. Today the buttonhole is used to hold a flower, though a sprig of ivy would not be out of place. Well-tailored suits have a loop inside the lapel to hold the stem. It is incorrect to pin a flower to a lapel without a buttonhole. A hole can easily be added by a tailor, the only exception being the shawl-collared dinner jacket, whose lapel never fastened. The buttonhole flower should look as though it was picked from the neighbor's garden, not arranged by a florist. Small roses and thistles are smart. Orchids are camp. Wearing miniature flags is a recent custom among American politicians, and other countries are following suit.

33.3 BANDANNAS

The word "bandanna" is derived from the Hindi word *badhnu*, an Indian method of selectively dyeing cloth by tying it in knots. It now refers to cotton squares printed with patterns of paisley or polka dots. Bandannas are bigger than handkerchiefs, typically 22 inches square as opposed to 16. They are kept in a front trouser pocket or the breast pocket of a jacket; beware of using a back pocket unless you are familiar with the semiotics of the camp "hanky code" or of gang allegiance. In the song "Drop It Like It's Hot," Snoop Dogg explains one instance of the latter: "I keep a blue flag hanging out my backside / But only on the left side, yeah that's the Crip side."

Bandanna uses: babushka · bandage · bandanna doll · Barbie parachute · belt (two tied together) · bib · blindfold · bottle apron · cat cape · cheese-cloth · coffee filter · cold compress · cravat · diaper · dish cloth · dog kerchief · dust mask · gag · gang allegiance · garotte · gift wrap · glasses cleaner · handcuffs · handkerchief · headband · hobo pack · kindling (for fire) · lunch box · muffler · napkin · neckerchief · origami · picnic cloth · pillow cover · pirate costume · placemat · polish rag · pot holder · poultice · scarf · shoe shine cloth · shoo away bugs · sit upon · sling · smokescreen mask · splint · strainer · sweat band · tie ponytail · towel · touch football · tourniquet · washcloth · whip · Wild West costume · wrap breakables

33.4 BELTS AND SUSPENDERS

Men, unlike women, do not have pronounced hips, and their trousers must be fixed at the waist. This is done by a belt, suspenders, or side fasteners.

Belts are the most common, but also the most recent and informal. With a suit they are acceptable but discouraged; with formal dress they won't do. Men's belts are threaded through the belt loops in a counterclockwise fashion, unlike women's, which are threaded clockwise. If the belt is leather, it should match the shoes: black belts with black shoes, tan belts with tan shoes, and so on. Informal belts can also be made of cotton or silk.

Suspenders keep the trousers fixed but not snug. They attach to the trousers' waistband at the front left, front right, and back center. They should always be attached by buttons, sewn on to the inside or outside waistband, never by clips. Suspenders are sometimes worn with suits, especially with formal clothes. The most popular and handsome variety are plain and colored and made of felt, woven silk, or artificial silk.

Side fasteners are adjustable (not elastic) bands on both sides of the trousers which can be used to vary the size of the waist by one or two inches. They are customary on better suits. If present, there should be no belt loops.

❦34 JEWELRY

A man's jewelry, like his clothes, should be plain, masculine, and conspicuously inconspicuous. It should be limited to a few functional items, either explicitly useful, like a watch or cuff links, or as a mark of specific status, like a wedding band. The use of jewelry to adorn – and this includes necklaces, bracelets, earrings, and piercings – is an essentially feminine concept.

34.1 RINGS

Wedding rings · Although the association of rings and marriage is ancient, before the Second World War only women wore wedding rings. Married soldiers away from home took to the idea of wearing a band as a symbol of their fidelity. Today the wearing of men's wedding bands varies from country to country. In America most men wear them, in Britain just under half, and in Europe somewhere in between. The ring itself should be a plain gold band, not silver or platinum. It is worn on the same finger as the women's, that is, the third finger of the left hand, although in many other countries it is worn on the third finger of the right hand.

Signet ring · These are traditionally worn by men whose family has its own coat of arms, which are engraved on the ring in metal or semiprecious stone. The ring was originally used to authenticate documents. Signet rings are usually worn on the small finger of the left hand.

34.2 WATCHES

Men's watches are unusual in being the only article of dress that men, as opposed to women, wear because of brand recognition. A man's suit, by contrast, never outwardly advertises its maker; it must be judged by its merits: cloth, cut, and fit. For this reason there is something mildly effete about paying large sums of money for famous watches. It is not expensive to produce a handsome, accurate, robust timepiece and it remains in the best taste to wear one of whatever make.

As regards design, thinner watches tend to be more elegant than thick ones; leather bands than metal; black bands than brown; analog than digital; minimal movement than complex. While most watches must occasionally be removed to avoid damaging them, there is something to be said for a sturdy timepiece which can be worn without concern while swimming or climbing a tree. It is no good to let one's dress dictate one's behavior.

34.3 EARRINGS

For men, earrings, nose rings, and other facial piercings are nearly always counter-cultural, rather than functional or aesthetic, forms of jewelry. They are intended to set the wearer apart from mainstream society politically, philosophically, or sexually.

A simple stud earring is the most common male piercing: a circularly symmetric decoration fixed directly to the piercing post and usually worn in the earlobe. Traditionally, a stud worn in the left ear indicates a straight man, and one worn in the right ear a gay man, although this convention remains less in force today than it did when such distinctions were coded. More recently, some men are known to wear identical earrings in both ears, as is customary for women – a practice of questionable manliness.

34.4 LAPEL PINS

Lapel pins are small emblems, often in the shape of a flag, that are worn on the left jacket lapel. Despite the name, they are not actually pinned to the cloth, but worn in the buttonhole in place of a flower. Flag lapel pins became popular after the September 11 terrorist attacks in 2001, and are especially common among politicians, for whom the absence of a pin is often more notable than its presence.

34.5 CUFF LINKS

Cuff links join double cuffs, sometimes called French cuffs. Their popularity varies considerably among countries. In Britain they are popular at work with a suit or jacket with men of all stripes, but are also sometimes worn casually with a pair of jeans. In America they are mostly worn at business or formal occasions or by fops. Gordon Brown wears them daily, Sarkozy more often than not, and Obama only at his more important meetings.

One of the simplest types of cuff links, and also the smartest, is two silver or gold metal ovals joined by a chain. Silk knots are an inexpensive and handsome alternative. Also notable are dumbbell-shaped links, made of metal or glass, and "bachelor's cuff links," which come in two separate halves and snap together. There are countless other varieties, some of which have ingenious designs. But there is a fine line between the smart and the common, and the inexperienced are advised to stick to the plainest designs. Double-sided links tend to be more formal than single-sided ones; metal and enamel than silk and glass; unadorned than novelty. In all cases it is acceptable to detach the link from one side of the cuff and roll up the sleeves.

34.6 COLLARS, TIES, AND FORMAL CLOTHES

Men's dress, especially formal dress, makes use of an array of hardware in the form of links, pins, and fasteners which can confuse even the most mechanically minded. While they are sometimes made of precious metals and materials, they should be of the most plain and sober design. Here is a guide.

Collar stiffeners, also known as *collar bones*, are inserted into the collars of better shirts with purpose-built slots sewn in to keep the points of the collar from curling. Collar stiffeners are typically made of plastic, sometimes metal, best of all bone. In a pinch, a safety pin can be used instead.

A *collar pin* or *collar bar* is a sturdy metal safety pin or rod which clasps both sides of the collar. Pins pierce the collar; bars pass through holes in specially made collars and are secured with screw-on ends. Both pass under the tie, forcing the knot forward and causing the tie to billow outward.

A *tie bar* is used to keep the necktie in place, usually for the sake of safety or formality. It is a hairpin-shaped piece of metal or other material which slides over the shirt and tie, keeping the tie immobilized. *Tie clips* are similar to tie bars but are spring-loaded. Both are hopelessly dated.

Tie tacks, on the other hand, have recently become fashionable after Princes William and Harry started wearing them to weddings (p 66). They are made of a circular metal disk with a pin on it which passes through the tie and attaches to a base secured to the second button hole of the shirt.

Studs close the front of formal shirts in place of buttons and resemble miniature dumbbells. When worn with a tuxedo (p 68), they are silver or silver and black (onyx); with white tie (p 70), gold or gold and white (mother-of-pearl). Studs for white tie vests are plain mother-of-pearl.

Collar studs attach detachable collars to the shirt. Like studs, they have a dumbbell shape, but with one end small and the other broad and flat. Two collar studs are used to attach a collar: a short one for the back, and a long one for the front, which also replaces the top shirt button.

OUTDOORS

Izaak Walton · No man is born an Artist nor an Angler. (*The Compleat Angler*, 1653)

Chuck Noland · Aha! Look what I've created! I have made fire! (*Castaway*, 2000)

Roger Scruton · My life divides into three parts. In the first I was wretched; in the second ill at ease; in the third hunting. (*On Hunting*, 1998)

Ed: Look, what is it that you require of us? *Mountain man*: Well we, uh, 're-quire' that you get your[selves] up in them woods! (*Deliverance*, 1972)

Ernest Shackleton · Men wanted for hazardous journey. Low wages, bitter cold, long hours of complete darkness. Safe return doubtful. Honour and recognition in event of success. (Supposed newspaper advertisement for Shackleton's South Pole expedition. It has never been verified.)

Samuel Johnson · Knotting ought to be reckoned, in the scale of insignificance, next to mere idleness. (*Dictionary*, 1755)

Capital City Fly Fishers · *Piscator non solum piscatur* ("There is more to fishing than catching fish," motto)

Ernest Hemingway · To me heaven would be a big bull ring with me holding two barrera seats and a trout stream outside that no one else was allowed to fish in... (letter to F. Scott Fitzgerald, 1925)

Sir Robert Baden-Powell · No man can be really good, if he doesn't believe in God and he doesn't follow His laws. This is why all Scouts must have a religion. (*Scouting for Boys*, 1908)

Michael Vronsky · You have to think about one shot. One shot is what it's all about. A deer's gotta be taken with one shot. (*The Deer Hunter*, 1978)

❦35 SURVIVAL

35.1 KNIFE

The most essential survival tool is a knife. With it you can construct numerous other tools for obtaining food, building shelter, and making fire. It is considered so vital that it is usually omitted from lists of survival tools. A knife is used foremost to carve wood; second to prepare food; and third as a tool for other tasks. Two knives are ideal: a pocket knife with one or two strong blades for the bulk of carving and cutting; and a multi-tool knife for more specific tasks. The best multi-tools are made by Leatherman and Gerber and by Victorinox and Wenger (acquired by Victorinox) for the Swiss Army.

35.2 SURVIVAL TOOLS

Whether camping, hiking, or lost, the difference between an agreeable or arduous time in the wilderness comes down to a handful of key tools. In the *SAS Survival Handbook* (Books, p 194), John Wiseman lists the following 12 essential items. Carefully chosen, the total weight need not exceed 8 ounces.

matches	needles and thread	snare wire
candle	fish hooks and line	flexible saw
flint	compass	medical kit
magnifying glass	beta light	surgical blades

35.3 NOTES

Matches · The ability to create fire is the most important survival skill, and the first four items in this list are aids to fire starting. Matches should be kept in a watertight container. Their heads can be dipped in candle wax as a means of making them water resistant, to be scratched off when needed.

Candle · In the *Complete Book of Camping*, Leonard Miracle makes a strong case for a candle: "Lighted with a match, it will burn long enough to dry out and ignite the most stubborn campfire fuel. It will light the inside of a tent…[and], propped under a can or a pan, a thick candle will cook food or boil coffee water when no other fuel is available. The same thick candle burning inside a tin can is a tiny heater that will substantially raise the inside temperature of a small tent. Melted candle wax rubbed into the fabric will stop a minor tent leak or seal the seams of a leather hunting boot."

Flint · Virtually everlasting, a flint (meaning artificial flint, called ferrocerium, not the rock flintstone) is used to make sparks by striking it with steel. The sparks are longer lasting and more substantial than those produced by flintstone, offering a reasonable chance of igniting common tinder.

Magnifying glass · Used to start a fire by concentrating the sun's rays onto dark tinder (Fire, p 86). It is also an aid to removing splinters and stings.

Needles and thread · Carry several sizes of needles, including a large one for sewing coarse objects with fishing line. Nylon thread is better than cotton.

Fish hooks and line · You are more likely to catch small fish than big ones, so include small hooks. Braided nylon line (25 lb test) is preferable to monofilament because it is less susceptible to damage and can double as binding material for tent and backpack repairs and for lashing together sticks.

Compass · Floating compasses, though heavier, are generally superior to dry ones. Make sure it has luminous markers so that it can be read in the dark.

Beta light · Also known as self-powered lighting or radioluminescence, a beta light will emit light for over 10 years (the half-life is 12.3 years). The light is caused by the beta decay of the unstable hydrogen isotope tritium.

Snare wire · A snare is a wire noose used to trap passing animals by the neck or leg: struggling causes the wire to tighten, thus securing the prey. But note that setting effective snares requires considerable expertise. As well as an aid to catching animals, snare wire is also useful as an all-purpose fastener.

Flexible saw · There are two types: wire saws and chain saws. Both have handles at the endpoints. A wire saw is a piece of wire with an abrasive finish, whereas a chain saw is a chain with teeth attached to the links, similar to that found on a motorized chain saw but lighter. At five ounces, chain saws are the heavier of the two, but offer much greater cutting efficiency.

Medical kit · "What you include depends upon your own skill in using it," advises Wiseman. He suggests the following: analgesic, intestinal sedative, antibiotic, antihistamine, water sterilizing tablets, anti-malaria tablets, potassium permanganate, butterfly sutures, and plasters. In addition to sterilizing water and wounds, potassium permanganate is combustible when combined with sugar in the ratio one part to two and struck by a rock.

Surgical blades · While these are meant to fit special metal handles, they can be held by hand or if necessary attached to improvised wooden handles.

❦36 FIRE

36.1 FIRE STARTING

Primitive methods of starting a fire, such as the bow and drill or striking rocks, are attractive in principle but require considerable effort and optimization. Literally weeks of practice and experimentation are needed to ignite carefully selected tinder from sparks thrown off by striking flint. Some more practicable and ingenious methods of fire starting are described here.

Compact OED · One of the easiest ways of starting a fire is by using a magnifying glass. A well-suited specimen is conveniently included with the compact edition of the *Oxford English Dictionary*. Held steady a couple of inches above the ground, it concentrates the parallel rays of the sun into a sharp point capable of igniting most dark tinder (see Firewood, opposite).

Saran wrap · If the *OED* is not at hand, a simple but effective lens can be constructed from water and Saran wrap. With the four corners held together, fill a 12-inch-square piece of wrap with water and twist the corners so as to create an approximate sphere. With some manipulation, the sun's rays can be concentrated into a point sufficiently tight to ignite tinder placed below.

Magnesium · This lightweight metal is extremely flammable (though not explosive) as a powder or in the form of shavings, but resistant to combustion in bulk. A small block of the metal, along with a flint for making sparks, can be bought as an extreme-weather fire starter. Form a pile of magnesium shavings, at least ½ inch in diameter, by scraping the soft metal with a knife. Then strike the back of the knife against the flint to cast sparks onto the shavings. Once ignited, the magnesium will burn for a short time with an intensely hot white flame. It should immediately be covered with tinder.

Coke can · In principle the sun's rays can be concentrated by a number of hand mirrors, each reflecting the rays onto the same spot. The continuum limit of such a collection of small nearby mirrors is a parabolic mirror. True parabolic mirrors, found in some telescopes, can be hard to come by. Much more common, and just as effective once modified, is the bottom of

a Coke or other aluminum can. The concave bottom already has the right shape, but its dull outer surface must be polished. This is best done in steps, starting with an abrasive polish, such as coffee grinds or steel wool, then finishing with a finer paste like chocolate or toothpaste. Apply the polish with a cloth or toothbrush, finishing with the cloth alone. The choice of polishes is not crucial, so long as the final polish is fine. Use the can to ignite tinder suspended by a thin stick so as not to obstruct the sun's rays.

36.2 TINDER AND FIREWOOD

Tinder is easily combustible material for the purpose of starting a wood fire – dry paper or leaves or finely cut bark or wood. When starting a fire using concentrated light, it is important to use dark tinder, which absorbs light, rather than fair tinder, which reflects it.

Once a fire is started, additional tinder and kindling should be added little by little to keep the fire going. After a base of coals has collected, just about any wood can be used to keep the fire going indefinitely, even green or wet wood which, if placed close by, will quickly dry. Nevertheless, some trees make better firewood than others. The chief desired properties are high heat production and low smoke emission and ash deposit. The energy output of firewood is measured in British thermal units (Btu). A Btu is the amount of energy necessary to heat one pound of water one degree Fahrenheit; it will light a 60-watt lamp for 18 seconds. A cord is the standard unit for measuring firewood: it is a stack of parallel logs 8ft × 4ft × 4ft, or the equivalent volume. The energy output per cord in millions of Btu (MBtu) for different species of trees is listed below. A good guide is the weight of the wood – energy output is almost directly proportional to density. Slow-growing trees, such as oaks and most fruit trees, tend to be the densest.

36.3 BEST TREES FOR FIREWOOD

Species	MBtu/cord				
Oak, Live	35	Fir, Douglas	25	Fir, White	20
Eucalyptus	33	Juniper, Western	25	Pine, Ponderosa	20
Locust, Black	30	Walnut, Black	25	Alder	19
Beech	29	Cherry	23	Cedar, Incense	19
Dogwood	29	Elm	23	Fir, Red	19
Birch	27	Hemlock, Western	23	Redwood, Coast	19
Oak, White	27	Magnolia	23	Pine, Sugar	18
Tanoak	27	Sycamore	23	Willow, Black	18
Ash	25	Maple, Big Leaf	22	Aspen	17
		Sweetgum	21	Cottonwood	16

❦37 KNOTS

Knots comprise all practically useful and decorative complications in line or rope, though not periodic ones, such as braids and lace, which are called weaves. Most common knots can be grouped into three categories:

Knots · Any complication tied into a single line itself.

Hitches · Used to attach a line to an object.

Bends · Used to join two lines.

The simplest knot is the overhand, which is the first half of a reef or square knot. When tied around an object, it is called a half-hitch. While the reef is the most familiar of knots, it is often confused with the practically useless granny knot. The bowline, sometimes called the king of knots, offers a simple, strong fixed loop in the end of a line. A more foolproof and very dependable alternative is the figure-eight knot, used in rock climbing.

Knots in everyday life

Some of the knots below are used in a man's daily rituals. A half-hitch is used to tie a sweater around the waist. An ascot is tied with a reef knot before pinning the overlapping ends. The usual four-in-hand necktie knot (p 74) is the buntline hitch. The seemingly complicated bow tie knot (p 76) is just the reef bow, which is also the knot used to tie shoelaces. When a bow tie or shoelace knot is offset by 90 degrees, there is a simple explanation: it has been tied with a granny bow (not shown) rather than a reef bow.

37.1 ESSENTIAL KNOTS

Knots

Reef or square knot .... Common knot for tying packages, bandages, etc.
Granny knot............. Common, useless result of a mistied reef knot.
Reef bow......... Easily untied knot used for shoelaces, gifts, and bows.
Surgeon's knot......... Less likely to slip while tying than the reef knot.
Bowline .... Essential knot for a fixed loop at the end of a rope.
Figure-eight loop.... Easily remembered fixed loop for critical situations.
Butterfly knot .... A fixed loop along a rope. Useful as a handle.
Spanish bowline .... Two adjustable fixed loops along a rope.
Sheepshank ..... Reduces excess length in a rope without using the ends.

Hitches

Timber hitch ..... Useful under constant tension, e.g., when hauling logs.
Clove hitch............. Used for attaching line to round posts or sticks.
Constrictor hitch....... A surprisingly secure knot around trees or posts.
Buntline hitch .... A sturdy slip knot that will resist jerking.
Tautline hitch .... Easily adjusted to keep line taut. Useful for tents.
Clinch or half-blood knot ... Joins monofilament line to a hook or swivel.

Bends

Sheet bend ...... If one rope is thicker, it should be the one from the right.
Carrick bend........... For ropes of equal width, especially heavy ones.

Reef knot

Granny knot

Reef bow

Surgeon's knot

Bowline

Figure-eight loop

Butterfly knot

Spanish   bowline

Constrictor hitch

Clove hitch

Buntline   hitch

Tautline   hitch

Sheet bend

Carrick bend

Timber   hitch

Sheepshank

Clinch

❦38 GUNS

38.1 RIFLES

The principal difference between a rifle and a shotgun is that the former has rifling, or helical grooves, along the interior of the barrel, causing the bullet to spin along its axis rather than tumble through the air. Additionally, the bullet forms an airtight seal with the chamber walls, meaning that much more of the energy released from the propellant is transferred to the bullet.

Cartridges

Rifles are described by the size of cartridge to which the chamber is fitted. A rifle cartridge has four parts: the bullet, powder, primer, and case. The case is usually made of brass and is reusable. Only the bullet, a heavy metal cylinder (usually lead, sometimes copper-jacketed) is emitted from the gun when it is fired. Twelve of the most popular hunting cartridges are shown below, where "dimensions" measures the bullet diameter by case length.

Cartridge	Dimensions (mm)	Uses
.22 Long Rifle	5.66 × 15.0	target, varmint
.223 Remington	5.66 × 44.7	varmint
.243 Winchester	6.17 × 51.9	varmint, medium game
6.5×55 Mauser	6.70 × 55.0	medium game
.270 Winchester	7.06 × 64.5	medium and large game
7mm Remington Magnum	7.21 × 63.5	medium and large game
.308 Winchester	7.82 × 51.2	medium and large game
.30-30 Winchester	7.85 × 51.8	medium and large game
.30-06 Springfield	7.84 × 63.3	medium and large game
.338 Winchester Magnum	8.61 × 63.5	large game
.416 Rigby	10.6 × 73.7	large African game
.45-70 Government	11.6 × 53.5	large African game

Left to right:
.22 to .45-70.

38.2 SHOTGUNS

A shotgun emits a group of metal spheres, called shot, which spread out in a cone. Shotguns are used to hunt nearly all birds, some deer, and smaller mammals. They are much more effective at hitting moving targets than rifles but are less useful at long ranges due to the poor aerodynamics of the shot.

Gauge

Shotguns are sized by gauge, which is related to the diameter of the bore: a shotgun is said to be *n*-gauge if *n* lead spheres which perfectly fit the bore weigh a pound. The diameter in inches is related to gauge as follows: diameter = $1.67 \text{ in}/\sqrt[3]{\text{gauge}}$. Thus a 12-gauge shotgun has an inside diameter of 0.729 in, which is the diameter of a sphere of lead weighing $\frac{1}{12}$ of a pound.

The more common shotgun sizes are listed below. The 0.410-in is universally known as a 0.410-gauge rather than the more logical 68-gauge.

Gauge	Diameter (in)	Notes
10	0.775	Long-range duck and geese or deer
12	0.729	Most common of all, for duck, geese, and turkey
16	0.663	Not at present common
20	0.615	Versatile, excellent first gun
28	0.550	Lightweight gun for small birds
68	0.410	For clay pigeon shooting, not used for hunting

Shot size

Shot falls into two classes, depending on size. Buckshot is the larger of the two and is used for small mammals; birdshot is the smaller and is used for fowl. Different sizes of buckshot and birdshot are coded as shown below.

Buckshot size	Diameter (mm)	No/oz (lead)	Birdshot size	Diameter (mm)	No/oz (lead)	No/oz (steel)
000	.36	6	BBB	.190	42	61
00	.33	8	BB	.177	55	72
0	.32	9	B	.160	71	103
1	.30	11	1	.150	86	125
2	.27	15	2	.140	106	154
3	.25	19	3	.130	132	192
4	.24	21	4	.120	168	243
F	.22	27	5	.110	218	317
T	.20	36	6	.100	291	423
			7	.090	399	
			8	.085	472	

❦39 CODES AND SIGNALS

Signaling is an essential skill in navigating at sea, aircraft control, radio communication, and survival in extreme environments. A more recent application of signaling and codes is text messaging, which shares many characteristics with telegraphy. The authoritative handbook of signaling is *The International Code of Signals*, published by the US National Geospatial-Intelligence Agency. Here is an introduction to codes and text messages.

39.1 MORSE CODE

The most universally recognized code is Morse code, in which characters are represented by a series of short and long intervals, called dots and dashes. The most frequently used letters are given the shortest series; the least frequent are given the longest. Phrases are sent according to the following rules:

1 The duration of a dot is one unit.
2 The duration of a dash is three units.
3 The duration between two consecutive dots or dashes is one unit.
4 The duration between two characters is three units.
5 The duration between two words is seven units.

Messages can be transmitted by sound or visually. When using light to signal, it is better to make the dots shorter rather than longer, a flash of light being easily recognizable. Note that the distress signal SOS is by convention ···———···, without the three-unit separation between characters.

A	·—	P	·——·	4	····—
B	—···	Q	——·—	5	·····
C	—·—·	R	·—·	6	—····
D	—··	S	···	7	——···
E	·	T	—	8	———··
F	··—·	U	··—	9	————·
G	——·	V	···—	.	·—·—·—
H	····	W	·——	,	——··——
I	··	X	—··—	?	··——··
J	·———	Y	—·——	!	—·—·——
K	—·—	Z	——··	'	·————·
L	·—··	0	—————	"	·—··—·
M	——	1	·————	/	—··—·
N	—·	2	··———	—	··——·—
O	———	3	···——	@	·——·—·

39.2 SOME STANDARD MORSE SIGNALS

The following signs are called prosigns, which means that, like SOS, they should be sent without the usual space of three units between characters.

Make ready to receive	CQ or AA
I am ready to receive	K
Wait	AS
Error; I will repeat	EEEEEEEE
Repeat	IMI
Message received	R
End of message, signing off	AR

39.3 MORSE SIGNALING BY HAND FLAGS OR ARMS

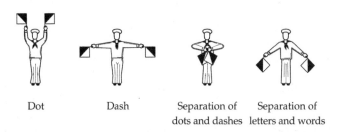

| Dot | Dash | Separation of dots and dashes | Separation of letters and words |

39.4 NATO PHONETIC ALPHABET

When transmitting letters and numerals by voice, and when it is important to avoid errors due to similar-sounding characters, it is customary to use a so-called spelling alphabet: in place of each letter is said a code word which starts with that same letter. The internationally accepted alphabet, called the NATO phonetic alphabet, is shown below. Note that the words "alfa" and "juliett" are intentionally misspelled to avoid mispronunciations.

A	Alfa	J	Juliett	S	Sierra	1	Unaone
B	Bravo	K	Kilo	T	Tango	2	Bissotwo
C	Charlie	L	Lima	U	Uniform	3	Terrathree
D	Delta	M	Mike	V	Victor	4	Kartefour
E	Echo	N	November	W	Whiskey	5	Pantafive
F	Foxtrot	O	Oscar	X	X-ray	6	Soxisix
G	Golf	P	Papa	Y	Yankee	7	Setteseven
H	Hotel	Q	Quebec	Z	Zulu	8	Oktoeight
I	India	R	Romeo	0	Nadazero	9	Novenine

✋40 TOOLS

Here are the 50 most useful tools for domestic repairs and building projects.

40.1 10 ESSENTIAL TOOLS

Adjustable wrench · Perhaps the most elegant tool of them all, it can fill in for countless wrenches and sockets.

Chisels · A small set of wood chisels (¼, ½, ¾ inch) is indispensable. Ideally hit with a carpenter's wooden mallet, not a hammer.

Drill · While a hand-held drill may be convenient for small jobs, it cannot compete with the efficiency of a cordless electric drill.

Hammer · There are several kinds: claw, ball peen, and tack. A 16-ounce claw hammer with a hickory or fiberglass handle is the most versatile.

Hand saw · There are many kinds of saw, but for quick results and cutting long straight lines, a hand saw is the best one.

Measuring tape (25 foot) · At least 1 inch wide and marked with imperial and metric units. Wider tapes will remain erect at greater distances.

Screwdriver · Flathead and Phillips in a few sizes each. Keep similar bits for the cordless drill.

Slip-joint pliers · Of the many varieties of pliers available, these are the most versatile for everyday use.

Spirit level · Of the torpedo sort. Determines true horizontal, vertical, and 45-degree angles, for jobs from hanging pictures to framing a house.

Utility knife · As well as for cutting cardboard, insulation, and carpet, its sharp edge is useful for scoring. The best come with breakable blades.

40.2 40 BASIC TOOLS

Allen wrench	compass	plumb bob
awl	crow bar	random orbital sander
bar-clamps	drill bit set	reciprocating saw
bench vice	electrical tape	sandpaper, various
bevel gauge	files (wood and metal)	sharpening stone
bullnose nippers	glass cutter	socket set (imperial
carpenter's pencil	hacksaw	and metric)
carpenter's square	hand plane	staple gun
caulking gun	interchangeable-tip	surform shaver
C-clamps	screwdriver	tin snips
chalk line (100 foot)	locking pliers	tool belt
channel-lock pliers	nail set	tool box
circular saw	needle-nose pliers	wire-stripper
cold chisel	pipe wrench	wooden mallet

☙41 BOY SCOUTS

The Boy Scouts was founded in England by Sir Robert Baden-Powell (B-P) in 1907. Scouting can now be found in nearly every country, with a world-wide population of over 28 million boys and young men. The United States has the largest membership, with one in seven males under 20 a Scout.

41.1 HISTORY

Scouting has its origins in B-P's military training manual, *Aids to Scouting for NCOs and Men*, published in 1899. When B-P shot to fame with his legendary defense of the town of Mafeking during the Second Boer War, his manual was widely adopted by youth organizations throughout Britain. Encouraged to adapt it for a younger audience, B-P wrote *Scouting for Boys* (Books, p 194), the basis of what is today called the *Boy Scout Handbook* in the US. B-P put his ideas into practice at a camp he organized for 20 boys on Brownsea Island in 1907. Scouting was suddenly taken up by adolescents throughout the country and the British Empire at an extraordinary rate. On the advice of the King, B-P retired from the Army in 1910 to devote his energy to the organization, which 12 years later numbered one million. American newspaperman William Boyce, after visiting London and learning about the nascent movement, founded the Boy Scouts of America in 1910.

Knowing his days were numbered, in 1941 B-P wrote his "Last message to Scouts," found among his possessions after his death. It ended:

> I have had a most happy life and I want each one of you to have as happy a life too. I believe that God put us in this jolly world to be happy and enjoy life. Happiness doesn't come from being rich, nor merely from being successful in your career, nor by self-indulgence. One step towards happiness is to make yourself healthy and strong while you are a boy, so that you can be useful and so can enjoy life when you are a man.
>
> Nature study will show you how full of beautiful and wonderful things God has made the world for you to enjoy. Be contented with what you have got and make the best of it. Look on the bright side of things instead of the gloomy one.
>
> But the real way to get happiness is by giving out happiness to other people. Try and leave this world a little better than you found it and when your turn comes to die, you can die happy in feeling that at any rate you have not wasted your time but have done your best. "Be Prepared" in this way, to live happy and to die happy – stick to your Scout promise always – even after you have ceased to be a boy – and God help you to do it.
>
> Your Friend Baden-Powell

41.2 SCOUT METHOD

Central to Scouting is the so-called Scout Method, a philosophy of education based on learning by doing, the formation of small groups, and the stage-wise completion of activities. Considerable attention is given to Scoutcraft, a collection of skills for proficiency out of doors. They include such things as chivalry, edible wild plants, fire building, first aid, nature lore, patriotism, physical fitness, signaling, swimming, tracking, tying knots, and using an axe. Advancement in these and related skills is marked by earning activity badges, an important aspect of day-to-day Scout activity.

41.3 ELEMENTS

Motto

Be Prepared, after B-P's initials, which means "you are always in a state of readiness in mind and body to do your duty," wrote B-P in *Scouting for Boys*.

10 Essentials

Water bottle • Extra clothing • First-aid kit • Map and compass • Matches and fire starter • Pocketknife • Rain gear • Sun protection • Flashlight • Trail food

Oath

On my honor I will do my best
To do my duty to God and my country
and to obey the Scout Law;
To help other people at all times;
To keep myself physically strong,
mentally awake, and morally straight.

Law

A Scout is trustworthy, loyal, helpful, friendly, courteous, kind, obedient, cheerful, thrifty, brave, clean and reverent.

41.4 SECTIONS

The Boy Scouts of America is divided into three divisions: Cub Scouts (7–10 years old), Boy Scouts (11–17 years), and Venturing (14–20 years). Cub and Boy Scouts offer several levels of advancement, shown below.

Cub Scouts (7–10 years)
Bobcat → Tiger → Wolf →
Bear → Webelos → Arrow of Light

Boy Scouts (11–17 years)
Scout → Tenderfoot → Second Class →
First Class → Star → Life → Eagle Scout

41.5 MERIT BADGES

A primary focus of Scouting is learning new skills and performing new activities, marked by a variety of merit badges. There are 121 merit badges as of summer 2008. To become an Eagle Scout, 21 must be earned, including those marked ★ below. (Only one of cycling, hiking, or swimming, and one of emergency preparedness or lifesaving, are required.) For more details, visit meritbadge.org and www.usscouts.org/advance/docs/MrDsReview.html.

American Business
American Cultures
American Heritage
American Labor
Animal Science
Archaeology
Archery
Architecture
Art
Astronomy
Athletics
Auto Mechanics
Aviation
Backpacking
Basketry
Bird Study
Bugling
★Camping
Canoeing
Chemistry
Cinematography
★Citizenship in the Community
★Citizenship in the Nation
★Citizenship in the World
Climbing
Coin Collecting
Collections
★Communications
Composite

Materials
Computers
Cooking
Crime Prevention
★Cycling
Dentistry
Disabilities Awareness
Dog Care
Drafting
Electricity
Electronics
★Emergency Preparedness
Energy
Engineering
Entrepreneurship
★Environmental Science
★Family Life
Farm Mechanics
Fingerprinting
Fire Safety
★First Aid
Fish and Wildlife Management
Fishing
Fly-Fishing
Forestry
Gardening
Genealogy
Geology
Golf
Graphic Arts
★Hiking

Home Repairs
Horsemanship
Indian Lore
Insect Study
Journalism
Landscape Architecture
Law
Leatherwork
★Lifesaving
Mammal Study
Medicine
Metalwork
Model Design and Building
Motorboating
Music
Nature
Nuclear Science
Oceanography
Orienteering
Painting
★Personal Fitness
★Personal Management
Pets
Photography
Pioneering
Plant Science
Plumbing
Pottery
Public Health
Public Speaking
Pulp and Paper
Radio

Railroading
Reading
Reptile and Amphibian Study
Rifle Shooting
Rowing
Safety
Salesmanship
Scholarship
Sculpture
Shotgun Shooting
Skating
Small-Boat Sailing
Snow Sports
Soil and Water Conservation
Space Exploration
Sports
Stamp Collecting
Surveying
★Swimming
Textile
Theater
Traffic Safety
Truck Transportation
Veterinary Medicine
Water Sports
Weather
Whitewater
Wilderness Survival
Wood Carving
Woodwork

❦42 TREEHOUSES

A treehouse is an ideal location for a study, a high-altitude deck for barbecues, or a men's den for private drinks with the guys. Despite the fascination with treehouses innate in all men, few understand the principles of constructing a stable, comfortable, and long-lasting living space in a tree.

42.1 PRELIMINARIES

We first begin with some legal considerations. There are two potential external obstacles to bear in mind: planning permission and neighbors. First, planning permission is not generally required if (i) a treehouse does not overlook an adjoining property and (ii) it can be classified as a temporary structure. For the sake of (ii), electricity and plumbing are not advised – an extension cord to the tree can serve most power needs.

Second, a treehouse will most likely be visible from a distance, and unhappy neighbors are likely to complain. The best approach is to involve potentially difficult neighbors from the start – it is harder to complain about something you have already known about. It is also wise to make the treehouse as handsome as possible. Any material other than natural wood, such as paint or plastic, looks conspicuous in a tree and should not be used.

Finally, a word on height. Treehouses are fun because they are high. There is little fascination in building a ground-level house *among* the trees; what makes a treehouse special is that it is up *in* the trees. Needless to say, a treehouse three feet above the ground is mildly disappointing. As a rule of thumb, any treehouse that can be reached by a man on the ground is questionably a treehouse. Just how high should a treehouse be? Here is the relation between value, height, and how much the treehouse costs:

$$\text{fun} = \text{height} \times \text{expense}$$

By this measure, you will have the same amount of fun in a $1000 treehouse six feet off the ground as in a $500 treehouse 12 feet off the ground.

42.2 FOUNDATION

Building a treehouse is little different from building any other outdoor shelter, apart from the foundation, which poses three concerns. First, a tree is a living thing, and the points of treehouse support must be strong but not injurious. Second, the foundation must rest on a limited number of contact points. Contrary to intuition, it is best to keep the number of support points as small as possible, usually three or four. Third, trees move, mostly owing to swaying in the wind rather than growth, so the contact points must not be vulnerable to a relative shift in the trunks or branches.

Once the foundation has been built, further work on the walls and roof can be done as with a conventional deck or outdoor workshop. Many of the grandest treehouses have stairs or a bridge leading to them, but this seems to go against their spirit, which is one of elevation and exclusion of the outside world. A simple rope ladder is the best way to access the house. Once in, you can pull it up behind you if you want to keep others out.

Bolts

To understand how best to attach the treehouse to the tree, a cursory knowledge of tree biology is helpful. The living part of a tree is the bark and outermost layers (the outer ½–2 inches, depending on species and size) which carry resources to the branches and foliage. The interior, called heartwood, is dead but remains strong. Accordingly, the most damaging injury is one which disrupts a significant fraction of the bark along a circumference; the least harmful is a hole perpendicular to the surface, such as a bolt.

A cable tied around a tree will eventually cut off its supply line, literally strangling it. Screws and nails, while individually safe, are not suitable for two reasons: they do not penetrate deep enough into the tree to hold fast; and too many minor wounds in a cluster can lead to compartmentalization, in which the tree blocks off the damaged region and lets it decay. Heavy bolts, at least ¾ inch thick, are the best solution. These are threaded and screwed into pre-drilled holes. Purpose-built bolts, called Garnier limbs (right), are 1¼ inch thick and are rated at 8,000 lb. They are available at www.treehouseworkshop.com, but are expensive.

Tree movement

The distance that a tree sways increases with height, while the force it can exert decreases with height. In other words, a tree acts as a lever, with small but powerful motions closer to the base. Relative movement of 1 inch during a storm can seriously damage the foundation. Tree growth, on the other hand, is not normally a concern. Growth in height takes place at the tips of the branches, not in the trunk or branches themselves. Growth in girth, which occurs everywhere in the tree and gives rise to annual rings in the wood, is a much slower process.

There are three approaches to minimizing the effects of tree motion. The first is to build on a single trunk, shown on p 100. The second is to build near enough to the ground for the amount of motion between trees or branches to be negligible. The third, and preferable, method is to incorporate floating contacts between the foundation and the bolts, described on p 100.

42.3 FOUNDATION DESIGN

Choosing which trees or limbs to build on is something of an art. Coniferous (needle-bearing) trees tend to have long, vertical trunks with few sturdy or accessible branches, and treehouses built on them use either a single trunk or multiple trunks close together. Deciduous (seasonal leaf-bearing) trees allow more imaginative possibilities. A forked branch can act as a convenient floating support point (a beam can rest on it without being fixed).

The three foundation configurations below make use of one, three, and four trunks or branches. Note that the first requires four bolts and diagonal supports. The frames are made of two 2 × 6-inch beams. The regions of the beams where they rest on the bolts should be covered with steel brackets or sheet metal. If the bolt ends do not already protrude, nuts can be welded to them to keep the supports from sliding off. A more secure and permanent solution is the arrestor bracket, which attaches to the bottom of the frame and is made to fit Garnier limbs; these are available online.

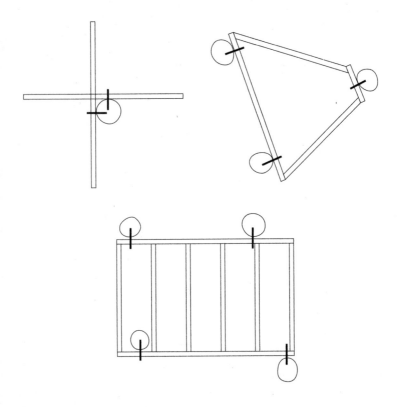

DRINKING

George Best · I spent 90% of my money on women, drink, and fast cars. The rest I wasted.

Richard Braunstein · The hard part about being a bartender is figuring out who is drunk and who is just stupid.

Samuel Johnson · A man who exposes himself when he is intoxicated has not the art of getting drunk. (Boswell, *Life of Johnson*, 1791)

Christopher Howse · Real ale fans are just like train-spotters, only drunk.

Ernest Hemingway · An intelligent man is sometimes forced to be drunk to spend time with his friends.

Abraham Lincoln · I believe, if we take habitual drunkards as a class, their heads and their hearts will bear an advantageous comparison with those of any other class. There seems ever to have been a proneness in the brilliant and warm-blooded to fall into this vice. (Address to the Washingtonian Temperance Society, 1842)

Peter the Great of Russia · Of all wine, Irish wine is the best.

The Massachusetts Spy · The cordial drop, the morning dram, I sing, / The mid-day toddy, and the evening sling.

Frank Sinatra · I feel sorry for people who don't drink. When they wake up in the morning, that's as good as they're going to feel all day.

Pablo Picasso · Drink to me. (last words)

Benjamin Franklin · He that drinks fast, pays slow. · Never praise your cyder or your horse. · There's more old drunkards, than old doctors. · Beer is proof that God loves us and wants us to be happy. (*Poor Richard's Almanack*, 1732–1757)

❦43 BARTENDER'S BIBLE

43.1 ESSENTIAL DRINKS CABINET

What should be stocked in a man's drinks cabinet? Two bottles each of red and white wine and one of a sparkling wine are essential, as is a six pack each of your preferred lager and ale. The principal masculine liquor is bourbon or whisky, and a bottle of each, along with ice and soda water for mixing, come next. For making cocktails, gin, vodka, and rum should be on hand, all of which work well with many different mixers and flavors. Of the liqueurs, the oldest two (Chartreuse and Benedictine) should be stocked for drinking neat, along with a triple sec (Cointreau) for mixing. The aromatics vermouth and Angostura are used in small doses for flavoring cocktails, and tonic water, sugar, and lemons are important ingredients in them.

Beer and wine	*Spirits*	*Other alcohol*	*Non-alcohol*
2 bottles red wine	whisky	Chartreuse Verte	ice
2 bottles white wine	bourbon	Benedictine	soda water
1 bottle sparkling wine	vodka	Cointreau	tonic water
6 bottles lager	gin	dry vermouth	sugar syrup
6 bottles ale	light rum	Angostura bitters	lemons

43.2 SERVING SIZE

Typical drinks servings are listed below. The ethanol per drink shows the relative strength of typical servings of drinks. A natural definition for a unit of alcohol is 15 ml ethanol, which is the amount of ethanol contained in one sixth of a bottle (a typical glass) of wine. A shot of spirits contains slightly more ethanol, 17 ml. A bottle of wine and a bottle of spirits contain 90 and 280 ml ethanol, respectively, which suggests that a bottle of spirits is a better value if it costs less than 3.1 times the price of a bottle of wine.

Measure	ABV	*Proof*	*Drinks/ bottle*	*Vol/ drink (ml)*	*Ethanol/ drink (ml)*
12-oz can of beer	5%	10	–	355	17.8
pint of beer (US)	5%	10	–	473	23.6
glass of wine	12%	24	6	125	15.0
glass of port or sherry	20%	40	10	75	15.0
shot of spirits	40%	80	16.4	42.6	17.0
shot of cask-strength whisky	60%	120	16.4	42.6	25.6
shot of absinthe	70%	140	16.4	42.6	29.8
shot of Everclear	95%	190	16.4	42.6	40.5

43.3 MEASURING DRINKS

The most common measure for mixed drinks is the shot. Despite the recent preponderance of the 40-ml shot, the more historically correct and generous definition is 1½ oz, which is 44.4 ml. This matters little when cocktail recipes (p 128) are given in relative terms (so many parts of this, so many parts of that) rather than absolute ones, as is the case in this book.

Measurement	fl. oz	ml	gill	4	118
dash	⅟₄₈	0.616	cup	8	237
teaspoon (tsp)	⅙	4.93	can of Coke	11.2	330
tablespoon (tbsp)	½	14.8	pint	16	473
fluid ounce or pony	1	29.6	bottle of spirits	23.7	700
shot	1½	44.4	bottle of wine	25.4	750

43.4 PROOF

The association of the word "proof" with alcoholic strength derives from an ingenious test of whether or not a spirit is stronger than a certain threshold, namely, 57.15% alcohol by volume. This is the concentration of a spirit above which a gunpowder paste made with it will still ignite, thus proving its potency. Today three methods are used to quantify alcoholic strength:

Alcohol by volume (ABV)	milliliters ethanol per 100 milliliters solution
Proof	twice the alcohol by volume times 100
British proof	approximately ⅞ proof; rarely used now

Thus a bottle of whisky at 40% ABV is 80 proof or 70 British proof. The strongest spirit that can be produced using conventional distillation is 95% (190 proof), available in certain American states under the name Everclear.

43.5 BOILERMAKER

This is a combination of two drinks served separately but drunk together: a shot of spirit or liqueur and ¾ pint of beer. The two are drunk in quick succession (the shot first, followed by the beer) or mixed together in the form of a depth charge: the shot glass and its contents are dropped into the beer and the whole thing is drunk at once. Some popular combinations include:

Traditional	1 shot whiskey	¾ pint beer (lager)
"Carbomb"	½ shot Jameson + ½ shot Baileys	¾ pint Guinness
"Jägerbomb"	1 shot Jägermeister	½ pint Red Bull

☕44 GLASSES

Different drinks require different glasses, not only by tradition but also because of variations in serving size, serving temperature, and volatility. All glasses should be made of clear glass or crystal. Crystal is cut lead glass, that is, glass with 12–30% lead oxide by weight, which gives the glass a higher refractive index and makes it sparkle. The different kinds of glasses, shown opposite, are not numerous, and can be divided into three categories.

44.1 STEMLESS GLASSES

Stemless glasses are cylindrical or have an inverted, slightly conical shape, with flat bottoms. The largest is the *pint glass*, which is mostly used for serving beer on draft. It is standardized to hold a pint of beer (473 ml in the US, 568 ml in the UK), plus room for the head. In the UK underfilling a pint is heavily frowned upon – selling pints 10% short can lead to prosecution. The *pilsner* is used to serve many bottled beers, and has a circular foot attached to the base for stability. The *beer mug* is thick-walled and sturdy and comes in various sizes. The *highball* and *collins* are used for water, juice, and long cocktails, the only difference being that a highball has parallel sides and a collins sloping sides. The *old-fashioned* is stockier and sturdier with a heavy glass base; it is used for neat spirits and short cocktails. Smallest of all is the *shot glass*, in which neat spirits and shooters are served without ice.

44.2 STEMMED GLASSES FOR WINE

There are many varieties of wine glass, but only a few are necessary to drink any given wine at its best. The spherical *red wine glass* in various sizes is the most familiar, and is sometimes used as a general-purpose vessel for other types of wine. The *white wine glass* is cylindrical near the top. Because it is intended to keep the wine cold, large examples are rarely seen. The *champagne flute*, designed to stay cold and minimize carbonation loss, has a small circumference at the top, unlike the largely obsolete champagne bowl with its shallow sides. The *sherry glass* is used for the fortified wines sherry and port which, being stronger, require smaller vessels. Finally, the *tasting glass* is medium-sized and has a small opening to concentrate a wine's aromas.

44.3 STEMMED GLASSES FOR SPIRITS AND LIQUEURS

Of the stemmed glasses used for spirits, liqueurs, and cocktails, the *brandy snifter* is the largest, though it is never filled anywhere near capacity. Its contents are warmed by the hand, on which the bowl rests. The familiar V-shaped glass is known as a *martini* or *cocktail* glass. It is used for short cocktails served without ice (with ice, use an old-fashioned). Liqueurs are served in a *cordial*, a small stemmed vessel similar in volume to a shot glass. A *hurricane* is a curvaceous glass used to serve cocktails made with lots of crushed ice. Finally, a *toddy* is for hot drinks, such as Irish coffee. It is in the shape of a tall mug attached to a stem and base, designed to keep the drink warm.

Pint glass   Pilsner   Beer mug   Highball

Collins   Old-fashioned   Shot glass   Red wine glass

White wine glass   Champagne flute   Sherry glass   Tasting glass

Brandy snifter   Martini or cocktail glass   Cordial   Hurricane   Toddy

❦45 BEER

Beer is an alcoholic beverage made from fermented grain. Drinks fermented from other sources have other names: fermented honey is called mead; apple juice, cider; grape juice, wine; and pear juice, perry. The ingredients of beer are generally limited to water, malted barley, hops, and yeast. Barley is a grain, like wheat, and it is malted by allowing it to germinate (sprout). This releases enzymes which convert its starches to sugars. Hops are the seed vessels of a vine-like plant, and they impart flavor and bitterness. Yeast causes fermentation – the conversion of sugar to alcohol – of which carbonation is a natural by-product.

Beers can be grouped by the kind of yeast used in fermentation. Naturally occurring wild yeast is used to make *lambics*. More often the yeast is cultivated: if it is top-fermenting, the beer is called *ale*; if bottom-fermenting, *lager*.

45.1 LAMBICS

Lambics are neither top-fermented nor bottom-fermented, but instead rely on wild yeast native to the area they are brewed in, usually around Brussels. This is one of the oldest styles of brewing, and lambics have a complex, yeasty, tart, dry taste. *Fruit beers* are made from lambics by the addition of fruit, the sugars of which lead to a refermentation. *Kriek* and *framboise* are made by the addition of cherries and raspberries, respectively.

45.2 LAGERS

Bottom-fermentation is a more recent innovation than top, and consequently the styles of lager are not as broad as they are for ales. Telltale signs of lager are a translucent color, a clean, crisp taste, and low (4–6%) ABV.

Pilsners
Often referred to simply as lagers, these have a light-gold color and pronounced hop flavor. Ideally, Pilsners are 5% alcohol by volume, or just under.

Pale lagers
These have minimal malt or hop character and are straw- to gold-colored. Sometimes called session beers, their chief advantages are mild flavor and low alcoholic content, which means they can be drunk in large quantities. They are aggressively marketed and their parent companies leverage bars to sell them at the exclusion of less mass-market but more distinctive beers.

Bocks
These are a strong, darker variety of lager with minimal hop flavor which

originated in the German town of Einbeck. They are dark gold to chestnut and their robust character makes them popular from autumn to early spring. *Doppelbock* and *Eisbock* are stronger varieties still, the latter being strengthened by freezing and removing the ice (water freezes before alcohol).

45.3 ALES

Ale, which is top-fermented, is a much older style of beer than lager, with complex roasted and fruity flavors and potentially higher ABV. There is an enormous range of varieties, some of which evade easy classification.

Anglo-American ales

Bitter refers to a lightly carbonated, pale-ale-style beer, usually served on draft, and accounts for a large fraction of the ale sold in Britain. *Old ale* is stronger with a malty taste and is often sweet. *India pale ale (IPA)* was originally made for export to India, with a strong presence of hops as a preservative for the long voyage. *Barley wine* usually refers to a brewer's most potent ale, typically 8% ABV or higher, strong in color and often sweet. *Winter warmer* is sometimes used to describe similar, slightly weaker versions.

Porter and stout

These are made from dark-roasted malt or barley and are dark brown to black. They have a toasted, nutty taste. *Porter* is the lighter-bodied of the two, and it has had a revival after a period of decline. *Stout*, which is more complex and filling, can be further divided into *dry stouts* and *sweet stouts*.

Belgian-style ales

Sometimes called Belgian speciality beers, this is a diverse category of ales usually produced in and around Belgium. They tend to have distinctive flavors, more alcohol, and include many of the world's most highly esteemed beers. Some better-known breweries are Leffe, Rodenbach, and Duvel. *Abbey ales* are made by breweries associated with a monastery or imitative of that style, such as L'Abbaye des Rocs and Karmeliet. *Trappist ales* are brewed within the walls of a Trappist monastery under the complete control of the resident monks and are internationally renowned. *Dubbels* are double-fermented and are strong (over 6.5% ABV) and dark with a malty, fruity taste. *Tripels* are stronger yet and tend to be pale and hoppy.

Wheat beers

Beers made from wheat in addition to barley are called wheat beers or white beers. They are usually light yellow and opaque and are often flavored with orange peel or coriander. One of the most refreshing styles of beer, they are popular in warm weather, sometimes with a slice of lemon.

45.4 NOTABLE BEERS FROM AROUND THE WORLD

	Lambic		
Beer	*Style*	*Origin*	*ABV*
Cantillon Gueuze-Lambic	Lambic	Belgium	5.0
Kriek Girardin	Kriek	Belgium	5.0
Lindemans Cuvée René	Lambic	Belgium	5.0

	Lager		
Amstel Herfstbock	Bock	The Netherlands	7.0
Anchor Steam Beer	Steam beer	California	4.9
Bitburger Premium Pils	Pilsner	Germany	10.0
Budweiser Budvar (Czechvar)	Pilsner	Czech Republic	5.0
Paulaner Salvator	Doppelbock	Germany	7.5
Pilsner Urquell	Pilsner	Czech Republic	4.4
Samuel Adams Boston Lager	Lager	Massachusetts	4.9
Tsingtao	Pilsner	China	4.2
Victory Prima Pils	Pilsner	Pennsylvania	5.3

	Ale		
Adnams Broadside	Old ale	England	6.3
Alaskan Smoked Porter	Porter	Alaska	6.1
Bass No. 1	Barley wine	England	10.5
Beamish Irish Stout	Dry stout	Rep. of Ireland	4.0
Brains SA	Bitter	Wales	4.2
BridgePort IPA	IPA	Oregon	5.5
Burton Bridge Porter	Porter	England	4.5
Chimay Blue	Trappist ale	Belgium	9.0
De Koningshoeven (La Trappe)	Trappist ale	The Netherlands	6.5
Duvel	Belgian-style ale	Belgium	8.5
Fuller's 1845	Winter warmer	England	6.3
Fuller's London Pride	Bitter	England	4.7
Guinness Extra Stout	Dry stout	Rep. of Ireland	4.2
Hoegaarden Witbier	Wheat beer	Belgium	5.0
Leffe Brune	Abbey ale	Belgium	6.5
Murphy's Irish Stout	Dry stout	Rep. of Ireland	4.0
Orval	Trappist ale	Belgium	6.2
Sierra Nevada IPA	IPA	California	6.9
Theakston Old Peculier	Old ale	England	5.6
Westvleteren 8	Trappist ale	Belgium	8.0
Young's Bitter	Bitter	England	3.7
Yuengling Original Black & Tan	Porter	Pennsylvania	5.2

45.5 MOST POPULAR BEERS: PALE LAGERS

Pale lager is by far the most-consumed style of beer. Originally derived from the pilsner style, it has minimal character and aroma and is drunk very cold. It is relatively pale in color and is about 5% alcohol by volume (ABV).

Despite its popularity, pale lager receives little attention from beer writers and aficionados. Michael Jackson, the world's foremost beer authority until his death in 2007, mentions none of the 20 pale lagers below in his *Great Beer Guide*, a compendium of 500 classic brews. This is partly because pale lagers are *not* among the world's best beers, as the low scores below suggest. But it is also the result of beer snobbery, in which popular and inexpensive beers are unfairly penalized in favor of complex and challenging beers. In truth, pale lagers are among the most thirst-quenching and refreshing beers, and the mild pilsner flavor of some can be a stepping stone to more robust brews.

The beer scores below are the consensus scores, out of 100 points, of user ratings on www.ratebeer.com, the most-visited beer information website.

	Beer	*Origin*	*ABV*	*Score*
	Budweiser	Missouri	5.0	1
★	Busch	Missouri	4.6	0
	Carlsberg	Denmark	5.0	11
	Cobra	England (prev. India)	5.0	7
	Coors	Colorado	5.0	2
	Corona Extra	Mexico	4.6	2
	Fosters	Australia	4.9	7
•	Grolsch Premium Lager	The Netherlands	5.0	18
•	Harp	Republic of Ireland	4.3	31
	Heineken	The Netherlands	5.0	8
★	Keystone Light	Colorado	4.2	0
	Labatt Blue	Canada	5.0	8
	Michelob	Missouri	5.0	5
	Miller High Life	Wisconsin	4.7	2
	Molson Canadian	Canada	5.0	7
	Old Milwaukee	Wisconsin	4.9	0
•★	Pabst Blue Ribbon	Wisconsin	5.0	3
	Peroni	Italy	4.7	9
	Stella Artois	Belgium	5.2	17
•	Yuengling Traditional Lager	Pennsylvania	4.9	30

KEY • Value: a good beer for its price.
   ★ Inexpensive: a beer for drinking games and college carousels.

45.6 SERVING TEMPERATURE

There is a widely held myth that all beer should be served ice cold. The truth is that different styles of beer are best served at different temperatures, ranging from 40 to 60°F. A general rule of thumb is that, as with wine, lighter beers should be colder than darker beers, though there are exceptions. Cellar temperature refers to the temperature of an (ideal) underground cellar, which was the temperature of most beer before refrigeration.

Temperature	°F	Beer styles
Ice cold	<40	Some pale lagers; beer not worth tasting
Cold	40–45	Fruit beer, pilsner, pale lager, wheat beer
Chilled	45–50	Lambic, porter, stout
Cellar	50–55	Bock, bitter, old ale, IPA, abbey ale, dubbels
Cool	55–60	Barley wine, Trappist ale, tripels

45.7 BEER WITH FOOD

North America and northern Europe have had a long tradition of drinking beer with food, just as southern Europe has tended to combine its food with wine. The right combination, such as oysters and stout, can be superb. Here is an overview of which beers complement which foods and moods.

Main courses		
	Beef	Strong ale, bitter, stout
	Chicken	Pilsner, wheat beer
	Chili/curry	Pale lager, pilsner, India pale ale
	Fish	Pilsner
	Game	Old ale, Trappist ale, tripels
	Pizza	Vienna-style lager, pale lager
	Pork	Pilsner, India pale ale
	Sausage	Bitter, dark lager, doppelbock
	Shellfish	Dry stout, porter
	Soup	Gueuze (meat); bitter (vegetable)

Desserts		
	Cheese	Porter (mild); Trappist ale (strong)
	Chocolate	Dry stout, sweet stout
	Fruit	Wheat beer
	Pies, tarts	Wheat beer, fruit beer

Other		
	Nightcap	Trappist ale, barley wine
	Smoking	Bitter (cigarettes); Trappist ale (cigars)
	Thirst quenching	Wheat beer, pale lager, Belgian red ale

❦46 WINE

Wine is the alcoholic beverage made from fermented grapes. It is not the most diverse type of alcohol – spirits are made from a much broader variety of plants. Nor is wine the oldest – beer brewing predates winemaking. Nevertheless, more is written about the variety, history, and drinking of wine than any other drink. Certainly it is much harder to see wine's big picture, partly because there is a continuum of styles, partly because the defining characteristics of a given style can be hard to describe in words.

46.1 GRAPE VARIETIES

The simplest classification of wines is not by geography (where the grapes are grown and the wines are made) but by the variety of grapes used to produce them. Some are made from a single grape, others are blended from two or more varieties. Traditionally, six dominant grapes, called noble grapes, were used to make the best wines in the world: the white grapes Sauvignon Blanc, Riesling, and Chardonnay; and the red grapes Pinot Noir, Cabernet Sauvignon, and Merlot. Today the list of top grapes is longer, due especially to innovative New World winemaking. Below are the most important.

White wine grapes

Chardonnay · This is the basis of the burgundy white wines Chablis, Côte d'Or, and Mâcon. It is blended with Pinot Noir and Pinot Meunier to make champagne. When only Chardonnay is used, champagne is called *blancs de blancs*. It is a reliable and resilient grape and is planted in such disparate climates as those of Portugal and England and Texas and Canada. It was the first grape widely used in varietal, as opposed to geographic, labeling.

Gewürztraminer · Also known as Traminer, this grape produces wine with a distinct spicy, aromatic aroma which makes it suitable for stronger foods. It can be a frustrating grape to cultivate and is largely grown in cool climates.

Muscat · Possibly the oldest domesticated grape variety of all, from which all others have descended. The grapes can be white or black, and are used to make a wide array of wines, all of which have a common distinct taste.

Pinot Noir · In addition to its use in making red wine (see overleaf), it is blended to make champagne and sparkling wines imitative of that style.

Riesling · The premier grape of Germany, and the chief grape used for fine wine production in that country. It is drinkable young but also ages well.

Sauvignon Blanc · This is the sole grape used to make Sancerre and Pouilly-Fumé. With Sémillon, it is used to make Graves and Sauternes. Often described as grassy and reminiscent of green fruits, especially gooseberries.

Sémillon · Rarely used to make wine on its own, it is mostly blended with Sauvignon Blanc to make Sauternes and other excellent dessert wines and dry wines of varying quality. When used for dessert wines, the grape is subjected to *Botrytis cinerea* while on the vine, a fungus better known as "noble rot," which causes the grape to shrivel and concentrates its sugar and flavor.

Red wine grapes

Cabernet Franc · Mostly grown in France, where it is blended to make red Bordeaux. It tends to be lighter than its dominant cousin, Cabernet Sauvignon, with which it is often blended when produced in California.

Cabernet Sauvignon · One of the most widely planted grape varieties, this is the basis of red Bordeaux, where it is blended with Cabernet Franc and Merlot, and of much Californian red wine. Its taste is sometimes compared to black currants, and its powerful character generally requires aging.

Gamay · Notable mainly as the grape solely responsible for the light, fragrant red wine Beaujolais. It is also used, less successfully, in Switzerland.

Merlot · A plump and plummy grape, Merlot is the basis of the red wines Pomerol and St.-Emilion and is the most used black grape in Bordeaux.

Pinot Noir · This grape is solely responsible for red burgundy. It gives unpredictable results but is spectacular at its best. The grape is grown extensively outside France but with less consistent results. Although its taste varies considerably, it tends to be fruity, light in body, and low in tannins.

Syrah · Known as Shiraz in Australia and South Africa, this robust, full-bodied grape is used to make the Rhône wines Côte Rôtie and Hermitage. It is also blended with other grapes because of its strong, smoky taste.

Tempranillo · Used to make Rioja and other Spanish reds, it is the premier red grape of Spain but until recently was little grown outside that country.

Zinfandel · Of European origin but largely produced in California, this adaptable and fruity grape is used to make reds and pale rosés. DNA fingerprinting has shown it to be same as the Primitivo grape of southern Italy.

46.2 WINE CUSTOMS

Opening a bottle

This is one of the most satisfying of all drinking rituals. The best corkscrew is the simplest: a metal spiral attached to a perpendicular wooden handle in the form of a T. See that you get a real spiral like a drill bit rather than a wound wire helix. A T-shaped corkscrew offers no leverage but depends solely on strength. The usual technique is to place the bottle between the legs, just above the knees, and hold the neck with one hand while pulling the corkscrew with the other. If your shoulders are not up to strength, a regime of upright rows (p 23) will help. In the absence of a corkscrew, pushing the cork *in* with a blunt tool works surprisingly well. Depress it slowly to avoid spraying wine when it gives way. Pouring the first glass is awkward because the cork gets in the way, but subsequent glasses are easy.

Opening a champagne bottle

The pressure in champagne and sparkling wine bottles increases with temperature and agitation, so very cold bottles handled carefully release their corks with the least force. First, remove the foil to expose the wire cage. Untwist the cage with your thumb over the cork to prevent its spontaneous expulsion. The trick to removing the cork quietly is to hold it fixed with one hand, with your thumb on top of it, while with the other hand slowly turning the bottle. Alternatively, to project the cork as far as possible across a room or away from a picnic, keep the bottle still and gently massage the cork with your thumb and forefinger lightly wrapped around its base.

Order of wines

The *Larousse Encyclopedia of Wine* gives the following conventions: "White wine before red, young before old, light before heavy, dry before sweet, minor before fine or rare. White wines accompany the first courses in a meal, red ones the main or later courses." Exceptions are champagne and sweet white wines, which can be served with dessert. Sherry makes a fine pre-prandial drink and is thought to complement smoking. If multiple wines are on offer at dessert, they rotate around the table clockwise in order of their fineness: port first, then claret (Bordeaux) or other red wine, then dessert wine.

Decanters

These are sometimes used as attractive replacement vessels for bottled wine and are essential for wines that throw a deposit, such as vintage ports and many old reds. Different decanters are used for different drinks: those for red wine are round and uncut so that the wine can be seen; those for port are round and sometimes cut; those for spirits are generally square and cut.

46.3 BOTTLE SIZES

Wine is sometimes sold in larger or smaller volumes than the usual 750-ml bottle. Different-sized bottles for champagne, Bordeaux, and port have by tradition different names, shown below. In the case of champagne, the wine normally undergoes secondary fermentation in standard bottles or magnums; these are decanted to fill the more unusually sized bottles.

Bottles	Liters	Champagne	Bordeaux	Port
¼	0.188	Split	–	–
½	0.375	Half bottle	Fillette	–
1	0.75	Bottle	Bottle	Bottle
2	1.5	Magnum	Magnum	Magnum
3	2.25	–	Marie-Jeanne, approx.	Tappit Hen
4	3	Jeroboam	Double Magnum	Jeroboam
6	4.5	Rehoboam	Jeroboam	–
8	6	Methuselah	Imperial	–
12	9	Salmanazar	–	–
16	12	Balthazar	–	–
20	15	Nebuchadnezzar	–	–
24	18	Solomon or Melchior	–	–
36	27	Primat	–	–

46.4 JOHNSON SYSTEM OF WINE SCORING

One of the problems with the growing trend of attaching objective scores to wines is that individual tastes are highly subjective. In *Hugh Johnson's Pocket Wine Book*, the author proposes a system of individual scoring based on the most straightforward of tests: how much of it would you drink? "You should assume that you are drinking without compunction," writes Johnson, "without your host pressing you or the winemaker glowering at you."

one sniff . . . . the minimum score
one sip . . . . not thoroughly unpleasant
two sips . . . . faint interest
half glass . . . . curiosity
one glass . . . . tolerance, general approval
two glasses . . . . you quite like it
three glasses . . . . you find it more than acceptable
four glasses . . . . it tickles your fancy
one bottle . . . . thorough satisfaction
two bottles . . . . irresistible
a full case . . . . you are not going to miss out on this one

46.5 WINE TASTING

Wine tasting is the consideration and determination of a wine's quality or identity. For many, the most difficult aspect of tasting is expressing taste in terms of language. Taste can be divided into mouth sensation, such as crisp or flabby, and aroma, such as fruity or spicy. The aroma wheel, below, provides a universal vocabulary for describing the aroma of wine. The words are meant to be objective rather than subjective: thus "citrus," which refers to a specific substance, rather than "bright," which does not. The wheel contains 12 main groups, 27 subgroups, and 87 specific descriptors.

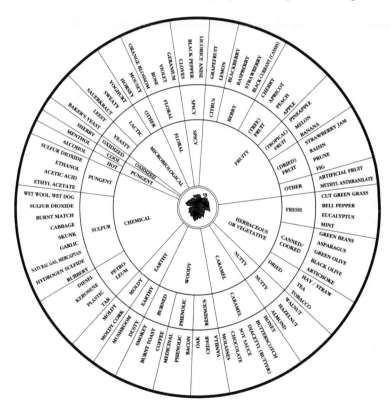

The wine aroma wheel was originally published in A. C. Noble et al., "Modification of a standardized system of wine aroma terminology," *American Journal of Enology and Viticulture*, **38**, 143 (1987). This updated aroma wheel is copyright 1990, 2002, A. C. Noble, www.winearomawheel.com.

❦47 SPIRITS

Spirits are the result of the distillation of wine or other fermented (alcohol-containing) liquids. Distillation is a way of separating two liquids that are mixed together on the basis of their different volatilities: alcohol is more volatile than water, and when the mixture is heated the alcohol will vaporize more readily. When the vapor is condensed back into a liquid, having become more pure, it will be higher in alcohol than the original mixture.

Spirits can be divided into families according to the source of the mash which is fermented: grape, fruit, grain, or sugar, all considered below. Some spirits, such as vodka, are so highly distilled that the choice of mash has little effect on the end product. After distillation, most spirits are diluted with water and bottled at 40–50% ABV (alcohol by volume), which is 80–100 proof, although some are considerably stronger than this. Unlike other types of alcohol, with spirits it is difficult to give specific indications of strength because they vary from spirit to spirit and producer to producer.

47.1 GRAPE SPIRITS

Spirits distilled from fermented grape juice are called brandy. Other fermented fruit juices, once distilled, are called fruit brandies. The more popular brandies have specific appellations: Cognac and Armagnac are the best known. Cognac is produced around the small French town of Cognac and Armagnac is produced in the Gascony region. Occasionally brandy bottles are marked VS, VSO, or VSOP, which mean Very Special, Very Special Old, and Very Superior Old Pale. These marks, however, are not backed up by an industry standard and cannot be considered serious indications of quality or age. Like all high-proof liquors, brandy, once bottled, ceases to develop.

The greatest by-product of the wine-making process is pomace, the leftover skins, stems, and seeds of the pressed grapes. These remains are used to make pomace brandy, a spirit with a long reputation for being a harsh and unsophisticated drink. Today, however, many distinctive, subtle versions are produced. Pomace brandy made in Italy is called grappa; that made in France is called marc; and that made in Portugal is call Bagaceira.

47.2 FRUIT SPIRITS

A broad spectrum of spirits is made from fruits and succulent plants, of which apple and agave are the most popular. Applejack is the traditional American name for apple brandy distilled from cider, potent if not always palatable. In the UK this is called cider brandy. Calvados, a more refined drink originating in France, is made directly from fermented apple juice or apple and pear juice and aged in oak casks before bottling. Tequila and mezcal both come from the fermented juice of the agave family of succulents, tequila from the blue agave and mezcal from the maguey plant. Despite their similar origin, the two spirits have different methods of production and are notably different in taste. It is mezcal, not tequila, which sometimes comes with a worm in the bottle, the "worm" in fact being a moth larva.

47.3 GRAIN SPIRITS

The most widely drunk spirits are distilled from grains, such as barley, corn, and rye. The purest of these is vodka, essentially water and ethanol, which can in principle be made from anything containing starch or sugar. In practice grain or potatoes are most often used. Poteen is similar to vodka, but more flavorful and, until recently at least, harsher. It is made in Ireland, usually from potatoes or grain. Despite being made privately for centuries, poteen could not be legally produced in Ireland until 1989, nor sold domestically until 1997. Gin, by which is meant London dry gin, is simply neutral grain spirit flavored chiefly with juniper and redistilled. Sloe gin is not a spirit but a liqueur, made by infusing sloe berries, a small wild plum, in gin and sugar. Aquavit, sometimes called schnapps, is made like gin: neutral grain spirit is infused with caraway seeds and other spices and redistilled. It is traditionally drunk neat and cold. Malt whisky, described in detail on p 119, is made exclusively from barley, yeast, and water. The mash used in bourbon (p 122) must include 51% corn; the mash in rye whiskey, 51% rye.

47.4 SUGAR SPIRITS

Of the spirits made from sugar, rum is the best known. It is produced from sugar cane or, more often, molasses: the dark, viscous fluid that remains after sugar is crystallized out of sugar cane juice. Whether rum is light or dark depends on how long it is aged in the barrel and how much caramel is added. The taste of dark rum is much more robust than light rum, and the two cannot be used interchangeably. Cachaça (pronounced ka-shah-sa) is made directly from sugar cane juice rather than molasses and has a flavor distinct from rum. It is the best-selling spirit in Brazil and is the basis of the excellent – some would say world's finest – cocktail, the caipirinha (p 128).

47.5 NOTABLE GRAPE SPIRITS

Spirit	*Source*	*Origin*
Armagnac	white grapes	Gascony (France)
Brandy	grapes	France

Bagaceira	grape pomace	Portugal
Cognac	white grapes	southwest France
Grappa	grape pomace	Italy
Marc	grape pomace	France
Metaxa	grapes	Greece
Pisco	Muscat and other grapes	Peru, Chile

47.6 NOTABLE FRUIT SPIRITS

Applejack	cider	New England (USA)
Arrack	coconut sap	Southeast Asia
Calvados	apples (or apples and pears)	Normandy (France)
Cider brandy	cider	England
Kirsch	cherries	Alsace (France), Germany, Switzerland
Kislav	watermelons	Russia
Mezcal	maguey plant	Mexico
Mirabelle	yellow plums	Alsace-Lorraine (France)
Palinka	plums, apples, apricots	Austria, Hungary, Romania
Quetsch	purple plums	Central Europe
Raki	grapes, figs, plums	Turkey
Slivovitz	plums	Balkan countries
Tequila	blue agave	Mexico

47.7 NOTABLE GRAIN SPIRITS

Aquavit	grain, potatoes (with caraway seeds)	Scandinavia
Bourbon	corn	southern USA
Gin	grain (with juniper)	The Netherlands
Jenever	rye, wheat, malted barley	The Netherlands, Belgium
Malt whisky	barley	Scotland
Poteen	grain or potatoes	Ireland
Rye whiskey	rye	USA
Schnapps	grain, fruit	Austria, Germany
Shochu	rice, grain, potatoes	Japan
Vodka	grain, potatoes	Russia, Poland

47.8 NOTABLE SUGAR SPIRITS

Batavia arrack	sugar cane	Indonesia
Cachaça	sugar cane	Brazil
Rum	molasses	Caribbean

❦48 WHISKY

To be called a single malt Scotch, a whisky (spelled whisky in Scotland and the UK; whiskey in America and Ireland) must satisfy three conditions:

Single · It must be produced at a single distillery, although it may be mixed from separately aged casks. The alternative is called *blended*.
Malt · It must be made entirely from malted (sprouted) barley, to which only yeast and water can be added. Other whiskies and bourbons (p 122) may contain additional grains, such as corn or rye.
Scotch · It must be distilled and aged in Scotland. There are curiously few single malt distilleries elsewhere in the world; Michael Jackson (Books, p 193) names six, located in Australia, Ireland, Japan, New Zealand, and Pakistan.

48.1 119 SINGLE MALTS

Unlike wine or other spirits, the world of single malt Scotch is small and demarcated and can be approached with a view to comprehensive familiarity. There are 119 distilleries which now produce or have recently produced single malt Scotch whisky. Each brand of spirit has a distinctive, characteristic taste. Some of the distilleries, such as Rosebank, are closed but previous production is still being aged and is available on the market. The 119 distilleries are summarized here. For each, the following details are listed:

Distillery · If the distillery has changed name, the most recent name is given.
District · One of nine regions of Scotland in which the distillery is located.
Classification (Cls) · One of 12 similarity classes to which each whisky was assigned in a statistical study (p 121). A dash (–) indicates it was omitted.

Distillery	District	Cls	Distillery	District	Cls
Aberfeldy	Midlands	A	Benriach	Speyside	F
Aberlour	Speyside	B	Benrinnes	Speyside	B
Allt-á-Bhainne	Speyside	–	Benromach	Speyside	F
Ardbeg	Islay	I	Bladnoch	Lowlands	E
Ardmore	Speyside	C	Blair Athol	Midlands	C
Arran	Island	–	Bowmore	Islay	I
Auchentoshan	Lowlands	D	Brackla	Speyside	K
Aultmore	Speyside	F	Braeval	Speyside	–
Balblair	N Highlands	E	Bruichladdich	Islay	H
Balmenach	Speyside	K	Bunnahabhain	Islay	F
Balvenie	Speyside	B	Caol Ila	Islay	E
Banff	Speyside	L	Caperdonich	Speyside	L
Ben Nevis	W Highlands	D	Cardhu	Speyside	F
			Clynelish	N Highlands	C

Cnoc	Speyside	–	Highland Park	Island	B
Coleburn	Speyside	D	Imperial	Speyside	L
Convalmore	Speyside	K	Inchgower	Speyside	F
Cragganmore	Speyside	G	Inchmurrin	W Highlands	E
Craigellachie	Speyside	K	Inverleven	Lowlands	E
Dailuaine	Speyside	K	Jura	Island	I
Dallas Dhu	Speyside	K	Kinclaith	Lowlands	E
Dalmore	N Highlands	B	Knockando	Speyside	F
Dalwhinnie	Speyside	F	Knockdhu	Speyside	K
Deanston	Midlands	H	Ladyburn	Lowlands	H
Drumguish	Speyside	–	Lagavulin	Islay	I
Dufftown	Speyside	I	Laphroaig	Islay	A
Edradour	Midlands	E	Linkwood	Speyside	J
Fettercairn	E Highlands	H	Littlemill	Lowlands	E
Glen Albyn	Speyside	J	Loch Lomond	W Highlands	–
Glenallachie	Speyside	F	Lochnagar	E Highlands	L
Glenburgie	Speyside	E	Lochside	E Highlands	B
Glencadam	E Highlands	L	Longmorn	Speyside	G
Glen Deveron	Speyside	F	Longrow	Campbeltown	I
Glendronach	Speyside	K	Macallan	Speyside	B
Glendullan	Speyside	B	Mannochmore	Speyside	–
Glen Elgin	Speyside	L	Millburn	Speyside	B
Glenesk	E Highlands	K	Miltonduff	Speyside	F
Glenfarclas	Speyside	I	Mortlach	Speyside	K
Glenfiddich	Speyside	H	North Port	E Highlands	J
Glen Flagler	Lowlands	–	Oban	W Highlands	B
Glen Garioch	E Highlands	L	Pittyvaich	Speyside	–
Glenglassaugh	Speyside	G	Port Ellen	Islay	C
Glengoyne	W Highlands	J	Pulteney	N Highlands	E
Glen Grant	Speyside	J	Rosebank	Lowlands	G
Glen Keith	Speyside	K	St. Magdalene	Lowlands	J
Glenkinchie	Lowlands	F	Scapa	Island	A
Glenlivet	Speyside	B	Singleton	Speyside	B
Glenlochy	W Highlands	I	Speyburn	Speyside	D
Glenlossie	Speyside	J	Springbank	Campbeltown	F
Glen Mhor	Speyside	H	Strathisla	Speyside	B
Glenmorangie	N Highlands	C	Strathmill	Speyside	–
Glen Moray	Speyside	G	Talisker	Island	C
Glen Ord	N Highlands	K	Tamdhu	Speyside	J
Glenrothes	Speyside	K	Tamnavulin	Speyside	G
Glen Scotia	Campbeltown	F	Teaninich	N Highlands	L
Glen Spey	Speyside	H	Tobermory	Island	H
Glentauchers	Speyside	H	Tomatin	Speyside	K
Glenturret	Midlands	B	Tomintoul	Speyside	G
Glenugie	E Highlands	A	Tormore	Speyside	K
Glenury Royal	E Highlands	I	Tullibardine	Midlands	F

48.2 WHISKY CLASSIFICATION

Below is a classification of 109 distilleries producing single malt Scotch whisky, based on a mathematical study of Jackson's 1989 tasting notes. (At the time of their analysis, the authors had information on only 109 of the 119 distilleries listed on pp 119–120.) The dendrogram is best considered as a tree, viewed from above. The trunk is the center point from which the branches emanate. Two whiskies (leaves) which join near the outer edge are similar in taste: for example, Glenlivet and Glendullan at four o'clock. The closer to the center a path between two whiskies travels, the less similar they are.

The two main branches from the center divide the spirits into two classes: 69 "full-gold-colored, dry-bodied, and smoky" whiskies (A–H) and 40 "amber, aromatic, light-bodied, smooth palate, and fruity finish" whiskies (I–L). Farther out, 12 sub-branches are labeled A–L; these are the 12 similarity classes in the table above. Drawn from data in F.-J. Lapointe and P. Legendre, "A classification of pure malt Scotch whiskies," *Applied Statistics* **43**, 237 (1994).

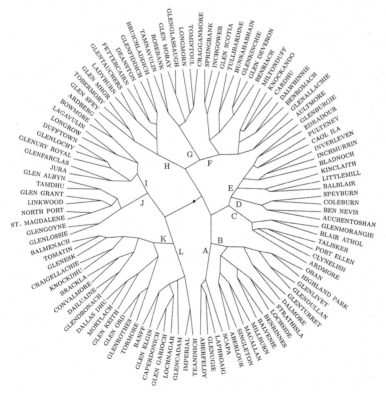

❦49 BOURBON

Bourbon – and the Scottish whisky (p 119) which inspired it – is the definitive man's drink: potent, dry, and characterful. Unlike vodka, gin, and rum, it has a complex taste that repays familiarity with a single brand as well as the exploration of others. Curiously, more so than any other form of alcohol, it separates the sexes: few women find it palatable, fewer pleasant.

Bourbon is indigenous to the United States, where it was perfected to its present form during the first half of the 19th century by James Crow. It is James Bond's preferred tipple in Ian Fleming's original novels (25% of his drinks are bourbon or whisky). We know that it continues to be drunk in the late 23rd century, when Dr. McCoy offers it to Captain Kirk in *Star Trek V*.

49.1 TYPES OF AMERICAN WHISKEY

The word "bourbon" is often used as an all-inclusive term for American whiskey, in addition to its technical definition given below. There are a number of different types of American whiskey, each with a distinct style and prescribed method of production protected by law. Here is an explanation.

Bourbon • Bourbon was defined as America's "native spirit" by an act of Congress in 1964. To be called bourbon, a whiskey must be made from between 51% and 80% corn, be aged in new charred oak barrels, and be at least 40% ABV when bottled. While bourbon can be produced in any American state, only Kentucky can put its name on the label. An essential step in making bourbon is the addition of sour mash, which is the leftover mash used to make the previous batch of whiskey. The taste of bourbon is distinct from Scotch whisky, which tends to be more flavorful. It is bourbon, rather than Scotch, which is called for in most whiskey-based cocktails.

Rye whiskey • This type of whiskey must be made from at least 51% rye (a type of grain, like wheat and barley). Rye whiskey tends to be more flavorful than bourbon, comparable to Irish whiskey or, some say, Scottish Islay.

Tennessee whiskey • This is a whiskey, made from 51% of any one grain but usually corn, which has undergone the so-called Lincoln County Process: filtering the whiskey through charcoal. The charcoal is typically made from maple wood, broken into pellets, and packed into a column. Filtering removes impurities (or unwanted flavors) and adds mild flavors of its own.

Corn whiskey • This little-produced spirit must be made from at least 80% corn. It is briefly aged in uncharred barrels or not aged at all, producing a potent but not subtle drink. It is usually used for mixing or getting merry.

49.2 HOW TO DRINK IT

Bourbon, like Scotch, is best drunk neat (undiluted), apart from a dash of water or a couple of ice cubes. If the bourbon is fine, and you want to appreciate its taste, you should dispense with the ice, which reduces its volatility and your sensitivity of taste. The addition of water, in the proportion of ⅟₂₀ to ¼ parts water to one part whiskey, is held by many, including purists, to bring out the flavor of the drink. While this may be true, a chemical explanation would be of interest, since bourbon is already diluted with water once, when it is removed from the barrel in its stronger ("barrel strength") form. When mixing whiskey cocktails, it is best to use an ordinary make.

49.3 NOTABLE AMERICAN WHISKEYS

Bourbon	Produced in	Age (yrs)	ABV
Buffalo Trace	Kentucky	–	45
Four Roses Yellow Label	Kentucky	5	40
Jim Beam White/Black Label	Kentucky	4/8	40/43
Knob Creek	Kentucky	9	50
Maker's Mark	Kentucky	–	45
Old Fitzgerald	Kentucky	6	43
Old Forester	Kentucky	–	43
Old Rip Van Winkle Handmade	Kentucky	10	45 or 53.5
Rebel Yell	Kentucky	–	45
Weller Special Reserve	Kentucky	7	45
Wild Turkey 101	Kentucky	8	50.5
Wild Turkey Rare Breed	Kentucky	6, 8, 12	"barrel"
Woodford Reserve Distiller's Select	Kentucky	–	45.2

Rye whiskey	Produced in	Age (yrs)	ABV
Old Potrero 18th Century Style	California	–	62.6
Van Winkle Family Reserve Rye	Kentucky	13	47.8
Wild Turkey Rye	Kentucky	–	50.5

Tennessee whiskey	Produced in	Age (yrs)	ABV
Jack Daniels Old Number 7	Tennessee	–	40–50
George Dickel No. 8/12	Tennessee	–	40/45

KEY When the age is not listed (–), it means it is not known or is not advertised on the bottle. By law, bourbon must be aged in the barrel for at least two years. Bourbons aged more than two and less than four years must show their age on the bottle, so an unlabeled bottle is at least four years old.

❦50 LIQUEURS

A liqueur is a spirit flavored with fruit, herbs, or spices – collectively called botanicals – to which sugar is added. This final distinction is important: modern gin, which is grain spirit flavored with juniper, is not a liqueur, but 18th-century gin, which was sweet, is. To be called a liqueur the product must, by European law, contain not less than 100 grams of sugar per liter and be at least 15% ABV. Most liqueurs are 25–40% ABV, but some are much stronger: Elixir Végétal de la Grande-Chartreuse is 71%, although in France it is considered a pharmaceutical product rather than an alcoholic drink.

Liqueurs are drunk in one of three ways. First, they are an essential ingredient in countless cocktails (p 128), where they are used to add sweetness and flavor to the drink. Second, they are drunk neat, usually from a cordial or shot glass, occasionally from an old-fashioned glass over ice. Third, they are diluted with water and ice to make a refreshing long drink, especially the anise-flavored liqueurs, which turn cloudy white on dilution.

50.1 PRODUCTION AND CLASSIFICATION

There are three ways by which flavoring can be added to a base spirit to produce a liqueur. Maceration is the combination of cold spirits and botanicals left to blend over a period of time. Infusion is the mixture of warm spirits and botanicals; as with tea, the higher temperature enhances the process of extraction. Alternatively, the mixture of alcohol and flavorings can itself be distilled – a process simply called distillation. In this case only the essential oils and other volatile flavorings from the botanicals remain in the resulting spirit. In all cases, the liquor is sweetened by adding sugar.

Liqueurs may be divided into those that are flavored with herbs and spices, such as apricot kernels, attar of roses, and mint; and those that are flavored with fruit, including cocoa and coffee beans. In practice, many liqueurs are a mixture of the two. Because liqueurs are often flavored with dozens of different botanicals, they can have complex, subtle tastes which are not easily described. The ingredients are usually heavily guarded secrets, in some cases known by only a handful of people at any one time.

The best liqueurs are the longstanding proprietary brands, many of which have remained more or less unchanged for centuries. The two most famous, and arguably the oldest, liqueurs are Benedictine and Chartreuse.

50.2 NOTABLE HERB LIQUEURS

Name	Tasting notes	ABV
Chartreuse Elixir Végétal	medicinal, aromatic	71
Absinthe (La Fée)	aniseed, mint, lemon	68

Chartreuse Verte	aromatic, herbs, licorice	55
Pastis (Ricard)	star anise, licorice, black pepper	45
Benedictine	mixed spices, honey, citrus, cognac-based	40
Benedictine B & B	a mix of Benedictine and brandy	40
Chartreuse Jaune	honey, aromatic	40
Danzig Goldwasser	orange peel, anise, caraway seed	40
Drambuie	honey, orange, aromatic, malt whisky-based	40
Sambuca (Molinari)	aniseed, black licorice	40
Strega	mint, fennel, aniseed	40
Ouzo (12)	anise, cinnamon	38
Glayva	honey, spices, whisky-based	35
Irish Mist	Irish whiskey, honey, heather	35
Galliano	spice, aniseed, citrus, vanilla	30
Royal Mint Chocolate	after-dinner mints	28.5
Amaretto (Disaronno)	apricot kernels, almonds, baked cake	28
Parfait Amour	rosewater, orange, vanilla	25
Pimm's No. 1 Cup	citrus, spices, gin-based	25
Frangelico	hazelnut, caramel, butter	24
Advocaat (Warninks)	custard, brandy-and-egg-yolk-based	17.2

50.3 NOTABLE FRUIT LIQUEURS

Cointreau	sweet oranges, bitter orange peel	40
Grand Marnier	burnt oranges, orange peel, cognac-based	40
Southern Comfort	caramel, citrus	40
Triple Sec	oranges, orange peel	30–40
Mandarine Napoléon	candied orange peel, bitter marmalade	38
Jägermeister	mixed spices, licorice, medicinal	35
Limoncello (Villa Massa)	lemon drops, lemon peel	30
Kahlúa	coffee, dark chocolate, vanilla, sharp then sweet	26.5
Tia Maria	Jamaican coffee, milk chocolate	26.5
Sloe gin (Plymouth)	raspberries, forest fruits, gin-based	26
Campari	bitter orange peel, honey	25
Cherry brandy (Heering)	ripe cherries, almonds, brandy-based	24.7
Peach schnapps (Archers)	sweet peach flesh	23
Malibu	sweetened coconut, rum-based	21
Pisang Ambon	banana split, overripe bananas	21
Midori	honeydew melon	20
Passoã	passion fruit, citrus	20
Baileys	Irish whiskey, cream, dark chocolate	17
Tequila Rose	strawberries, tequila-based	17
Chambord	raspberries, honey, jam	16.5

♥51 COCKTAILS

A cocktail is an iced spirit modified by juices, liqueurs, sugar, aromatic wines, and bitters, which may or may not be diluted by a sparkling beverage or water. David Embury, the author of the definitive cocktail guide *The Fine Art of Mixing Drinks* (Books, p 194), defines a cocktail axiomatically:

1 It must whet the appetite, not dull it.   4 It must be pleasing to the eye.
2 It should stimulate the mind.   5 It must have sufficient alcoholic flavor.
3 It must be pleasing to the palate.   6 Finally it must be well iced.

From these axioms a number of properties of cocktails can be deduced. Axioms 5 and 6 tell us what a cocktail is not, namely, anything made without spirits or warm. Thus a kir (white wine and cassis) is not a cocktail, nor is an Irish coffee, which is hot. However desirable a cocktail may be after dinner, it must function as an aperitif before (axiom 1). The variety of cocktail glasses is partly explained by axiom 4, each type of drink being most tempting in its own shape of glass. Finally, a cocktail should taste nice (axiom 3), and recipes can be varied according to the principles given here.

51.1 CLASSIFICATION

Cocktails fall into three categories: short drinks, which are undiluted (apart from flavorings); long drinks, which are diluted with soda water or other carbonated drink; and punches, which are diluted with water. Of course, in practice all cocktails are to some extent diluted by adding ice, and are the better for it, but this implicit dilution is not considered in their definition.

Short drinks should be at least 50% spirit by volume, which is about as strong as port or sherry. Consequently, they are served in smaller portions, usually in martini or old-fashioned glasses. They may be further divided into sours and aromatics. Sours, which do not in general taste sour because sugar is added, have as a modifying agent lemon or lime juice. With aromatics the principal modifying agent is one of the bitters, such as Angostura or Peychaud, or an aromatic wine, such as vermouth.

Long drinks differ from short drinks by the addition of a neutral background beverage, generally soda water, but sometimes tonic water, ginger ale, or Coke. If it is made without citrus juice, it is a highball; with lemon juice, a collins; and with lime juice, a rickey.

Punches, which have the longest lineage, are made in large quantities. They are traditionally diluted with still water, although in many recipes this has been replaced by soda water or lemonade. Punches are typically served from a bowl containing a block of ice; ice is not added to each glass.

Ice

Ice is the most neglected ingredient in cocktails. Not only is it essential to have plenty of ice, but it should be of the correct consistency. The most finely broken is crushed, followed by cracked and cubed. Crushed ice is ground by machine, or made from cubes by pounding ice wrapped in a towel.

Quality over quantity

Most books on cocktails contain far too many recipes, many of them unpalatable. In fact there are not more than two dozen drinks from which nearly all others can be derived. Start, for example, with the Gimlet: it is made of four parts gin, two parts lime juice, and one part sugar syrup. If the gin is replaced with light rum, it is a Daiquiri. Add some crushed mint leaves and soda water and it becomes a Mojito. Substitute bourbon for rum and drop the soda and lime for a Mint Julep. Replace the mint with lemon and it is a Whiskey Sour. A good understanding of which flavors mix with others, and in what proportions, makes cocktail recipes altogether redundant.

Stirring versus shaking

The debate over stirring versus shaking should be laid to rest, as there is little difference between the two: shaking involves slightly less dilution if the ice is much colder than 0 °C (32 °F). The exception is drinks that froth, such as those made with egg whites, where shaking is essential. More important is whether to strain (keeping the ice out of the drink) or pour (leaving it in). Pouring is more common with long drinks. In all cases drinks should be as cold as possible, and to this end they are sometimes served in chilled glasses.

Muddling

Muddling is the mashing of ingredients in the base of an old-fashioned or highball glass with a 1-inch-thick wooden rod, called a muddler. It is usually done to citrus fruit, sometimes with sugar added, with the remains left in the glass. Bruising is a very light muddling often used for mint leaves.

Making many drinks

Apart from bartenders, most mixers need to make not one drink at a time but two or four or six. All of the drinks listed on pp 128–129 are given in terms of relative, rather than absolute, measures. This means that a cocktail can be made in as large a quantity as desired by changing the volume of a single part. As a rule of thumb, the typical amount of spirits (40% ABV) in a cocktail is 43 ml (Bartenders' Bible, p 102). For larger gatherings, it is often impractical to make drinks in small batches, and mass mixing is a must. The best method is to combine in a jug or large bowl all the ingredients except ice, sparkling beverages, and fruit, which are added one glass at a time.

51.3 INGREDIENTS

What are cocktails made from? The most useful ingredients must be those that come up most frequently in different cocktail recipes. An analysis of the 100 most popular cocktails yields a total of 94 different ingredients, distributed as follows (only the top 12 ingredients in each column are shown):

Spirits	%	Other alcohol	%	Non-alcohol	%
vodka	30	Angostura	14	ice	98
gin	18	Cointreau	12	sugar syrup	46
light rum	10	framboise	8	lime juice	28
tequila	8	champagne	6	lemon juice	22
bourbon	7	dry vermouth	5	soda water	12
cognac	7	sweet vermouth	5	orange juice	10
dark rum	6	blackberry liqueur	4	cranberry juice	8
Scotch whisky	4	cassis	4	apple juice	7
cachaça	3	Kahlúa	4	egg white	6
gold rum	2	peach schnapps	4	ginger beer	6
Pisco	2	Baileys	3	pineapple juice	6
Irish whiskey	1	Grand Marnier	3	Rose's lime cordial	5

Different cocktails are served in different glasses (p 104), and the distribution of glasses is also of interest. The same 100 cocktails are served in these:

Glass	%				
martini	33	old-fashioned	21	hurricane	3
highball	27	flute	6	shot	2
		pilsner	4	other	4

51.4 A DOZEN COCKTAILS FOR LIFE

These 12 classic drinks from the old world and the new have stood the test of time. Proportions can and should be adjusted to suit individual tastes. The glass and garnish for each cocktail are labeled Ⴧ and ♂, respectively.

Caipirinha
8 parts cachaça
¾ lime per glass
3 parts sugar syrup
Ⴧ old-fashioned, straw
Muddle sliced lime in glass. Add rest and crushed ice and stir.

Cosmopolitan
6 parts vodka
3 parts Cointreau
6 parts cranberry juice
1 part lime juice
Ⴧ martini, ♂ orange peel
Shake with crushed ice and strain into glasses.

Gimlet
4 parts gin
2 parts lime juice
1 part sugar syrup
Y martini, ♕ lime slice
Shake with crushed ice and strain
into glasses.

Manhattan
5 parts bourbon
1 part dry vermouth
2 dashes Angostura per glass
Y martini, ♕ orange peel
Shake with crushed ice and strain
into glasses.

Margarita
2 parts tequila
1 part Cointreau
1 part lime juice
Y martini, ♕ lime slice
First salt glass rims. Shake with
crushed ice and strain into glasses.

Martini
7 parts gin
1 part dry vermouth
Y martini, ♕ lemon peel
Shake with crushed ice and strain
into glasses.

Mint Julep
3 parts bourbon
1 part sugar syrup
10 mint leaves per glass
1 dash Angostura per glass
Y highball, straw
Bruise mint leaves with bourbon.
Add rest and crushed ice and stir.

Mojito
4 parts light rum

4 parts soda water
½ lime per glass
10 mint leaves per glass
1 part sugar syrup
Y highball, straw
Muddle sliced lime and mint in
glass. Add rest and crushed ice; stir.

Old-fashioned
5 parts bourbon
1 part sugar syrup
2 dashes Angostura per glass
Y old-fashioned, ♕ orange slice
Shake with crushed ice and pour
(with ice) into ice-filled glasses.

Sidecar
2 parts cognac
1 part lemon juice
1 part Cointreau
Y martini, ♕ lemon peel
Shake with crushed ice and strain
into glasses.

Singapore Sling
8 parts gin
4 parts cherry brandy
2 parts lemon juice
1 part sugar syrup
1 dash Angostura per glass
Y highball, straw, ♕ cherry
Shake with crushed ice, pour (w. ice)
into glasses and top with soda water.

Whiskey Sour
2 parts bourbon
1 part lemon juice
1 part sugar syrup
2 dashes Angostura per glass
Y old-fashioned, ♕ lemon slice
Shake with crushed ice and pour
(with ice) into glasses.

❦52 FLASKS

Portable spirits are a boon whenever your drinks cabinet is out of reach: out of doors, when liquor is not available, and in the bar, when it is too expensive. In principle any container can be used to store the drink, so long as it is concealable, sturdy, and leak-proof. The best flasks hold between 4 and 8 ounces and are made of pewter (an inexpensive alloy of tin with copper and antimony) or silver, with a screw-on cap of the same material.

52.1 FLASK CAPACITY

A typical flask holds 6 ounces, or ½ a can of beer, so the spirit inside should be strong. (Spirits are better than liqueurs because they are not sticky.) Below is the amount of beer and wine equivalent to a flaskful of different drinks.

6-oz flask of	12-oz cans of beer (4% ABV)	Bottles of wine (12% ABV)
Sherry	2.2	0.36
Bourbon/brandy	5.0	0.79
Cask-strength whisky	6.9	1.1
Everclear	12	1.9

52.2 FLASK ETIQUETTE

When should a flask be carried? In principle, one can be kept in the breast or trouser pocket at all times. In the field and street it usually can be drunk from with impunity. In bars, where it is a money saver, it is best used clandestinely. In a private house it should be avoided, on the presumption that your host will provide sufficient alcohol. Better to bring a bottle if in doubt.

52.3 FLASK STYLES

The simplest styles tend to be the best. For easy pocket storage, an undecorated 6-oz rectangular flask (left) or a 4-oz circular one (right) is ideal. If you find yourself in a pinch, a small plastic drinks bottle will do the job.

SMOKING

Arnold Schwarzenegger • I have inhaled, exhaled everything.

Klinger • A good cigar is like a beautiful chick with a great body who also knows the American League box scores. (*M*A*S*H*)

Winston Churchill • My rule of life prescribed as an absolutely sacred rite smoking cigars and also the drinking of alcohol before, after, and if need be during all meals and in the intervals between them. (*Triumph and Tragedy*, 1953)

Anonymous • Thus dost thou every taste and genius hit, / In smoke thou'rt wisdom; and in snuff thou'rt wit.

Joseph Cullman (former head of Philip Morris) • Some women would prefer having smaller babies. (*Face the Nation* interview, 1971)

A. A. Gill • When on occasion I'm asked by groups of aspiring writers what they should do to get on, my advice is always, emphatically, smoke… It's a little-known, indeed little-researched, fact of literature and journalism that no nonsmoker is worth reading. (*Sunday Times*, 1999)

Cigarette slogans
The length you go to for pleasure (*Benson & Hedges*)
I'd walk a mile for a Camel (*Camel*)
If you smoke, please smoke Carlton (*Carlton*)
Blow some my way (*Chesterfield*)
Just what the doctor ordered (*L & M*)
Reach for a Lucky instead of a sweet (*Lucky Strike*)
Come to where the flavor is (*Marlboro*)
Alive with pleasure (*Newport*)
Wherever particular people congregate (*Pall Mall*)
Springtime…it happens every Salem (*Salem*)
You've come a long way, baby (*Virginia Slims*)
Tastes good like a cigarette should (*Winston*)

❦53 HOW TO START SMOKING

Everyone knows how to quit smoking and the advantages it offers, but there is very little information available on how to start smoking. Most apparent pro-smoking pamphlets and websites are either tricks – they contain anti-smoking propaganda in disguise – or spoofs – they are meant to be funny rather than useful. The result is that first-time smokers have to learn how to smoke through trial and error, without reliable information about the benefits, customs, and relative risks associated with different types of tobacco. Here are some pointers on why and how to pick up the habit.

53.1 ADVANTAGES OF SMOKING

At a time when smoking bans are being put into effect across America and around the world, it is tempting to think that there is no worse time to start than now. In truth it may be as good a time as ever. When a morally neutral act is banned, more people often turn to it than would have otherwise; a classic example of this is foxhunting in Britain. Moreover, like underage drinking in America, illicit activities are more likely to be perceived as fashionable. A persecuted minority mixes more freely among itself, and a ban does nothing if not add to social cohesion among smokers.

There are a number of advantages associated with smoking which may for some offset the known disadvantages. Smoking can be an effective method of weight control, as Lucky Strike cigarettes put into profitable effect with their famous slogan, "Reach for a Lucky instead of a sweet." Smoking appeals to man's innate fascination with fire, particularly in the case of cigars and pipes, which offer little in the form of a chemical kick. Smoking is manly and suggests gravitas, notwithstanding its popularity with women relatively recently in its long history. Finally, for many smoking is an essential means of relaxation. It brings reflection, and with reflection more considered judgment, if not wisdom. A Bushongo man, having learned to smoke on a journey away, said this of smoking on his return:

> When you have a quarrel with your brother, in your fury you may wish to slay him: sit down and smoke a pipe. When the pipe is finished you will think that perhaps death is too great a punishment for your brother's offences, and you will decide to let him off with a thrashing. Relight your pipe and smoke on. As the smoke curls upwards you will come to the conclusion that a few hard words might take the place of blows. Light up your pipe once more, and when it is smoked through you will go to your brother and ask him to forget the past.
>
> M. W. Hilton-Simpson, *Land and Peoples of the Masai*, 1911

53.2 WHICH TOBACCO?

The first step towards habitual smoking is to decide which kind of tobacco to take up. There are five popular kinds: cigarettes, cigars, pipes, chewing tobacco, and snuff (pp 134–141). Each possesses its own sub-culture and suits some personalities better than others.

In order of health risk, cigarettes are the most dangerous, because they alone are inhaled and bring tar in contact with the lungs. Chewing tobacco, which offers a hundred-fold reduction in risk, is a distant second; then cigars and pipes, which are not inhaled; then nasal snuff, the safest tobacco of all. Cigarettes and chewing tobacco offer the most nicotine and are consequently the most addictive.

Different tobaccos have different social connotations. Cigarettes are socially neutral, although the individual brands are not. Cigars, the most expensive tobacco, are often associated with the bourgeoisie, though this is less true after the cigar boom of the 1990s. Pipes, once a young man's essential accessory, have for some time been out of favor with the young. Today they are often smoked in solitude or as an aid to contemplative work. Chewing tobacco is generally considered the most uncouth, though there are exceptions, such as snus, which is widely popular in northern Europe. Snuff, the least expensive and today least popular form of tobacco, was historically associated with both the lower and upper classes, less so the middle.

53.3 ADVICE FOR BEGINNERS

A new smoker must at all times be in possession of his tools of the trade. It is frustrating to be separated from your essential smoking kit, so get into the habit of putting everything you need in the same pocket and always check it as you leave the door.

You will invariably receive pressure from others to either not take up smoking or refrain from smoking in their presence, particularly at dinners and parties. The best response to this is a defensive one: surround yourself with other smokers, which makes taking up smoking much more enjoyable. Two or three smokers together at a party are a social attraction; walk up to them and light up and you will be sure to be taken in with open arms.

Early on try different brands of cigarettes to find which one most suits your taste; old smoking habits die hard. If you are smoking cigars, start with an inexpensive brand, as most beginners will appreciate an ordinary cigar no less than an expensive Cuban. It is also wise to begin with a small ring gauge – a cigarillo or a panatela, for example – and work your way up to bigger cigars with experience, if at all. Like big game hunters, men who smoke big, expensive cigars should have learned the ropes with lesser ones.

❦54 CIGARETTES

54.1 TOP-SELLING CIGARETTE BRANDS

Although there are many brands of cigarettes available, smokers are a loyal bunch and rarely try other makes. In Ian Fleming's novel *Thunderball*, James Bond switches from his Balkan and Turkish Morland specials to low-tar Duke of Durhams only after being sent to a health clinic by his medical officer. For curious smokers, it is useful to be reminded what the alternatives are. Below are the ten most popular brands in America and in Britain.

US market share, by brand		*UK market share, by brand/type*	
Marlboro	35.4%	Lambert & Butler KS	13.5%
Doral	6.3%	Benson & Hedges Gold	7.3%
Newport	6.2%	Mayfair King Size	7.1%
Camel	5.3%	Richmond Superkings	6.6%
Winston	5.2%	Richmond King Size	4.9%
Basic	4.9%	Marlboro Gold King Size	4.4%
GPC	4.7%	Regal KS	3.5%
Kool	3.3%	Royals King Size Red	3.4%
Salem	3.2%	Superkings	3.3%
Virginia Slims	2.6%	Silk Cut Purple	3.2%
SOURCE www.tobacco.org		SOURCE www.ash.org.uk	

54.2 CIGARETTE CUSTOMS

Lighting · Compared to lighting a cigar or a pipe, lighting a cigarette looks easy. But there is a certain knack to inhaling at just the right moment from the right part of the flame to light up with a swift and elegant motion. The beginner lingers too long, burning too much of his cigarette in the process. When you don't have matches or a lighter at hand, it is possible to light one cigarette from another lit one by bringing the tips together and inhaling.

Sharing · When offering a cigarette to someone else, do not hand over the cigarette itself, but let him take a cigarette from the pack. It is customary to pull one partially out, as shown, before offering it.

Packing · Pack the cigarettes by firmly rapping the unopened pack on the palm of your hand; this compresses the tobacco for a supposedly better smoke and gives the impression of a man who knows what he's doing. But it must be done with an air of insouciance – mid-conversation, for instance.

54.3 CIGARETTE HOLDS

A person's first impression of a smoker depends not so much on his choice of cigarette as on the way he holds it. Below is a catalog of good grips.

Classic cigarette · This standard hold for cigarettes will not draw attention as being too negligent or too much studied.

Gentry · A variation on the classic grip that conveys gravitas (or pomposity). It need only be used momentarily to produce the desired effect.

Twee · This affected hold is a quick giveaway of (i) a new smoker hoping to impress or (ii) a man who bats for the other team.

Comfort · This ingenious hold can be used for cigarettes and cigars. The middle finger acts as a natural rest for one's heavier smokes.

Classic cigar · Used by the majority of cigar smokers, this natural grip can handle anything from cigarillos to the highest of ring gauges.

Chap · What this hold suffers from in functionality it makes up for in aesthetics. Note that the cigarette must not be held too close to the butt.

Bounder · Apart from damaging the cigarette, this unusual hold enables any smoking ruffian to throw a punch at a moment's notice.

Stealth · At a distance, this clever hold conceals a cigarette from smoking-ban vigilantes. At closer proximity the smoke may prove incriminating.

Woman's · European women frequently use cigarettes as a fashion accessory, and this elegant hold is bound to attract a few catcalls.

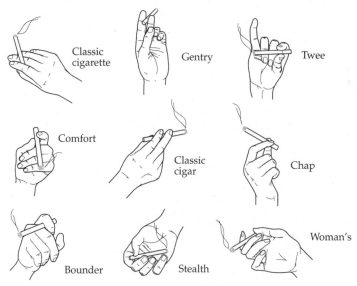

❦55 CIGARS

55.1 CIGAR SIZE

The first thing to consider when smoking a cigar is not the brand but the size. Size affects the intensity of flavor, prescribes the occasion, and determines the duration: a typical cigarillo can be smoked in under 10 minutes, while a giant may last more than two hours. The length of a cigar is measured in inches and the diameter, or ring gauge, in 64ths of an inch. Although there is no prescription as to which cigars should be smoked by whom, it is loosely accepted that "the ring gauge should match your age." Thus a 24-year-old man might smoke a ⅜-inch cigarillo, a 32-year-old a ½-inch panatela, and a 48-year-old a ¾-inch Churchill. The smallest cigarillos tend to have ring gauges in the low 20s, which is probably the earliest age to be seen smoking cigars. A young man with a big cigar looks faintly ridiculous.

55.2 SIZE CHART

There is a longstanding tradition of associating names with certain cigar sizes, and some names have specific meaning in the cigar industry. But there is no set convention, and some names conflict or are redundant. Below is an attempt to rationally divide the entire cigar size range, taking into account present usage. Measurements between sizes belong to the larger size.

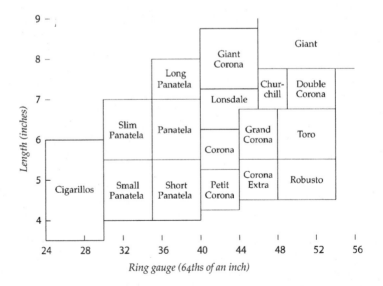

Typical dimensions of each size are as follows:

Size	Inches × 64ths of an inch		
Cigarillo	4 × 26	Lonsdale	6.5 × 42
Small Panatela	5 × 32	Giant Corona	7.5 × 44
Slim Panatela	6 × 34	Corona Extra	5.5 × 46
Short Panatela	5 × 38	Grand Corona	6.5 × 46
Panatela	6 × 38	Robusto	5 × 50
Long Panatela	7.5 × 38	Toro	6 × 50
Petit Corona	5 × 42	Churchill	7 × 48
Corona	5.5 × 42	Double Corona	7.5 × 50
		Giant	8.5 × 52

55.3 CIGAR CUSTOMS

Storage · Left in the open air, a cigar will dry out, making the wrapper brittle and liable to crack and the cigar itself smoke hot and fast. The best way to circumvent this is to store cigars in a humidor, which is any softwood-lined box with a wet sponge or a small pot of water inside. A cheap hygrometer, which measures humidity, is found in many commercial humidors, but this gadget is unnecessary so long as the sponge is kept wet, or pot filled.

Grip · The most common mistake of a cigar novice is to hold a cigar as if it were a cigarette – between the middle and index finger. Instead it should be held between both the middle and index fingers and the thumb (p 135).

Ash · The ash on a cigar is much sturdier than the ash on a cigarette, and it is not necessary to flick it in an ashtray nearly as often. With better cigars the ash is robust enough to extend as much as an inch. Knowing just when the ash is about to fall, and flicking it off beforehand, is an acquired skill.

Extinguishing · Whereas a cigarette will burn continuously whether it is smoked or not, a cigar will die in several minutes when it is left unattended. For this reason it is not necessary to snub out a cigar when you have finished smoking it, which is thought to be inelegant; instead, leave it to die.

Removing the band · There is no consensus as to whether the paper band at the base of the cigar should be removed. In general it is not necessary because a cigar is not normally smoked to the end, which has a bitter taste.

Lighting · To ensure that the cigar is evenly lit, hold it at a 45-degree angle an inch above the flame of a match while rotating it until the edge begins to smoke. Then light the cigar in the usual way by inhaling from the flame.

❦56 PIPES

The attraction to pipe smoking is largely not based on nicotine – like cigars, pipes are not inhaled – but association and ritual: the routine filling of the bowl; the warmth of the briar; the subconscious fascination with fire. Pipe smoke itself is more instinctively pleasant than the smoke from rolled tobacco. Cigars are typically smoked in company, pipes in solitude.

Pipes can be made from briar, meerschaum, clay, corncob, or calabash. Of these, briar is by far the most popular. It is the hardened root burl of the Mediterranean heath tree. Meerschaum is a soft, white, clay-like mineral which is carved. Calabash is the gourd of an evergreen tree. The most distinctive feature of a pipe is whether the stem is bent or straight. Bent stems are easier to hold in the mouth (they exert less torque on the teeth) while straight are presently smarter. The style of stem does not determine the shape of the bowl, which comes in many varieties. Pipe authority Richard Carleton Hacker (Books, p 192) classifies bowls into eight types, as follows.

56.1 TYPES OF PIPE

Apple · An elegant, spherical, comparatively squat bowl.

Billiard · Classic shape; height of bowl equals length of shank.

Bulldog · A beveled top with carved ridge and diamond-shaped stem.

Canadian · A long shank and short bit, thus more difficult to make.

Dublin · Wider at the top than base, with a flat or concave rear.

Freehand · A freeform style inspired by the individual briar stock.

Pot · The shortest and broadest of bowls, with a rounded bottom.

Poker · A flat-bottomed, clean-cut, cylindrical bowl.

56.2 INSTRUCTIONS FOR LIGHTING A PIPE

The main skill in smoking a pipe is knowing how to fill and light it. This determines how easily the pipe draws, how long the tobacco lasts, and how much dottle (ash and partially burnt tobacco) remains at the end. Bear in mind that pipes, like cigars, go out from time to time and must be relit.

1 Fill the bowl of the pipe until it slightly overflows by dropping in loose strands of tobacco, taking care to disentangle clumps.
2 Using a pipe tool or the head of a nail, tamp down the tobacco with light force until it has been reduced to about half its volume.

3 Again, drop loose tobacco into the bowl until it overflows.

4 Tamp the tobacco until it is just below the surface of the bowl.

5 Light the pipe, ideally with a horizontal match, and take in several short puffs of smoke. Stop and wait for the coals to die out. This is known as the charring light.

6 Tamp down once more, creating a layer of charred tobacco. This essential step ensures that the bowl of tobacco lights evenly.

7 Light the pipe a second time, as before, and continue to draw.

56.3 BREAKING IN A NEW PIPE

A well-used briar pipe will have accumulated over time a thick layer of charred soot and resin on the inside of the bowl. This coating, or cake as it is often called, is crucial to the normal function of the pipe: it insulates the wood from the heat of the burning tobacco and, like a bed of coals, stores heat, ensuring a more even burn. New pipes do not have the benefit of this protective layer, and much care should be taken when breaking them in, as smoking such a pipe too hot can burn deep into the briar. Some experts suggest applying a thin layer of honey to the inside of a new bowl, which will carbonize and encourage the development of a cake. After smoking half a dozen pipefuls, a thin cake will have emerged, which will continue to accumulate with use.

56.4 CLEANING A PIPE

Ideally, a pipe should be cleaned after every one or two smokes, although in practice it is common to move on to other pipes and then clean them all in parallel. Two things are essential for cleaning a pipe: a pipe tool and pipe cleaners. Pipe tools come in a variety of designs; a typical and inexpensive one is a folding multi-tool with a circular tamper, a spoon, and a thin rod for picking. Pipe cleaners are long, thin wire brushes.

The first step in cleaning is to use the spoon to scrape out any dottle and residue from the bowl, taking care not to remove much, if any, of the insulating cake described above. Knowing just how firmly to scrape, and therefore how much of the cake to remove, is learned with experience.

The second step is cleaning the air hole. To do so, first separate the stem from the bowl by gently twisting the stem out; this should never be done before the pipe has cooled completely, because the wood tends to expand with heat. Then fully insert a pipe cleaner into the air hole of each half. Repeat this process, each time with a new pipe cleaner, until the cleaner emerges with little or no residue, which may take a few cleaners for the stem and twice as many for the bowl. Soiled pipe cleaners have a tendency to make a whole room reek, so they should be disposed of immediately, ideally in a fire.

❦57 CHEWING TOBACCO

Chewing tobacco is the popular name of several kinds of tobacco that are not smoked but put directly into the mouth: dipping tobacco (dip), snus, and chewing tobacco. Dip and snus, the most popular kinds, are finely cut tobacco and are placed between the lower or upper lip and the gums. They are not chewed but are left in the mouth for several minutes to over an hour.

57.1 DIPPING TOBACCO AND SNUS

Dipping tobacco · Dipping tobacco (dip) causes an excess of saliva to be produced, which is spat out regularly onto the ground or into a cup. Partly for this reason, it is popular with outdoorsmen; it also has a strong following among baseball players. Common brands include Copenhagen, Kodiak, and Skoal, which typically come in a flat, round pack. A telltale sign of a dip user is the faded ring left by the pack in the back pocket of his Wranglers.

Snus · Snus is similar to dipping tobacco, but the tobacco is less processed and it typically comes in small, single-portion pouches, like small tea bags. It is very popular in Sweden and Norway, and has become increasingly so in America with the introduction of smoking bans. Unlike dip, snus does not cause excessive spitting, which makes it much more practical to use.

57.2 SAFER THAN SMOKING?

It is widely recognized in the scientific literature that chewing tobacco and snus (collectively called smokeless tobacco) are immensely safer than smoking. In a recent study in the journal *BMC Public Health*,* the authors write:

> Compared to smoking cigarettes, use of Western smokeless tobacco products is associated with a very small risk of life-threatening disease (with estimates in the range of a few percent of the risk from smoking, or even less).

Nevertheless, the vast majority of public health authorities and policy makers state that the risk of smokeless tobacco is comparable to smoking cigarettes, or use misleading phrases such as "Smokeless tobacco is not a safe alternative to cigarettes." (By the same reasoning, hiking is not a safe alternative to cigarettes.) The *BMC* paper concludes: "These messages are clearly false and likely harmful, representing violations of ethical standards."

*C. Phillips, C. Wang, and B. Guenzel, "You might as well smoke; the misleading and harmful public message about smokeless tobacco," *BMC Public Health,* **5**, 31 (2005).

❦58 SNUFF

The introduction of indoor smoking bans throughout the world is of course cause for smokers' sorrow. But even this dark cloud brings with it some cause for hope: snuff. With the exception of fire, the smokeless tobacco offers all of the attractions of smoking: the kick, the kit, the ceremony, and the camaraderie. The clampdown on smoking might bring snuff use back to levels not seen since it was taken up by the 19th-century gentility and 20th-century coal miners. The motto of Wilson of Sharrow, snuff producers in England since 1737, is timely: "Smoke when you can, snuff when you can't."

Snuff is finely powdered tobacco leaf and stalk which is not ignited but sniffed directly into the nose. It comes in many varieties, falling roughly into three classes: natural, perfumed, and medicated. Perfumed snuff is scented with the essential oils of fruits or flowers; medicated, with menthol or eucalyptus or aniseed. First-time users might have a tendency to sneeze, but this dies off with experience. Snuff is stored in a snuffbox, a small lidded container with any one of a number of (preferably airtight) closing mechanisms. While snuffboxes of some value are available, an experienced snuff taker uses a sober metal or wooden box which can be lost without regret.

58.1 INSTRUCTIONS FOR TAKING SNUFF

There are two ways of taking snuff. The first is executed by placing a pinch of snuff in the depression on the back of the left hand, between the forefinger and outstretched thumb. From here it is sniffed into both nostrils or one nostril at a time. In the case of the latter it is helpful, if inelegant, to close the other nostril with the right hand. Note that to sniff is not to snort: unlike other powdered substances, snuff is not meant to reach the sinuses. The second technique is described in a mid-19th-century snuff pamphlet:

1 Take the snuff box in the right hand.
2 Pass it to the left hand.
3 Rap the snuff box.
4 Open the box and inspect the contents.
5 Present box to surrounding company with a courteous bow.
6 Receive it back with the left hand.
7 Gather up the snuff by striking the box side with middle and forefinger.
8 Take a pinch with the right hand.
9 Hold the snuff for a second or two between fingers before taking.
10 Carry the pinch to the nose.
11 Snuff with precision by both nostrils and without grimaces or distortion of the features.
12 Close snuff box with a flourish.

❦59 SMOKING ETIQUETTE

The introduction of indoor smoking bans in states across America is changing the way men smoke. There is more smoking in private residences and
out of doors, and the much-persecuted community of smokers is voicing its
solidarity. Here is a guide to smokers' rights and wrongs. Throughout this
section, the word "smoking" refers to the use of cigarettes, cigars, and pipes,
but not chewing tobacco and snuff, which are permissible everywhere.

59.1 INDOOR SMOKING

First, is it acceptable to ban guests from smoking in your house? James
Leavey, editor of the *FOREST Guide to Smoking* series, gives this advice:

> There are those who will not permit any smoking in their home. It is their
> prerogative but of course their smoking guests may consider this anti-
> social. It is very unkind to confront a heavy smoker in your home with the
> fact that he or she will have to suffer a smoke-free evening. Better to warn
> your guests when you invite them, so they can decide whether or not to
> turn down your invitation.

John Morgan, in *Debrett's New Guide to Etiquette and Modern Manners*, concurs. "If you as the host hate the habit, you can quite legitimately never invite smokers to your table. However, it is not appropriate to forbid a guest
to smoke in your house once he or she is there."

Second, when is it acceptable to light up in someone else's house? In an
ideal world, if you are known to be a regular smoker and have been in-
vited, you are welcome to smoke. In reality, you have to be on the lookout
for context clues. The presence of ashtrays is a sure sign that smoking is allowed. The possession of a personal portable ashtray, on the other hand,
does not confer a licence to just smoke anywhere. If you cannot see an ashtray, an unabashed "May we smoke?" is often answered in the affirmative.
Smoking while others at the table are eating is bad manners, although a
cigarette between courses is perfectly acceptable. Children, especially boys,
are known to enjoy being in the presence of all forms of fire and smoke.

59.2 OUTDOOR SMOKING

More and more smokers are forced to smoke outside bars and restaurants,
and certain special rules apply to this community in exile. The usual social
reservation between strangers is lifted: striking up a conversation with a
smoker you don't know is to be encouraged, and asking him for a cigarette

is perfectly acceptable. At work, dedicated smokers should coordinate their outdoor smoking breaks, and the same applies to bars and restaurants.

59.3 DEALING WITH NON-SMOKERS

What is the correct response to hostile or disapproving non-smokers in places where smoking is permitted? A gentle smoker would like, on the one hand, to avoid causing pain (in the words of Newman, p 204). On the other, he has a moral duty to resist non-smoking bullies. With regard to the first, he will realize when his habit is not welcome and adjust his behavior accordingly – standing near an open window, for example. With regard to the second, he will nip intolerance in the bud with a smug smoke ring or firm puff in the direction of the complainer. As host, if one guest shows annoyance at another's smoking, the easiest solution is to isolate not the smoker but the complaining guest: "Let's step outside for a chat on the balcony while John finishes his cigarette."

A less considered problem is the *apparent* non-smoker who persistently leeches off the secondhand smoke of others without lighting up himself. While this may or may not be intentional, ultimately it means that there is less secondhand smoke to go around. Like a man at the bar who never buys his round, a repeat offender should be encouraged to light up or leave.

59.4 ASHES, BUTTS, AND DOTTLE

The question of where you can dispose of ash, butts, and dottle is a tricky one (dottle is the burnt and partially burnt tobacco left in the bowl of a pipe). Certainly it is acceptable to flick your ash onto the ground or street out of doors. Dropping butts and dottle is an unattractive habit, but there are occasions when this is the only option. If there is no ashtray or bin nearby, it is acceptable in public, though not private, outdoor spaces. Indoors the policy is similar, but more stringent by one degree. When necessary, ash can be dropped on public, though not private, hard floors; butts and dottle must be properly disposed of. Carpets require special care – it is hugely annoying to find cigarette burns the morning after a swinging party.

59.5 LIGHTING UP

When the occasion arises, a man should light a woman's cigarette directly, but should offer the lighter to a man for him to light his own. The exception is when both men are lighting up simultaneously; in this case you light the other's first, then your own. Lighting cigars (p 137) and pipes (p 138) is a comparatively complex ritual and is always executed by the smoker himself.

59.6 SMOKING BANS

Unlike many countries, America has does not have a blanket ban on smoking in public places. Instead, individual states are left to decide to what extent smoking should be prohibited. The law differentiates between smoking in the workplace, restaurants, and bars. According to the American Nonsmokers' Rights Foundation, bans vary from state to state, as shown below. Bear in mind that even if smoking is not banned by the state, it may be banned by cities within that state. Note that the tobacco-producing states, such as Kentucky, North Carolina, and Virginia, do not ban smoking at all, and it is unlikely that they will do so in the near future.

Smoking bans by state

State	Work	Rest.	Bars	State	Work	Rest.	Bars
Alabama	O	O	O	Montana	●	●	O
Alaska	O	O	O	Nebraska	O	O	O
Arizona	●	●	●	Nevada	●	●	O
Arkansas	O	O	O	New Hampshire	O	●	●
California	O	●	●	New Jersey	●	●	●
Colorado	O	●	●	New Mexico	O	●	●
Connecticut	O	●	●	New York	●	●	●
Delaware	●	●	●	North Carolina	O	O	O
Florida	●	●	O	North Dakota	●	O	O
Georgia	O	O	O	Ohio	●	●	●
Hawaii	●	●	●	Oklahoma	O	O	O
Idaho	O	●	O	Oregon	O	O	O
Illinois	●	●	●	Pennsylvania	O	O	O
Indiana	O	O	O	Rhode Island	●	●	●
Iowa	●	●	●	South Carolina	O	O	O
Kansas	O	O	O	South Dakota	●	O	O
Kentucky	O	O	O	Tennessee	O	O	O
Louisiana	●	●	O	Texas	O	O	O
Maine	O	●	●	Utah	●	●	O
Maryland	●	●	●	Vermont	O	●	●
Massachusetts	●	●	●	Virginia	O	O	O
Michigan	O	O	O	Washington	●	●	●
Minnesota	●	●	●	West Virginia	O	O	O
Mississippi	O	O	O	Wisconsin	O	O	O
Missouri	O	O	O	Wyoming	O	O	O

KEY   ● banned   O not banned

COOKING

Lisa: Do you have any food that wasn't brutally slaughtered? *Homer*: Well, I think the veal might've died of loneliness. (*The Simpsons,* Faith Off, episode BABF06, 2000)

Lord Byron · All human history attests / That happiness for man – the hungry sinner! – / Since Eve ate apples, much depends on dinner. (*Don Juan,* Canto xiii)

National Cattlemen's Beef Association · Beef: It's what's for dinner. (Advertising campaign)

Esquire · The average woman, to this day, can't make a good cup of coffee. It must be that, basically, coffee is a man's drink. (*Esquire's Handbook for Hosts,* 1949)

Jonathan Swift · For this is every cook's opinion, / No savoury dish without an onion; / But, lest your kissing should be spoiled, / Your onions must be thoroughly boiled. ("Market Women's Cries")

Pink Floyd · If you don't eat your meat, you can't have any pudding. How can you have any pudding if you don't eat your meat? (*The Wall,* 1979)

Paul Erdős · A mathematician is a device for turning coffee into theorems. (Attributed; more likely by Alfréd Rényi)

Charles Pierce · The perfect lover is one who turns into a pizza at 4:00 a.m.

Gordon Ramsay · Parents of obese children should be fined. (*Daily Mail,* 2007)

Benjamin Franklin · Never spare the parson's wine, nor baker's pudding. · Three good meals a day is bad living. · After fish, milk do not wish. · Beware of meat twice boil'd, and an old foe reconcil'd. · He that would travel much should eat little. · Many dishes, many diseases. (*Poor Richard's Almanack,* 1732–1757)

❦60 COOK'S BIBLE

60.1 MEASURING

In American recipes, the cup is a standardized unit of volume equal to 8 US fluid ounces or approximately 237 ml. Also customary are the tablespoon (tbsp or Tbs), of which 16 make a cup; and the teaspoon (tsp), of which 3 make a tablespoon. Smallest of all is the dash; 8 dashes make a teaspoon. The relations between different measurements are shown here; all are exact apart from conversions to milliliters.

	ml	*tsp*	*tbsp*	*US fl. oz*	*cup*	*pint*	*quart*
							2
						2	4
					8	16	32
				2	16	32	64
tsp			3	6	48	96	192
ml		4.93	14.8	29.6	237	473	946
dash	0.616	8	24	48	384	768	1,536

60.2 COOKING

Cooking means to prepare food with heat, but there are many variations, depending on the temperature and how much water or oil is used to cook in.

Boiling is cooking in water at its boiling point, 212 °F. For most foods, the water should be boiling before the food is added. · *Simmering* is cooking in water just below boiling, 185–205 °F. · *Steaming* is cooking with the steam from water boiling but not in contact with the food. · *Stewing* is slow cooking at low temperature in a small amount of liquid. · *Frying* is cooking in oil or fat at a temperature over 212 °F. · *Deep frying* is frying in enough oil or fat to submerge the food. · *Sautéing* is frying at high heat with a small amount of oil, usually with the intention of browning. · *Grilling* is cooking on a rack over an open flame or heat source whereby the food does not cook in its own juices. · *Broiling* is cooking with high heat not in direct contact with the food, usually from a source above (in part thermal radiation).

60.3 TEMPERATURE

The conversion between temperature measured in Celsius, T(°C), and temperature measured in Fahrenheit, T(°F), is T(°C) = 5/9 × (T(°F) − 32). "Gas mark" is an older standard for measuring the temperature of gas ovens.

°F	200	225	250	275	300	325	350	375	400	425	450	475
°C	93	107	121	135	149	163	177	191	204	218	232	246
Gas mark				1	2	3	4	5	6	7	8	9

60.4 DICTIONARY OF HERBS AND SPICES

Many men neglect basic herbs and spices because they simply aren't familiar with them. These 20 should be in every bachelor's kitchen. Herbs tend to refer to the leaf of a plant; spices, to the the fruit, seeds, root, or bark.

Basil · Known as the king of herbs, best used fresh and added just before serving. Used to make pesto.

Bay leaf · From the bay tree, it has a sweet, aromatic taste. Used whole in tomato sauces and soups.

Chili powder · A mixture including ground chilies, cumin, coriander, and paprika, for making *chili con carne*.

Cilantro · The aromatic leaves of the coriander plant, which taste very different from the seeds. Use fresh.

Cinnamon · Brown bark of an evergreen tree, normally ground and used in baked goods and candy.

Crushed chilies · Crushed hot chili peppers, used to give piquancy to chili, curry, stews, sauces, and meat.

Cumin · A powder ground from roasted, dried seeds. Warm, earthy. Essential to chili and curry powder.

Curry powder · A mixture including coriander, cumin, fenugreek, and turmeric, used in various curries.

Horseradish · A white root which, when grated, is intensely pungent. Popular with beef and sausages.

Garlic · The bulb of a close relative of the onion plant, it is pungent when raw, mellow when cooked.

Ginger · The base of the ginger plant. Fresh ginger is typically used in savory cooking, dry ginger in sweet.

Mint · An aromatic herb with a cool aftertaste. When fresh, used to make the cocktails mojito and mint julep.

Oregano · An aromatic, bitter herb related to marjoram, most notably present in pizza and Italian cuisine.

Paprika · Ground mild chili peppers, used in chili and especially in goulash, a traditional Hungarian dish.

Pepper · Black pepper, best milled directly from peppercorns, which are dried pepper plant berries.

Rosemary · Dry or fresh evergreen leaves with a bitter taste, used for fowl and meat, especially pork.

Sage · A strong, pungent, peppery-tasting herb used especially to flavor poultry, sausage, and stuffing.

Salt · Technically not a spice but a mineral (NaCl), it is the most abundant and frequently used of spices.

Tarragon · One of the components of French *fines herbes*, aromatic and excellent with chicken or eggs.

Vanilla · Sweet, aromatic extract popular in desserts. Derived from the shriveled pod of a type of orchid.

❦61 BACHELOR'S KITCHEN

61.1 30 BASIC UTENSILS

A bachelor's kitchen is a minimal kitchen; in principle, a man could happily cook and eat with a knife, fork, plate, frying pan, and spatula. A few well chosen utensils will make you a better cook than a kitchen full of gadgets.

Cooking	*Preparing*	*Eating*
casserole	colander	bottle opener
coffee maker (p 154)	cutting board	bowls
frying pan, cast-iron	grater (four-sided)	can opener
frying pan, non-stick	knives	corkscrew (p 113)
microwave	measuring cup	cups
roasting pan	measuring spoons	cutlery
saucepan, large	mixing bowl	glasses (p 104)
saucepan, small	peppermill	knife sharpener
teapot	spatula	plates
toaster	vegetable peeler	wooden spoon, fork

61.2 UTENSILS NOTES

Cooking • You don't need many pots and pans, but it helps if they are good ones. A *casserole* is a earthenware dish used for baking stews and lasagne. A cast-iron *frying pan* is the traditional man's choice: it is indestructible and provides uniform heat owing to its high heat capacity. If wiped clean with little or no soap, it will build a carbonized layer which is excellent for frying on. A *roasting pan* should have 2-inch (5-cm) sides. *Saucepans* should be heavy stainless steel–coated copper or anodized cast aluminum. Keep a large one for chili, pasta, and vegetables; a small one for soups and sauces.

Preparing • A *cutting board* should be large and wooden rather than plastic. Wood is better for knives, better to look at, and better at killing bacteria. Three good *knives* are better than the motley hoard found in most kitchens: a 4-inch (10-cm) paring knife, a 6-inch (15-cm) chef's knife, and a long serrated knife for cutting bread and tomatoes. A *measuring cup* and *spoons* make cooking more of a science and less of an art. Keep two *spatulas*: a plastic or wooden one for non-stick pans and a metal one for all others.

Eating • *Cups* can be mugs or cups and saucers. Keep enough b*owls, cutlery, glasses,* and *plates* for eight. For each person, *cutlery* means two table knives, two forks, and a spoon; a set of serrated knives are useful for meat.

61.3 30 BASIC PROVISIONS

Men like to keep cooking simple, but don't let a paltry pantry prevent you from preparing a midnight snack, cookies on a rainy day, or dinner for an unexpected guest. In addition to items needed for particular meals, a sensible chef will always have the following basic ingredients in store. Whenever you go shopping, be sure to replenish anything that has gone missing.

Dry goods	*Perishables*	*Herbs and spices (p 147)*
bread	balsamic vinegar	basil
coffee (p 154)	butter	chili powder
cookies	cheese	cinnamon
crackers	eggs	crushed chilies (p 158)
flour	garlic	cumin
nuts	lemons	curry powder
pasta	milk	oregano
rice	mustard	paprika
sugar	olive oil	peppercorns
tea	onions	salt

61.4 PROVISIONS NOTES

Dry goods • Instant *coffee* is for boys, ground coffee is for men. *Nuts*, the closest vegetarian approximation to meat, are a vital pantry provision. Serve salted ones with drinks before dinner, which increases thirst. *Pasta* comes in many shapes and sizes: spaghetti (long, thin cylinders) and rotini (short spirals) are the most versatile. *Tea* comes in bags and loose: loose tea is put into a teapot or a small wire cage which acts as a reusable tea bag.

Perishables • *Balsamic vinegar* (along with olive oil) is an essential ingredient in the simplest and, many would argue, best salad dressing. Get a good Italian one. A few *eggs* can rescue even the most lacking of larders. They are essential for breakfast (p 156), baking, and spaghetti carbonara. *Lemons* have countless uses: to squeeze over fish; to mix many cocktails; to make a quick salad dressing. *Mustard*, which suits both fast food and fine, is the most essential condiment. The best oil is *olive oil*. It costs more, but its versatility is worth it: use it for frying; add it to pasta; serve it with bread.

Herbs and spices • These are the ten most essential, all of which can be stored dry; the exception is basil, which is often needed fresh. Use all ten regularly to develop an intuition for which ones mix with what. If you dispense them with measuring spoons, your cooking will be reproducible.

❦62 HANDBOOK FOR HOSTS

If you are planning a party by yourself, chances are you're a bachelor. Here are some suggestions for entertaining in the absence of a woman's touch.

62.1 HOW TO BE HAPPY THOUGH HOST

Look after yourself first

The first piece of advice usually given to an aspiring host is always look after your guests. To this should be appended: look after yourself first. It is less self-serving than it sounds. Guests take their cue from the host: if he is happy, so are they; if he is stressed, they will be too. Nothing makes a party wane like a weary host. But enjoying one's own party is not always easy, and many hosts exasperate themselves out of a false sense of duty to others. So, having thoroughly prepared beforehand, once your party begins, have a ball: go where you want, talk to whom you like, and let your guests sort out minor mishaps. As Jay Gatsby knew, the best parties don't need a host. Happy hosts hold more parties, which is bound to make everybody happy.

Worry less about the food...

The single biggest mistake men make when cooking for others is giving too much attention to food and too little to form. We rarely judge a dinner by how good the food is. Our perception is largely determined by our expectation, which in turn is shaped by signs and ceremonies. Here are a few to consider: (i) Stay with your guests. Better to have simple fare and the host at hand than fancy with the host in the kitchen. (ii) Sit everyone down at a table, and have a seating plan; a summary of seating plans is shown opposite. (iii) Offer more than one course. It is well known that women excel at multitasking and men at single-mindedness. Put this to your advantage: instead of serving several dishes in parallel, serve several courses in series, of one (cooked) dish each. (iv) Keep the lights low. Everyone looks more attractive in low light, and consequently their conversation is more intimate.

...But more about the drinks

If food tends to receive too much attention, drinks usually receive too little. A case of Budweiser does not serve every occasion equally well. Consider instead starting off with a well-known cocktail (p 128). Just as it's wise to vary the courses, so too should you vary the drink. If you wish to stick to beer, consider the broad spectrum of lagers and ales; a guide to serving beer with food can be found on p 110. Likewise, if you plan on serving wine, let your guests try different varieties, chosen with consideration for the food they will accompany. Nothing kills merriment so much as an empty glass; keeping guests' glasses filled is the one duty you mustn't neglect.

62.2 AN ANALYSIS OF SEATING PLANS

Everyone likes a seating plan at a sit-down dinner. Instead of shuffling around the table on the lookout for a well-placed seat, the host has a plan, and you're part of it. Good seating plans are hard to make because the number of possible plans grows quickly with the number of guests, so it is wise to draft one before anyone arrives. The numbers of different kinds of seating plans are shown below right, for tables of 4, 6, 8, and 10 persons.

While each guest has two immediate neighbors, one left and one right, the effective number of neighbors – the sum over everyone at the table, weighted by his proximity – can vary, as shown below left. Note that the center seats, not the end ones, offer the most opportunity for conversation.

KEY *Distinct* means distinct seating plans, not including rotations and reflections. When there is an equal number of men and women present, *boy-girl* means distinct plans where the sexes alternate. If all the guests are in couples, *couples apart* means boy-girl plans such that all couples are separated (not sitting next to each other). The *effective number of neighbors* assumes the opportunity for conversation decreases with the square of the distance between two people, and that the width of the table is equal to the distance between adjacent neighbors, both defined to be equal to one.

Effective number of neighbors

	1.2	
1.2		1.2
	1.2	

2.1	2.1
1.5	1.5
2.1	2.1

2.4 — 3.0 — 2.4
1.7   1.7
2.4 — 3.0 — 2.4

2.6 — 3.3 — 3.3 — 2.6
1.8   1.8
2.6 — 3.3 — 3.3 — 2.6

Number of seating plans

Distinct	Boy-girl	Couples apart
3	1	0
60	6	1
2,520	72	6
181,440	1,440	156

❦63 COOKING OUTDOORS

Cooking directly over fire, in its more refined form called grilling or barbecuing, is the simplest and most ancient method of cooking meat. For
many men it is also the most satisfying and best. While the kitchen has
been called the woman's province, the barbecue pit is very much the man's.

63.1 CHARCOAL, WOOD, OR GAS

Charcoal is the most common source of fuel for cooking outdoors. The black
briquettes are made by heating formed or solid wood pieces in the absence
of oxygen. You don't need charcoal to barbecue, however. It is also possible to cook meat over the coals left over from a wood fire – mesquite is a
popular choice. But be sure to use a hardwood rather than a softwood (leaf-
bearing rather than needle-bearing): softwoods tend to contain resins which
impart a bad taste to the meat. Gas grills forgo coals, but because they do
not smoke, it is advisable to add wet wood chips for flavor. Partially wrap
the chips in foil to keep them from flaming and to keep the grill clean.

63.2 WOODS FOR SMOKING

While any hardwood can be reduced to coal for barbecuing, some woods
impart desirable smoke flavors as they smolder, shown below. These can be
used as the source of the coals themselves. Alternatively, wet chunks of the
wood can be added to normal charcoal, where they will smolder and smoke.

Alder . . . . Traditional, light smoke for fish, especially salmon
Apple . . . . Mild, fruity taste, for chicken, turkey, ham
Hickory. . . . . Strong, sweet taste, excellent for pork, also beef and chicken
Maple. . . . . . Medium, sweet taste, excellent with ham, good with chicken
Mesquite. . . . . Popular but strong; use sparingly for beef and chicken
Oak . . . . Never overpowering; complements most meats
Pecan . . . . Excellent for smoking; good for beef, pork, chicken

63.3 OUTDOOR HAND THERMOMETER

Part of the art of barbecuing is getting the temperature right, which depends on how hot the coals are and how high the meat is above them. The
temperature at a given height can be estimated as follows. Once the flames
have died down, spread out the coals. Place the palm of your hand a fixed
distance above the coals and count the seconds you can keep it there without flinching. This translates into the temperature at that height as shown:

Seconds	Temperature range		Best for cooking
7–10	250–300 °F	121–149 °C	Slow-cooking beef, pork
5–7	300–350 °F	149–177 °C	Fish, shellfish, vegetables
3–5	350–400 °F	177–204 °C	Chicken, sausage
2–3	400–450 °F	204–232 °C	Hamburgers, ribs
1–2	450–550 °F	232–288 °C	Ribs, steak
<1	>550 °F	>288 °C	Good cuts of steak

63.4 RED MEAT DONENESS

Temperature and color

By tradition there are six levels of red meat doneness, listed below. But what they mean varies from region to region: a medium steak in Paris tends to be rarer than one in New York, which is rarer than one in Texas. Meat doneness can be systematized by measuring the temperature of the center of the steak or roast with a meat thermometer. For beef, doneness is defined in terms of temperature as follows. Keep in mind that the center will continue to cook (get hotter) even after cooking has stopped, as heat in the outside diffuses into the center. Always let the meat rest a few minutes before cutting into it.

Doneness	Temperature range		Appearance
Blue	110–120 °F	43–49 °C	Red throughout, cool in center
Rare	120–130 °F	49–54 °C	Red in center, otherwise pink
Medium-rare	130–140 °F	54–60 °C	Reddish-pink center, brown edge
Medium	140–150 °F	60–66 °C	Center half pink, outer half brown
Medium-well	150–160 °F	66–71 °C	Thin layer of pink in center
Well-done	160–170 °F	71–77 °C	No sign of pink whatsoever

Hand test

An alternative to a meat thermometer is the hand test, which is based on the feel of the steak when poked with the forefinger. Rare steaks have a pliant, squishy feel; well-done steaks are firm and springy to the touch. The feel of the meat can be compared to the feel of the pad below the thumb. When the feel of the two match, the doneness of the meat is as follows:

Rare   Medium-rare   Medium   Medium-well

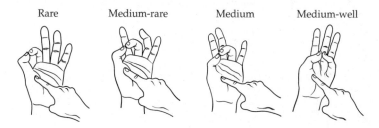

❦ 64 COFFEE

Coffee is made from the seeds of berries from the genus *Coffea,* a family of shrubs and small trees. The flavor of the seeds, or beans, bears little resemblance to the flavor of coffee until the seeds are roasted, which changes their chemical structure.

The two main types of coffee beans are *C. arabica* and *C. robusta* (also known as *C. canephora*). Arabica is the more flavorful and less bitter of the two, and consequently the more expensive. Within these two species there are many varietals, such as Colombian, Java, Jamaican Blue Mountain, and Kopi Luwak. The last is made from berries that have been consumed by the Asian palm civet, a small mammal. The beans pass through the digestive tract intact and are used to make the most expensive coffee in the world.

64.1 COFFEE BREWING

Coffee is the result of the infusion of ground coffee beans in hot water. Its concentration and taste depend on the temperature of the water, how finely the coffee is ground, the amount of time the water and coffee are in contact, and the pressure at which they are mixed. How best to mix the two has been the subject of much ingenuity and invention.

The simplest way to make coffee is to mix coarse-ground beans with boiling water in a jug and, after letting it stand, pour it through a handheld strainer into a cup. In principle, this can be done without a strainer because the coffee will eventually settle at the bottom of the cup; in practice this results in a somewhat grainy drink.

The French press, or *cafetière,* is similar, but the strainer is built into the pot in the form of a plunging sieve. Once the grounds are saturated, the plunger is pressed down, leaving the grounds at the bottom and the coffee on top.

Alternatively, medium-ground coffee may be held in a paper filter and the coffee poured over it. Because the coffee and water are in contact for a short time, only the most soluble components of the coffee will dissolve, and the taste is noticeably less harsh than the above two methods.

The Moka Express, invented in Italy in the 1930s, is an elegant two-piece coffee maker. Placed on the stove, it takes advantage of the steam pressure which builds in the lower chamber to force water through finely ground coffee into the upper chamber. The higher pressure yields a cup in between that obtained by the filter method and a professional espresso machine, below.

An espresso machine is a high-precision piece of equipment which forces hot water through compact, finely ground coffee at high pressure. The result is the famous espresso, a strong, distinctive coffee marked by the telltale presence of a crema, or fine golden froth, at the surface of each cup.

64.2 CHEMEX COFFEE MAKER

James Bond is a heavy coffee drinker. In Ian Fleming's *From Russia with Love*, we are given a glimpse of Bond's morning ritual: "Breakfast was Bond's favourite meal of the day. When he was stationed in London it was always the same. It consisted of very strong coffee, from De Bry in New Oxford Street, brewed in an American *Chemex*, of which he drank two large cups, black and without sugar." De Bry is no longer in business, but the simple and elegant Chemex coffee maker can still be obtained.

The Chemex (www.chemexcoffeemaker.com) was invented by German-born American Peter Schlumbohm in 1941. It has no moving parts but consists only of a heat-resistant glass vessel with an hourglass shape. A filter is placed in the upper half, where the coffee brews before passing to the lower half. It was voted one of the 100 best industrial designs of modern times and is on permanent display at the Museum of Modern Art in New York.

64.3 CAFFEINE CONTENTS

Coffee is one of the best sources of caffeine, the natural stimulant found in the seeds and leaves of a number of trees and shrubs. The typical caffeine content of various substances are shown below. The amount of caffeine in coffee and tea depends significantly on bean and leaf variety and on production and preparation. Note that, for comparison, the serving sizes used below are 8.4 fl. oz (250 ml) or 1.4 oz (40 g); in practice these can vary considerably. The average daily caffeine intake is 280 mg per person.

Lethal dose for 50% of people (mg caffeine)	10,000
Coffee and tea	*mg caff./250 ml*
Coffee, brewed (typical)	140
Coffee, instant (typical)	100
Tea, black (typical)	85
Tea, fruit (typical)	80
Tea, green (typical)	60
Coffee, decaffeinated (typical)	5
Soft drinks	*mg caff./250 ml*
Red Bull	82.5
Jolt Cola	50.0
Mountain Dew	39.1
Diet Coke	32.8
Dr Pepper	29.6
Pepsi-Cola	26.4
Diet Pepsi-Cola	25.4
Coca-Cola	24.0
Chocolate	*mg caff./40 g*
Unsweetened choc. (typical)	35
Hershey's Special Dark	29.2
Semi-sweet choc. (typical)	25
Milk chocolate (typical)	10
Hershey's Bar	9.4
Kit Kat	5.7
Caffeine tablets	*mg caff./pill*
Vivarin	200
Stay Alert gum	100
No Doz	100
Pro Plus	50

❦ 65 BREAKFAST

There are few things more rousing in the morning than a cooked breakfast. The cheerless, so-called Continental breakfast – coffee diluted with milk and a croissant – is unlikely to summon you from slumber. Fruit is for women, cereal for children; a working man needs a hearty meal to start the day.

65.1 FULL ENGLISH BREAKFAST

"To eat well in England," noted W. Somerset Maugham, "you should have a breakfast three times a day." The most splendid cooked breakfast is the full English, which is made up of a generous selection of the following items:

eggs	hash browns	fried potatoes
toast	grilled tomatoes	pancakes
bacon	fried mushrooms	coffee (p 154)
sausage	baked beans	orange juice

While it may not be practical to prepare a full English breakfast every day, with practice you will be able to whip up bacon and eggs without thinking. Here are some essential recipes which should help you rise and shine.

65.2 SCRAMBLED EGGS JAMES BOND

In the Ian Fleming short story "007 in New York," included in more recent editions of *Octopussy and The Living Daylights* (James Bond, p 180), we are presented with the recipe of Bond's favorite any-time meal – breakfast:

> He would have one more dry martini at the table, then smoked salmon and the particular scrambled eggs he had once (Felix Leiter knew the head-waiter) instructed them how to make.

> For four individualists:
> 12 fresh eggs   Salt and pepper   5–6 ounces fresh butter
> Break the eggs into a bowl. Beat thoroughly with a fork and season well. In a small copper (or heavy-bottomed saucepan) melt 4 ounces butter. When melted, pour in the eggs and cook over a very low heat, whisking continuously with a small egg whisk. While the eggs are slightly more moist than you would wish for eating, remove the pan from heat, add the rest of the butter and continue whisking for half a minute, adding the while finely chopped chives or fines herbes. Serve on hot buttered toast in individual copper dishes (for appearance only) with pink champagne (Taittinger) and low music.

65.3 ESQUIRE OMELET

The most elegant way of preparing eggs is to make an omelet. *Esquire's Handbook for Hosts* (Books, p 194) offers these instructions for making a perfect specimen. Just before folding in half you may add your favorite filling.

Crack into a bowl two eggs (for each person) and season them with a pinch of salt and a half pinch of pepper. Beat it unmercifully for five minutes, until the whites and yolks are completely mixed; the more the eggs are beaten, the lighter the omelet will be; and beat it with a silver fork. Do not use fancy kitchen utensils like an egg beater unless you are callous to the contempt of professional chefs.

Take a frying pan and put into it a teaspoonful of best olive oil; do not use butter as it might burn. Heat the oil in the pan until it becomes terribly hot on the brisk flame. When the oil starts to smoke, fume and crackle, pour the eggs into the pan and agitate them gently for no longer than forty to fifty seconds; never dry them out by leaving them longer on the range, as a dried-out or burned omelet is uneatable. Now remove the pan to a somewhat less hot spot on the range and fold the omelet with your fork – the side nearest the handle first – into a half-moon shape. Smear a bit of butter over it; take the handle of the pan in your right hand, a hot plate with a napkin underneath it in your left, and with a rapid movement turn the pan right over the center of the plate. If you have done all this properly you may crow like a cock: "Ko-ko-ri-ko!" for that is how the French chefs greet a perfect omelet when it is ready. But do not forget that efficiency and quickness count above all, and that an omelet must always be made to order; it is better that the man wait rather than eggs.

65.4 MAKING BACON

Bacon is pork that has been cured (immersed in water mixed with salt and other preservatives), originally prepared as a means of preservation. There are two main kinds: bacon and Canadian bacon. Normal bacon has much more fat than Canadian bacon, and is recognizable by its marbled texture.

The best way to cook bacon is over low heat for a long time, which is the only way to reduce the fat without burning the meat. *Frying* is the most common method and should be done at low heat for 20–30 minutes. No oil is necessary because the bacon will quickly start to cook in its own grease, but it is important to turn it every few minutes. *Baking* is a much less common method but is believed by some to be the best. The bacon should be placed directly on an oven rack at 200–250 °F for one to two hours, with foil or a pan below to catch the drippings. It does not need to be turned.

❦66 CHILI

Chili is the archetypal male dish. It is easy to make, contains red meat, and is cooked in a single pot, from which it can in principle be eaten. It is not necessary to have fine ingredients to prepare an excellent specimen. It usually divides the sexes, men finding it addictive and women unremarkable.

66.1 DEFINITION OF CHILI

The best definition of *chili con carne* is a literal translation of its Spanish name: peppers with meat. These are the chief and essential ingredients. Chili originated in the American Southwest (but not what is now Mexico) as a simple, palatable preparation of staple foods. Early-19th-century recipes called for beef and suet and as much again a combination of chili peppers, onions, and garlic – alas, no tomatoes, which could not always be obtained. Today, the International Chili Society defines chili as any kind of meat or combination of meats, cooked with chili peppers, spices, and other ingredients, with the exception of beans and pasta, which are forbidden; the exclusion of beans is particularly contentious. This definition regulates its annual cook-off – the largest chili, and indeed food, competition in the world.

66.2 CHILI PEPPERS

Chili peppers, sometimes called chilies or peppers, are the fruit of the genus *Capsicum*, which contains many species that are used as a spice or food. Characteristic of chilies is their piquancy (hot taste). This is caused by a substance in them called capsaicin: an irritant in the form of a single molecule, which produces a burning sensation when brought in contact with the mucous membranes of the mouth, nose, and eyes.

The piquancy of a chili pepper grows in proportion to the amount of capsaicin present. It can be quantified by the Scoville scale, which measures the factor by which a liquid extract of the pepper must be diluted until it can no longer be detected. For example, a pepper with a rating of 1,000 must be diluted as 1 part pepper in 1,000 parts water to be undetectable. A bell pepper, which contains no capsaicin, registers zero, whereas pure capsaicin registers 16 million Scoville units. More Scoville ratings are given opposite.

An alternative and less cumbersome system for measuring heat, first defined here, uses a scale of 1 to 24. It is the base-2 logarithm of the Scoville rating (see Beauty, p 38); adding 1 to the scale corresponds to a two-fold increase in piquancy. The units of this scale are called logarithmic Scoville units, or LSU for short. The minimum rating is 1 LSU for a bell pepper and the maximum is 24 LSU for pure capsaicin, with other chilies falling in between.

66.3 CHILI PEPPER SCOVILLE RATINGS

Chili or compound	Scoville units	LSU
Pure capsaicin	15,000,000–16,000,000	23.8–23.9
Pepper spray (self-defense)	2,000,000–5,000,000	20.9–22.2
Naga Jolokia (hottest known pepper)	860,000–1,000,000	19.7–19.9
Scotch Bonnet	100,000–320,000	16.6–18.3
Cayenne	30,000–50,000	14.8–15.6
Jalapeño	2,500–7,500	11.3–12.9
Tabasco sauce	2,500–5,000	11.3–12.3
Anaheim	500–2,000	9.0–11.0

66.4 2007 ICS CHAMPIONSHIP CHILI (JERRY BUMA)

3 lb tri-tip beef
1 medium onion, minced
1 small can green chilies, diced
3 cloves of garlic, minced
1 can (14½ oz) chicken broth
1½ tsp Tabasco
1 can (8 oz) Hunt's tomato sauce
2 tbsp Mexican hot chili powder
2 tbsp Mexican mild chili powder

2 tbsp California hot chili powder
2 tbsp California mild chili powder
3 tbsp ground cumin
1 tsp Mexican oregano
1 tsp sugar
2 tsp MSG
1 tsp black pepper
2 tsp salt

Serves 6. Method: Mix together spice mix (last 10 ingredients). Brown meat, combine with remaining ingredients and half of spice mix. Simmer two hours, add rest of spice mix and simmer for an hour, adding water to taste.

66.5 FINK'S CHILI

1½ lb cubed lean beef
3 tsp olive oil
¼ tsp salt
½ tsp black pepper
2 chopped chili peppers
1 small chopped onion
4 cloves chopped garlic
½ can (5 oz) chopped tomatoes

1½ tbsp chili powder
2 tsp ground cumin
1 tsp paprika
1 tsp sugar
½ tsp cayenne pepper
½ tsp oregano
1 beef stock cube
1 can (10 oz) red kidney beans

Serves 3. Method: Fry beef in 1 tsp oil over high heat. Add salt and black pepper. Fry chili peppers, onion, and garlic separately in 2 tsp oil. Combine with remaining ingredients except beans in saucepan and simmer for at least an hour, adding water to taste. Add beans 30 minutes before serving.

❦67 STEAK

The best steak is served rare or medium-rare. For some men this is an acquired taste, due as much to squeamishness as to anything else. It is a taste
worth acquiring, however, and the best way to do so is to cook or order
your steak one degree rarer than you would normally have it (medium instead of medium-well, for example). You will soon become accustomed to
this, and much the happier for it, and you may wish to repeat the process.

67.1 HOW TO COOK A STEAK

Although many men assume grilling is the best way to prepare steak, the
very best method is frying. The ideal frying pan is a heavy cast-iron one, for
two reasons. Because the thick iron base stores a lot of heat, it will stay hot
during the initial period of contact with the steak. Second, pans with non-
stick coatings are liable to be damaged at the high temperature required to
cook a steak. Good steak (T-bone, filet mignon), correctly cooked, should
speak for itself. The seasoning should be simple: salt, pepper, and olive oil
are the only necessary ingredients. Only pepper should be put on the steak
before cooking it; salt is best added afterwards because it draws out the
juices from uncooked meat via osmosis (this is the basis of salt curing).

Heat the pan at the highest possible setting; a gas stove is preferable to
an electric one because the pan gets hotter. First let the pan warm up, then
add a small amount of olive oil, one teaspoonful (4 ml). Let the pan continue
to heat until the oil begins to smoke, taking care not to let it catch fire. At this
point, drop the room-temperature steak onto the pan so that it lands flat. It
will make an awful noise and splatter, so be sure to wear a cook's apron.
The steak will immediately stick to the pan, which is what you want; do not
agitate it in any way. Leave it there for 1–3½ minutes (more precise times are
given below), then pull it off with a fork on each side with an upward motion and turn it over. (Scraping it off with a spatula is likely to break the thin
crust which keeps the juices of the steak from escaping.) Leave it to cook on
the second side for the same amount of time, adding salt to the cooked side.

When the time is up, pull the steak off again and place it on a plate with
the cooler side down, salting the second side. Cover it loosely with foil and
let it sit for 4 minutes before eating it. It is during this essential period that
the inner and outer juices equilibrate. The resulting steak will appear more
cooked by one degree than it would have had you cut into it immediately.

The amount of time to cook each side depends on how done it should be.
For a 1-inch (2.5-cm) thick steak, cook it approximately 1–1½ minutes per
side for rare, 2½ for medium, and 3½ for well-done. These times vary with
the cut of meat and pan temperature and should be adjusted accordingly.

67.2 CUTS OF BEEF

Brisket · This cut is the chest, rippled with fat, and tough if not marinated. It barbecues well when slow-cooked and is the source of "burnt ends."

Bottom sirloin · The largest part of the sirloin section, this produces good but somewhat tougher steaks than the top sirloin and the tenderloin.

Chuck · Being the shoulder, this well-used muscle is tough but flavorful. Usually ground to make hamburger, also used for slow pot-roasting.

Flank · The lower belly. Tough with much connective tissue, it is usually ground, apart from the flank steak, used to make London broil.

Rib · The source of ribs, often barbecued, and rib-eye roast and steaks. The prized center of the rib (rib eye) is a tender, marbled cut of beef.

Plate · The front belly, a tough, fatty, and inexpensive cut. The source of skirt steak and the hanger steak; the former is sliced to make fajitas.

Round · The large hind leg muscles, it is the source of round (rump) steak and rump roast which, being lean and slightly tough, is slow-cooked.

Short loin · The second most desired cut, and the source of T-bone and strip steaks. One side of the T-bone is tenderloin, the other, strip steak.

Shank · Being well worked, the legs are flavorful, tough, and sinewy, with a high collagen content. Used to make soups and broths; also ground.

Sirloin · This refers to the general cut behind the short loin, and includes the top and bottom sirloins and part of the tenderloin, all described here.

Tenderloin · A little-worked muscle, this is the most tender and desired cut of beef. It is the source of filet mignon and chateaubriand steaks.

Top sirloin · Superior to the larger, less desirable bottom sirloin, it does not include the prized tenderloin but is an excellent steak nonetheless.

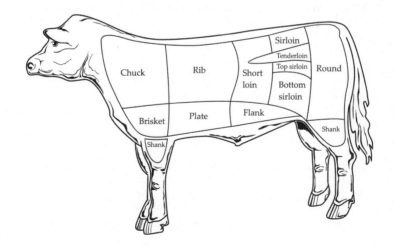

❦68 CARVING

The carving of birds and meat has long been an essential man's skill, often performed by the resident patriarch. But many men, unaccustomed to carving, are all too keen to pass this task on to someone else. Here is a guide.

68.1 KNIFE

The biggest hurdle in carving is not poor technique but poor equipment. A good carving knife is essential. The most important features are a long blade, at least eight inches, and considerable sharpness. Less important, but nevertheless useful, is a large carving board with a moat around the edge to keep the juices from running off. Carving in a roasting pan won't do.

Apart from relatively advanced sharpening machines, the best way to sharpen a knife is with a sharpening steel. This is a long, cylindrical piece of steel with thin metal ridges cut into it along the direction of the axis. The knife is slid against the steel with the sharp edge leading, a stroke on one side, a stroke on the other, and so on. Getting the right angle of inclination between the blade and the sharpening steel is important: if the angle is too big, the knife will be dulled; too small, and the cutting edge will not connect. About 20° is appropriate for most kitchen knives. As you do when polishing shoes, aim to sharpen lightly and often – once every two or three uses.

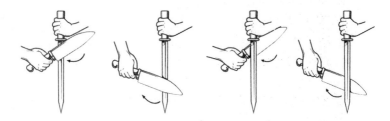

Now that you have the tools of the trade, you can follow these instructions for carving birds and meat from *Esquire's Handbook for Hosts* (p 194).

68.2 HOW TO CARVE BIRDS

Turkey

First sink the fork at a spot a couple of inches behind the point of the breast bone with one prong on either side of the bone; there is a special place for it, which was apparently designed to accommodate forks, and you will find it readily. Now slip the point of the knife under the far wing and make an upward cut for the joint that holds the wing to the turkey, a straight cut well towards the neck so as not to undershoot the joint. If the wing doesn't drop off, get the knife into the joint and break it if necessary. The leg or drumstick and the second joint should be removed in one piece. Make a straight cut for the joint that holds it to the turkey. Cut an inch or two above the "Pope's nose," going as far as you can; then slip the knife behind the joint and cut to the juncture again. This should separate the whole business from the body of the fowl. Once it is off, put the fork in the second joint and cut for the juncture of the drum stick and the second joint. Now one side of the bird is stripped of its appendages and you are ready to carve the breast. Put the fork in the same position in which you originally inserted it into the bird, and lay the bird on its side, legless side up, so that the slices of breast, as you carve them, will remain in position until you lift them off. If you permit the bird to remain upright, the slices would fall off to the side and, while this is all right with ham and certain other joints, it will not do with turkey: the breast will crumble and the slices be difficult and unappetizing to handle. So, lay the bird on the side and cut the slices with firm, even strokes. Slices should not be thick.

Duck

Young duck or duckling is carved in a similar manner to chicken or turkey. First, the wings are removed and then the breast is either sliced or, if it be a small bird, it is removed in one piece. Next the leg and second joint are removed, divided or served in one piece if it is small.

Goose

Remember that the breast of a goose, more than that of any other bird, is most highly esteemed, and the carver may not have to give much attention to any other part, though some people find the legs excellent.

Fowl

Roast and broiled fowl (chickens, capon, etc.) are cut in a manner similar to roast turkey.

Pheasant

The choicest parts of the pheasant are the breast and the wings, as is true of most fowl. Pheasant is carved exactly as turkey.

Partridge

The usual method is to cut the bird along the top of the breast bone and divide it into two equal parts: a half partridge is a fair portion for one person.

Grouse

Grouse may be carved in the same way as partridge. It is well to know that the backbone of the grouse is highly esteemed by many and considered, along with the same portion of many game birds, to possess the finest flavor.

68.3 HOW TO CARVE MEAT

Meat should always be cut across the grain, the one exception to this rule being the saddle of mutton which is always carved...parallel with the fibers or grain of the meat. Ham and beef should be cut in very thin slices, and lamb, mutton and pork in fairly thick ones.

Beef

A round of beef, or ribs rolled, are not so easy to carve as some joints. A thin-bladed knife is recommended. First, cut a thick slice off the outside of the joint at its top, so as to leave the surface smooth, then thin and even slices should be carved.

Veal

Breast of veal consists of two parts: the rib bones and the gristly brisket. These two parts should be separated: then the rib bones may be detached separately and served.

Mutton

Leg of mutton is comparatively simple to carve. The knife should be carried sharply down and slices taken from either side, as the guests may desire.

The saddle of mutton is a fine old English dish: it consists of two loins connected by the spinal bone. The meat is generally carved across the ribs in slices running parallel with the backbone and the grain of the meat, and with each portion is usually served a small piece of fat cut from the bottom of the ribs. Plenty of good gravy and red currant jelly should be served with this.

In carving a shoulder of mutton the joint should be raised from the dish and as many slices cut away as can be managed. After this the meat lying on either side of the blade bone should be served by carving it from the knuckle end. The joint can then be turned and slices taken off along its whole length.

Pork

A leg of pork is carved as a leg of mutton: the knife should be carried sharply down to the bone right through to the crackling. A loin of pork, if it is properly prepared at the butcher's, may be divided into neat and even chops and presents no particular carving problems.

Ham

Here the carver must be guided by whether he desires to practice economy or to serve immediately from the best part. Under the first supposition, he will commence at the knuckle and cut thin slices toward the thick part of the ham. If he prefers to serve the finest part first, he will cut across and down to the bone at the center of the ham.

Lamb

A leg or shoulder of lamb is carved as a leg or shoulder of mutton.

IDLING

Idleness: want of occupation; habitual indolence (*Oxford English Dictionary*)

Samuel Johnson • Every man is, or hopes to be, an Idler. (*The Idler*, 1758–1760)

Honoré de Balzac • In order to be fashionable, one must enjoy rest without having experienced work… Like steam engines, men regimented by work all look alike… The man instrument is a social zero.

Raymond Chandler • [Poker is] as elaborate a waste of human intelligence as you could find outside an advertising agency.

Ian Fleming • The scent and smoke and sweat of a casino are nauseating at three in the morning. (First sentence, *Casino Royale*, 1953)

Anonymous • You don't have to be a beer drinker to play darts, but it helps.

Izaak Walton • I love such mirth as does not make friends ashamed to look upon one another next morning. (*The Compleat Angler*, 1653)

Tom Hodgkinson • Characteristic of the idler's work is that it looks suspiciously like play. (*The Idler*, 1993–2007)

Samuel Johnson • The Idler, who habituates himself to be satisfied with what he can most easily obtain, not only escapes labours which are often fruitless, but sometimes succeeds better than those who despise all that is within their reach and think every thing more valuable as it is harder to be acquired. (*The Idler*, 1758–1760)

Benjamin Franklin • It is not lesiure that is not used. • The busy man has few idle visitors; to the boiling pot the flies come not. • A life of leisure and a life of laziness are two things. (*Poor Richard's Almanack*, 1732–1757)

❦69 SUPERLATIVES

Trying to agree upon the best of anything is sure to elicit endless debate. Here is a list of the world's best products, principles, and customs for men. Many can serve as points of reference even if they are unattainable for most.

Best advice . . . . Never apologize [1]
Best age of your bride at marriage. . . . . ½ your age + 7 (p 45)
Best American fashion export. . . . . Blue jeans; penny loafers [2]
Best beer . . . . Westvleteren 12 (one of seven Trappist ales)
Best beer, mass-marketed . . . . Grolsch
Best Bond novel (film). . . . . *From Russia with Love* (*Goldfinger*)
Best bottle to take to a drinks party . . . . Whisky and a candle [3]
Best bourbon, whisky. . . . . Booker's, Highland Park
Best (and worst) buttonhole flower . . . . Carnation [4]
Best car . . . . Bentley [5]
Hottest chili pepper . . . . . . Naga Jolokia (1 million Scoville units, p 159)
Best cigar . . . . Trinidad Fundadore [6]
Best cigarettes to be seen smoking . . . . Lucky Strike; Marlboro Red
Best cocktail. . . . . Caipirinha (p 128)
Least-documented common male ailment. . . . . Blue balls (p 13)
Second-best dandy. . . . . Count d'Orsay [7]
Worst drink to order in a pub or bar . . . . Half-pint [8]
Best drinking accessory . . . . Pewter or silver hip flask (p 130)
Best drinking game . . . . Beer pong (p 29)
Best endurance sport . . . . Tour de France; Iditarod Sled Dog Race
Worst fashion item . . . . . . sleeveless T-shirt (a.k.a. tank top, wife beater)
Best gun maker . . . . Holland & Holland (shotguns); Purdey (rifles)
Best jeans for men . . . . Levi's; Diesel
Best male fashion eras . . . . The late Plantagenet, Regency, and
1950s Edwardian revival periods [9]
Best men's film. . . . . *Deliverance* (1972)
Best regiment. . . . . Delta Force [10]
Best possible result on the US Army fitness test . . . . 75 push-ups in two
minutes, 80 sit-ups in two minutes, two-mile run in 13 minutes
Best shirtmakers . . . . . . Alexander Kabbaz (US); Turnbull & Asser (UK)
Best smoking accessory . . . . Parabolic mirror solar cigarette lighter
Strongest spirit . . . . Everclear [11]
Best sports biography. . . . . *Arnold: The Education of a Bodybuilder* (p 194)
Best tie . . Seven-fold tie, made from a single piece of silk with no lining
Best tie knot. . . . . Nicky (p 74) [12]
Best way to give up smoking . . . . Take up chewing tobacco (p 140)

69.1 SELECTED NOTES

1 "It is a good rule in life never to apologize. The right sort of people do not want apologies, and the wrong sort take a mean advantage of them," wrote P. G. Wodehouse in *The Man Upstairs*.

2 Soon after loafers became fashionable in the 1930s and 40s, copper pennies were inserted into the strap across the vamp. Fops prefer to use 1943 wartime steel pennies, issued when copper was scarce.

3 Between refills, force the lighted candle into the bottle. No one expects a vessel with a candle in it to contain anything drinkable.

4 "Best," argues fashion writer John Taylor, "because its calyx (the cup beneath the bloom from which the petals grow out) is bulky enough to be held firmly in place by the best buttonhole – which should be between 1 inch and 1⅛ inches long." Worst because it was last popular in the 1970s.

5 In Ian Fleming's novels, James Bond owns three Bentleys. The last is a Mark II Continental, battleship gray with black leather interior, "the most selfish car in England." Originally an English company, Bentley was acquired by Volkswagen Group in 1998.

6 Although the Trinidad has been privately produced by the El Laguito factory in Havana, Cuba, for many years as gifts of state, it became commercially available in limited quantities in 1998. It was made in a single size only, the Fundadore, at 7½ inches × 39 ring gauge, until 2003 when the Reyes, Coloniales, and Robusto Extra sizes were introduced.

7 The best, of course, was Beau Brummell, who turned men's dress away from finery and extravagance to understatement, restraint, and studied indifference, now so ingrained in masculine costume.

8 Despite being standard issue in France, ordering a half-pint is suspect in the Anglo-Saxon world. Order a pint or go home.

9 Not, as many argue, the 1930s, during which men's and women's fashion de-emphasized sex. The eras opposite "idealized the 'natural' but virile shape – emphasizing masculinity with shoulder focus and hose, breeches or trousers which revealed the shape of the leg," writes Taylor.

10 Technically a special operations unit rather than a regiment, Delta Force is the popular name of the US Army 1st Special Forces Operational Detachment-Delta. It was modeled on the British Special Air Service (SAS).

11 Everclear is nearly pure grain alcohol, or ethanol, which comes in two strengths: 151 proof (75.5% ABV) and 190 proof (95% ABV). The latter should never be drunk neat and is very flammable.

12 A symmetric knot, in between the four-in-hand and half-Windsor in size. The earliest-known description of the Nicky is by Italian tie-shop owner Ernesto Curami. It was rediscovered by David Kelsall as an improvement on the Pratt knot and reported in the *Sunday Telegraph* in 1991.

❦70 D A S T A R D ' S   T R I C K S

These tricks are dirty, but none of them relies on sleight of hand. They should enable any man to win a few drinks a week with a little practice.

Lift three matches

Put three matches on the table and bet your friend that you can lift all three with a fourth. To do so, assemble the matches into a tripod formation, with the flammable tips touching, as shown. Use the fourth match to ignite the tripod from below, blow all the matches out, and lift the three fused matches with the fourth one.

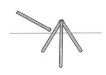

Guess a number

Tell your friend to "pick a random digit," and have him write it down. On a separate piece of paper, write the numbers 3, 5, and 7. Now bet him even money that his number is one of your three. If your friend chose his number randomly, he would win 70% of the time. But people don't choose random numbers; they pick numbers they *think* are random. The distribution of choices is shown below, taken from 1,770 participants (M. Kubovy and J. Psotka, *J. of Exp. Psychology: Human Perception and Performance*, **2**, 291 (1976)). The numbers 3, 5, and 7 are chosen 54% of the time, which is about the probability with which you should win the bet – a 17% return on investment.

0	1	2	3	4	5	6	7	8	9
1%	3%	6%	14%	9%	13%	11%	27%	12%	4%

Snaps is the name of the game

This excellent party trick is used to telepathically transmit a message from one person (the sender) to another (the receiver). Someone in the party tells all but the receiver a well-known person, place, or thing. The sender begins by saying: "Snaps is the name of the game." The word is "sent" to the receiver apparently by a mysterious sequence of finger snaps, but really by spelling it out, according to the following code: consonants are the first letter of every phrase said by the sender; and vowels correspond in rank to the number of snaps of the fingers: "a" = one snap; "e" = two snaps; "i" = three snaps; and so on. If the sender wishes instead to spell out the second word of the message, he begins with: "Snaps is the name of the game, OK?" For example, if the message is William Shakespeare, the game might go as follows: "Snaps is the name of the game, OK? – Silence, please. – Here we go. – [Snap] – Keep thinking. – [Snap Snap] – Sooner rather than later!" At this point (s-h-a-k-e-s) or soon after the receiver will likely guess the message.

Hold a lit cigarette by its ends

Without being noticed, press your thumb against
an ice-cold glass for 30 seconds. While doing so, bet
your friend that you can hold a lit cigarette length-
wise between two fingers, as shown. The trick is to
lightly hold it between thumb and forefinger with
the lit end against the thumb. You shouldn't feel a
thing, or burn your thumb, for several seconds.

Guess anyone's phone number

For this trick you need a phone book of at least 900 pages. Have your friend
pick a secret three-digit number, reverse the digits, and take the difference
between the two. For example, 123 reversed is 321, and the difference between them is 198. Now ask your friend to turn to the same page of the
phone book as the number he arrived at, go to the fifth entry, and read off
the first initial of the surname. Little does your friend know that the above
manipulation of his number can result in only one of ten numbers: 0 (in
this case you must start over), 99, 198, 297, 396, 495, 594, 693, 792, and 891.
You simply need to memorize – or write on a small card – the nine initials
from the nine pages (they will all be different) and their phone numbers.

Lift a glass from above

Bet your friend that you can lift a shot glass without touching its bottom or
sides. To do so, light a glassful of spirits or liqueur (at least 40% ABV) with
a lighter and extinguish it by placing your wet or licked palm directly on top
of it. If done quickly the flame will extinguish at once and the cooling gas
will create a partial vacuum, affixing the glass to your palm without pain.

Non-transitive dice

Consider the four unusual dice below, sometimes called Efron's dice, which
can be made from wooden or plastic cubes by writing or painting on the
numbers. With a friend, play the following simple game: your friend picks
a die and throws it, then you pick one of the remaining die and throw it,
and the highest number wins. Which die should your friend throw? The
answer is it doesn't matter which die he chooses. You should always choose
the die shown to the left of his (below); if he chooses the left-most die, then
you should choose the right-most die. In every case you will win with probability two-thirds. These dice are called non-transitive because, even though
die A beats die B, B beats C, and C beats D, die D nevertheless beats die A.

0					3					6					5			
4	4	4	4		3	3	3	3		2	2	2	2		1	1	1	5
0					3					6					5			

❦ 71 S P U D   G U N

This is the classic homemade potato gun. It is simple: it consists of a chamber in which a flammable gas is exploded and a barrel in which a fitted projectile is accelerated. And it is effective: at a range of 20 feet it will make a three-inch hole in half-inch board. It is made from PVC pipe and fittings and is typically used to shoot potato slugs. Here are complete instructions for building and operating your own, as well as a custom ballistics table. (Note that safety goggles and adult supervision are required when executing this project.)

71.1 M A T E R I A L S

There are many different ways to make a potato gun. The following is a sturdy, classic design that shoots 1½-inch-diameter (⅛ pound) slugs of potato. All of the parts below can be found in a hardware store for a total cost of about $50. Before you leave the store, make sure the pieces fit together as explained opposite to avoid any mistakes.

PVC is short for polyvinyl chloride, a tough resin used to make white pipes and fittings. PVC pipe tends to come in fixed-length pieces which must be bought whole, then cut down to size at the store or at home with a saw. The igniter is a piezoelectric sparker used for gas barbecue grills and makes a spark that is uncomfortable to the touch but not painful.

Gun

12-in × 4-in PVC pipe	PVC cement
36-in × 1½-in PVC pipe	BBQ igniter (replacement for gas
4-in PVC clean-out adapter	grill, with red button)
4-in PVC threaded plug	2-in × 2.5-in machine screws
4-in PVC coupler	2-ft insulated wire (14–18 gauge)
4-in × 1½-in PVC reducer bushing	Metal bracket and small wood
PVC primer (clear if you can find it)	screws to fit igniter (optional)

Tools

Drill and drill bits	Electrical tape
Handsaw	3-ft pole or stick (for loading)
Screwdriver	Wood file or sandpaper and block

Propellant

Popular propellants for firing include aerosol deodorants and aerosol hair sprays, although many other flammable aerosols will work. Aerosol deodorants ignite dependably but some varieties have been reformulated to be nonflammable, so check the can for a flammability warning to be sure it will work. Hair sprays tend to give less consistent results.

71.2 ASSEMBLY

PVC

If possible, have the 1½-inch and 4-inch pipe cut to size at the hardware store. If not, PVC can be easily cut with a handsaw. Make sure the ends are as square as possible. With a file or sandpaper, flatten the cut ends and remove any rough edges. To load potato slugs more easily, bevel the outside edge of one end of the 1½-inch barrel with a file or sanding block so that it tapers at a 30-degree angle to the inside rim (chamfering). Using the technique below, weld the PVC pipes and fittings together. There are four joints to weld: (i) the clean-out adapter to the 4-inch pipe; (ii) the coupler to the other end of the 4-inch pipe; (iii) the reducer bushing to the coupler; and (iv) the 1½-inch pipe to the reducer bushing. The threaded plug screws into the clean-out adapter. It will make a few revolutions before it starts to get tight; don't force it beyond this point. Let the cement dry for 24 hours before using the launcher.

PVC *welding*

PVC cement dissolves the surface of PVC pipe and fittings and literally causes the two pieces to fuse together. The primer and cement are volatile and flammable, so weld (glue together) outside or in an open garage. You will need to work fast because the cement dries quickly. First, read the primer and cement instructions. To weld, apply a coat of primer to the outside of the pipe and then the inside of the fitting. Then apply cement first to the outside of the pipe, then to the inside of the fitting, then again to the outside of the pipe. Insert the pipe into the fitting, making sure that it bottoms out by making a quarter or half turn and putting your weight into it.

Igniter

Drill two holes into the center of the chamber, as shown, with a drill bit just smaller than the diameter of the screws – it is essential that the fit be tight so that no gas can escape during combustion. The screws should be perpendicular to the chamber and at 90 degrees from each other. Drive the screws into the holes so that the tips are almost touching. If you wish, attach the igniter to the gun with a metal bracket and two small wood screws, as shown. (It is not crucial how or where you attach the igniter – you could even use tape – but the method suggested here works well.) Connect the ends of the igniter to the heads of the screws, using the insulated wire if necessary; some igniters come with wire attached, some don't. Wrap the wire around the screws clockwise and tighten the screws. Now the gap between the screws can be adjusted by slightly bending them. It should be between ⅛ and ¼ inch, such that when the igniter button is pressed you consistently get a spark. When this is done, cover the screws and exposed wires with electrical tape.

71.3 DIRECTIONS FOR USE

First, find a location to shoot your gun, bearing in mind that it can make a report considerably louder than a firecracker. An open field is ideal; downtown in a city, less so. For the first few launches, it is wise to look away and hold the gun entirely by the 4-inch base to test its structural integrity.

Loading

To load, cut a potato in half crosswise and place the flat end against the chamfered edge of the barrel. A sharp knock on the potato will cut out a cylindrical slug. A close-fitting slug is important because it keeps the rapidly expanding gas from escaping before the potato is expelled. Push the slug down with a ramrod (any blunt 3-foot pole will do) until it is at the bottom of the barrel.

Adding fuel and launching

The power of the gun is limited by the amount of oxygen in the chamber, which is fixed by the chamber volume. It is important to find the right balance between fuel and oxygen. If there is too little fuel, it will not ignite; if there is so much that most of the oxygen is expelled, again there will be no ignition. Make sure that the igniter is not in danger of being pressed. Remove the screw-on plug, spray fuel into the chamber for three to 12 seconds, and quickly screw the plug back on without overtightening. Start off with six seconds of fuel; if necessary, vary this as per below.

To launch, immediately after adding fuel take aim and press the igniter.

Troubleshooting

The most common problem is that the igniter is pressed but the gun does not fire. There are two possibilities: (i) There was no spark between the screw ends. To check this, you must first remove the threaded plug and the potato and let the fuel dissipate for several minutes. Blowing into the barrel can expedite this. *Testing the spark without letting the fuel dissipate is a common source of injuries.* Make sure you have a consistent spark every time you press the igniter. If not, reduce the gap between the screws. If this doesn't work, check the wiring. Do you have a spark when the ends of the wire leading from the igniter are close together? (ii) There was a spark but the fuel and air mixture did not ignite. You may have added too little fuel, or too much and retained too little oxygen. Try increasing and decreasing the amount of fuel you add by one second at a time. If that doesn't work, try a different fuel.

If the potato exits with a feeble thump instead of a bang, check that your slug fits the barrel closely, without gaps; if not, you may need to sharpen the chamfered barrel edge or use bigger potatoes. Alternatively, the fuel-air mixture may need to be adjusted by adding more or less fuel, as described above.

71.4 PLANS

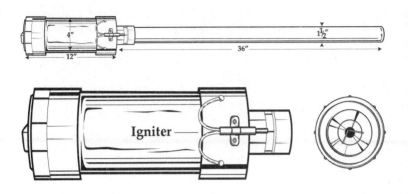

71.5 BALLISTICS

The muzzle velocity of a potato gun can be estimated by shooting the potato straight up into the air and measuring the time it takes to land. Air resistance significantly alters the dynamics of high-speed projectiles, and taking it into account requires more complicated physics than Newton's laws of motion. The calculation used for the table below assumes a ⅛-pound (57-gram) potato slug with a terminal velocity of 80 feet per second. Notice that the true muzzle velocity grows much more quickly with time than does muzzle velocity in the absence of air resistance. Also note that it is very difficult to shoot a supersonic potato (> 770 mph), even with advanced spud guns, and the simple gun described here will get nowhere near that speed.

Air time (s)	True muzzle velocity (ft/s)	(mph)	Were there no air resistance (ft/s)	Energy (J)
4	67	46	64	12
5	90	61	80	21
6	120	82	96	38
7	160	109	113	68
8	214	146	129	121
9	286	195	145	217
10	382	260	161	386
11	510	348	177	689
12	682	465	193	1,232
13	911	621	209	2,197
14	1,220	832	225	3,941

❦72 ORIGAMI WALLET

For a wallet to be practical, it must be able to securely store both dollar bills (6.14 × 2.61 in) and credit and business cards (3.37 × 2.12 in). Here are two designs for paper wallets, both of which are folded from square sheets of paper. They are practical enough to take the place of a leather wallet for daily use. Sturdier specimens can be made from heavier paper; one with a substantial cotton content will last longest. Black or brown paper looks best.

72.1 SIX-COMPARTMENT WALLET

This wallet is folded from a square piece of paper without any cuts or tape. It contains two compartments for bills and four for credit/business cards.

Directions

Start with a 14-in square sheet of paper, which will make a wallet which is 6.4 × 3.5 in, or 3.2 × 3.5 in when folded in half. Fold the paper as follows:

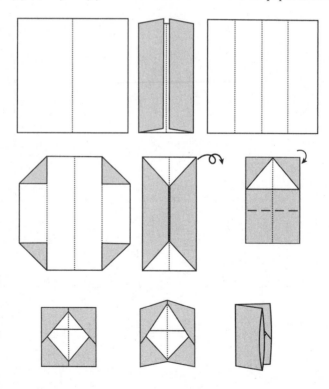

72.2 THREE-COMPARTMENT WALLET

This ingenious design is somewhat more complicated but produces a sturdier wallet. It has fewer compartments than the one opposite: one for bills and two for cards. It was created by origami designer Nick Robinson (www.nickrobinson.info). Again, there are no cuts and no need for tape.

Directions

Start with a 14-in square sheet of paper, which will make a wallet which is 3.5 × 3.5 in when folded in half (it must be stored folded to keep the cards secure, unlike the wallet opposite where they are confined). Fold as follows:

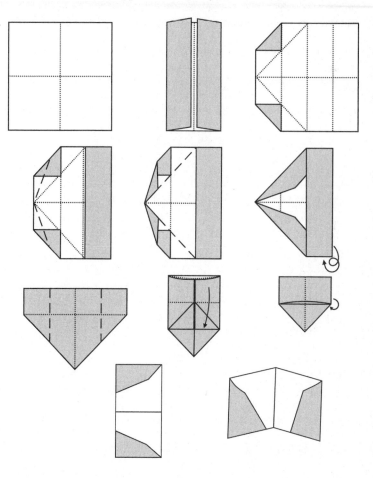

❦73 ERNEST HEMINGWAY

73.1 BIOGRAPHY

Hemingway was born in Oak Park, Illinois, on July 21, 1899. After finishing school he worked as a cub reporter for the Kansas City *Star*. He was determined to see action in the First World War, however, and after six months of journalism he served as an ambulance driver for the Italian Red Cross. He was wounded and decorated for his rescue of an Italian soldier.

Hemingway moved to Paris in the early 1920s, where he befriended other expatriate American writers, including Gertrude Stein and Ezra Pound. He wrote his first novels there, although it was not until *The Sun Also Rises* that he was established as a first-rate writer. War and outdoor pursuits – hunting, deep-sea fishing, and bullfighting – would become themes in Hemingway's life and writing. In the 1930s, he covered the Spanish civil war, which would be the basis of *For Whom the Bell Tolls*. He spent much of the Second World War on a boat off the Cuban coast, drinking and big-game fishing as much as looking to sink German submarines.

The Old Man and the Sea was the last of his books to appear during his lifetime, and soon after its publication he won the Nobel Prize in literature. But his physical and mental vigor deteriorated, and in 1961 Hemingway committed suicide, like his father, brother, and sister before him, with a shotgun wound to the head. He had married four times and produced three sons. "The world is a fine place and worth the fighting for," he had once written in *For Whom the Bell Tolls*, "and I hate very much to leave it."

73.2 WRITING

Hemingway's terse style, which has had such a significant and widespread influence on American literature, was marked by spartan word choice, limited use of qualifiers, and simple sentence structure – a conspicuous inconspicuousness, to use a description from men's dress. This simplicity was deceptive, however, and did not come easily (cf. Hemingway, p 185): he was an inveterate revisionist, sometimes reworking a manuscript dozens of times. He remains one of the few writers whose identity is apparent from the style of a single sentence.

Despite Hemingway's multifarious interests, reckless lifestyle, and frequent bouts with depression, he kept up a disciplined program of writing. For him the writer's life was a lonely one, and it depleted him. "I learned never to empty the well of my writing," he wrote in his memoir *A Moveable Feast*, "but always to stop when there was still something there in the deep part of the well, and let it refill at night from the springs that fed it."

73.3 BOOKS

A number of Hemingway's works were first published after his death in 1961. Several of these were unfinished and required significant pruning.

Novels and stories			
Three Stories and Ten Poems	1923	*True at First Light*	1999
in our time		*Under Kilimanjaro*	2005
(limited printing)	1924	*Nonfiction*	
In Our Time	1925	*Death in the Afternoon*	1932
The Torrents of Spring	1926	*Green Hills of Africa*	1935
The Sun Also Rises	1926	*A Moveable Feast*	1964
Men Without Women	1927	*The Dangerous Summer*	1985
A Farewell to Arms	1929		
Winner Take Nothing	1933	*Other*	
The Snows of Kilimanjaro	1936	*By-Line* (journalism)	1967
To Have and Have Not	1937	*88 Poems* (poetry)	1979
The Fifth Column and the		*Dateline: Toronto* (journalism)	1985
First Forty-Nine Stories	1938		
For Whom the Bell Tolls	1940	*Re-collected works*	
Across the River		*The Essential Hemingway*	1964
and Into the Trees	1950	*The Nick Adams Stories*	1972
The Old Man and the Sea	1952	*The Complete Short Stories*	
Islands in the Stream	1970	*of Ernest Hemingway*	1987
The Garden of Eden	1986	*The Collected Stories*	1995

73.4 BIOGRAPHIES

Of the many biographies of Hemingway, the five below are notable. The premier Hemingway website, www.timelesshemingway.com, says: "The bios by Lynn, Baker, and Meyers [are] 'the big three' and any serious EH scholar or enthusiast should have these works in his or her possession." *The New York Times* says Mellow's biography "stands with the best work done on the writer to date." Most ambitious of all is Reynolds's five-volume set.

Ernest Hemingway: A Life Story	Carlos Baker	1969
Hemingway: A Biography	Jeffrey Meyers	1985
Hemingway: Life and Work	Kenneth Lynn	1987
Hemingway: A Life Without Consequences	James Mellow	1992
The Young Hemingway (1986);	Michael Reynolds	1986–1999
Hemingway: The Paris Years (1989); *The American Homecoming* (1992); *The 1930s* (1997); *The Final Years* (1999)		

♛74 JAMES BOND

Of all 20th-century literary characters, the British spy code-named 007 has had the biggest influence on the modern perception of masculinity. James Bond is the central character of Ian Fleming's 14 books and the inspiration for 22 official films and countless other books and publications. The 3,000 pages penned by Fleming, however, remain the authoritative record of Bond, and in them can be found a detailed and coherent picture of the man.

74.1 BIOGRAPHY

James Bond was (likely) born in 1924, the son of Andrew Bond of Glencoe, Scotland, and Monique Delacroix of Switzerland. His family motto is *Orbis non sufficit* (The world is not enough). Bond's father was an arms dealer for Vickers, what is now part of BAE Systems Land & Armaments, and as a consequence much of Bond's childhood was spent abroad. When Bond was 11 his parents died climbing in the Aiguilles Rouges and he was taken in by his aunt Charmian Bond in Pett Bottom, Kent, a stone's throw from what is now the Duck Inn restaurant. A year later Bond entered Eton College, following his father's instructions, but had to be re-moved after two halves due to "alleged trouble with one of the boys' maids." He transferred to

Fleming's vision of Bond, from the *Daily Express.*

his father's old school, Fettes, where by comparison he prospered: he was an avid judo wrestler and lightweight boxer and spoke French and German, of which he had had early exposure abroad, with ease.

At 17 Bond finished school and began study at the University of Geneva; this was interrupted when he joined the Royal Navy Volunteer Reserve in 1941. By the end of the war he had achieved the rank of commander and his service record soon drew the attention of M (Miles), the director of the UK's Secret Intelligence Service, MI6. It was at this stage that Bond became "associated with certain aspects of the ministry's work." After his second assassination, Bond was awarded a double-o number, indicating a license to kill, and it is from this point that a number of his missions have been documented. In 1954 Bond was made a Companion of the Order of St. Michael and St. George (CMG). He was later offered a knighthood for his services to MI6 but refused for the sake of professional anonymity. At the end of *On Her Majesty's Secret Service*, Bond married Contessa Teresa di Vicenzo

(Tracy), daughter of Marc-Ange Draco; she was killed shortly after the wedding by Ernst Stavro Blofeld, Bond's longstanding nemesis. Nonetheless, Bond is known to have had at least one illegitimate child, through the Japanese agent Kissy Suzuki whom he first met in *You Only Live Twice*.

74.2 APPEARANCE

At 6 feet and 165 pounds, Bond is slim, almost wiry (body mass index = 22.4). He has blue-gray eyes, a rather cruel mouth, a long vertical scar on his left cheek, and short, dark hair which falls to his forehead in a wandering comma. On the back of his hand is a scar in the shape of the Russian character Ш, carved by a SMERSH agent in *Casino Royale*. His dress is simple but elegant: single-breasted blue serge or houndstooth check suits (probably from a tailor just off Savile Row; certainly not Italian) with a white shirt and slip-on shoes. His tie is black knit silk, evidently tied in a four-in-hand or half-Windsor (Bond thought the Windsor knot was "the mark of a cad"; see p 75). Alas, his bow tie is black satin rather than barathea.

Bond has few possessions, but they are fine: a wide, flat gun-metal cigarette case; a black oxidized Ronson lighter; and a Rolex Oyster Perpetual watch. Contrary to the films, Bond prefers Bentleys; in order, he drives a 1930 (or 1933) Mark IV convertible, a 1953 Mark VI, and a Mark II Continental, all of them gray with navy or black interior. He occasionally dines at the London gentlemen's club Blades, modeled after the real club Boodle's.

74.3 HABITS

Bond is an able amateur sportsman, particularly at skiing, golf, and hand-to-hand combat, the last being the subject of his book-in-progress, *Stand Firm*. He rode the Cresta Run from Top.

The British spy dislikes tea but frequently drinks coffee, brewed in an American Chemex. His taste in food is refined if unadventurous, with a preference for traditional English fare. His favorite meal is breakfast, for which we are given his recipe in the short story "007 in New York" (see p 156). Bond smokes approximately 60 cigarettes a day, usually a mix of Turkish and Balkan tobaccos, with three gold bands on the filter, indicative of his naval rank. He is a heavy drinker. Despite his cinematic preference for shaken vodka martinis, Fleming's Bond prefers whisky. Throughout the books his most common drinks are 25% whisky or bourbon, 11% sake, 10% champagne, and 6% vodka martini.

In *You Only Live Twice* Bond is missing, assumed dead. His secretary, Mary Goodnight, suggests for him this simple if simplistic epitaph: "I shall not waste my days in trying to prolong them. I shall use my time."

74.4 ORIGINAL FLEMING NOVELS

Ian Fleming wrote 12 novels and two collections of short stories about Bond, published annually between 1953 and 1966 (two were posthumous):

Casino Royale	1953	*For Your Eyes Only*	1960
Live and Let Die	1954	*Thunderball*	1961
Moonraker	1955	*The Spy Who Loved Me*	1962
Diamonds Are Forever	1956	*On Her Majesty's Secret Service*	1963
From Russia with Love	1957	*You Only Live Twice*	1964
Dr. No	1958	*The Man with the Golden Gun*	1965
Goldfinger	1959	*Octopussy and The Living Daylights*	1966

74.5 POST-FLEMING NOVELS

Since Ian Fleming's death, a number of authors, sanctioned by Ian Fleming Publications, have written Bond novels imitative of Fleming's original books. Some are adaptations of films into novel form ("novelizations").

Kingsley Amis

Colonel Sun	1968	(under the name Robert Markham)

John Gardner

License Renewed	1981	*License to Kill* (novelization)	1989
For Special Services	1982	*Brokenclaw*	1990
Icebreaker	1983	*The Man from Barbarossa*	1991
Role of Honour	1984	*Death Is Forever*	1992
Nobody Lives For Ever	1986	*Never Send Flowers*	1993
No Deals, Mr. Bond	1987	*SeaFire*	1994
Scorpius	1988	*GoldenEye* (novelization)	1995
Win, Lose or Die	1989	*COLD*	1996

Raymond Benson

Zero Minus Ten	1997	*High Time to Kill*	1999
Tomorrow Never Dies		*Doubleshot*	2000
(novelization)	1997	*Never Dream of Dying*	2001
The Facts of Death	1998	*The Man with the Red Tattoo*	2002
The World Is Not Enough		*Die Another Day*	
(novelization)	1999	(novelization)	2002

Sebastian Faulks

Devil May Care	2008	(writing as Ian Fleming)

74.6 BOOKS ON BOND

Of the many nonfiction books on Bond, three can be considered classics. Amis's book is a serious analysis of Fleming's novels; Pearson's is a biography of Bond on the assumption that he really existed; and Benson's is a comprehensive encyclopedia about the Bond books, films, and Ian Fleming.

The James Bond Dossier	Kingsley Amis	1965
James Bond: The Authorized Biography of 007	John Pearson	1973
The James Bond Bedside Companion	Raymond Benson	1984

74.7 FILMS

In the 22 official films, Bond has been played by six actors, though Fleming lived only to see Sean Connery. According to Vesper Lynd in the novel *Casino Royale*, we know that Bond resembled singer Hoagy Carmichael, and on this basis Timothy Dalton looks most like Fleming's vision of the spy.

Film	Bond actor	Bond girl actress	Year
Dr. No	Sean Connery	Ursula Andress	1962
From Russia with Love	Sean Connery	Daniela Bianchi	1963
Goldfinger	Sean Connery	Shirley Eaton	1964
Thunderball	Sean Connery	Claudine Auger	1965
You Only Live Twice	Sean Connery	Akiko Wakabayashi	1967
On Her Majesty's Secret Service	George Lazenby	Diana Rigg	1969
Diamonds Are Forever	Sean Connery	Jill St. John	1971
Live and Let Die	Roger Moore	Jane Seymour	1973
The Man with the Golden Gun	Roger Moore	Britt Ekland	1974
The Spy Who Loved Me	Roger Moore	Barbara Bach	1977
Moonraker	Roger Moore	Lois Chiles	1979
For Your Eyes Only	Roger Moore	Carole Bouquet	1981
Octopussy	Roger Moore	Maud Adams	1983
A View to a Kill	Roger Moore	Tanya Roberts	1985
The Living Daylights	Timothy Dalton	Maryam d'Abo	1987
License to Kill	Timothy Dalton	Talisa Soto	1989
GoldenEye	Pierce Brosnan	Izabella Scorupco	1995
Tomorrow Never Dies	Pierce Brosnan	Teri Hatcher	1997
The World Is Not Enough	Pierce Brosnan	Sophie Marceau	1999
Die Another Day	Pierce Brosnan	Halle Berry	2002
Casino Royale	Daniel Craig	Eva Green	2006
Quantum of Solace	Daniel Craig	Olga Kurylenko	2008

☙75 TEXT MESSAGES

Texting (also known as short message system, or SMS) is for many people the main form of non-spoken communication, exceeding letters and even emails. Part of the attraction of texting is its immediacy – messages are usually read by the recipient within seconds of sending. Unlike postal or electronic mail, a message is often neither essential nor interrogative, placing no responsibility on the recipient to respond. But because composing a text is a lot slower than typing or writing, it is in the interest of the sender to make it brief. Over the years a unique form of semi-coded expression with a haiku-like economy has evolved. It makes use of minimal punctuation and a number of conventions for the concise expression of words.

75.1 TEXT MESSAGE THEORY

The principal hurdle in entering text into a small device is the difficulty of incorporating a full-size keyboard. The solution has been to reduce the number of keys and take advantage of the limited range of words: not every arrangement of letters forms a word. The number of letter combinations grows with the number of characters N as 26^N: there are 26 possible one-letter combinations, 676 two-letter combinations, and so on. The number of English words, as found in the official Scrabble word list, grows much more slowly: there are three one-letter words, 96 two-letter words, etc. Roughly in between is the number of possible SMS numbers, which grows as 8^N: 8 one-digit numbers, 64 two-digit numbers, and so on (only the digits 2–9 are used). As the graph below suggests, apart from between two and four characters, most SMS numbers correspond to one or no words, and the chance for ambiguous input (textonyms, opposite) is low.

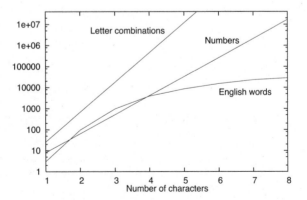

75.2 PREDICTIVE TEXT

Most cell phones provide an efficient means of entering words on the numeric keypad, known as predictive text. The user types in the number associated with each letter of the alphabet, as shown below, and the phone attempts to predict the word that the user wants. (Characters for 1 may vary.)

0	_ (space)	2	abc2	4	ghi4	6	mno6	8	tuv8
1	. , ? ! ' " 1	3	def3	5	jkl5	7	pqrs7	9	wxyz9

For example: 626 = man; 2427 = chap; 335569 = fellow. But more than one word can correspond to a number; 2427 also yields agar, bias, bibs, and char. Words with the same number are called textonyms. Textonyms require the user to scroll manually through the possibilities. Without scrolling, typing "Ask the cool barmaid for nine pints of beer" produces "Ask the book carnage for mind shots of adds." Some notable textonyms include:

46 = go, im, in	33284 = death, debug
627 = map, mar, nap, oar	746637 = phones, simmer, sinner
5477 = kiss, lips, lisp	7425464 = picking, shaking, sibling
22737 = acres, bards, barer, bares, baser, bases, caper, capes, cards, carer, cares, cases (the largest set of textonyms known)	

75.3 TEXT MESSAGE SHORTHAND

Text messages can be condensed in a variety of ways, described here. First, many common words can be abbreviated (periods are omitted):

&	and	md	made	t	the	w	with
bn	been	msg	message	thx	thanks	wd	would
cd	could	pls	please	tmr	tomorrow	wk	week
lk	look	spk	speak	v	very	wt	what

Some words can be replaced by single letters, which are read out in full:

b	be, bee	i	eye	p	pea, pee	u	you
c	see, sea	j	jay	r	are	y	why
g	gee	o	oh, owe	t	tea		

Similarly, some words can be replaced by punctuation marks or digits:

@	at	1	one, won	2	to, too	4	for	8	ate

Likewise, characters can replace some groups of phonemes within a word:

@	at	4	for	b	bee	r	ar	u	yoo
2	too	8	ate	n	en	s	ess	x	eks

A combination of abbreviation, replacement, and spelling yields, e.g.:

a4d	afford	b4	before	nter	enter	2day	today
any1	anyone	ch@	chat	gr8	great	tmw	tomorrow
rt	art	chx	checks	ls	less	ur	your

75.4 TEXT MESSAGE PARALANGUAGE

Machine-printed and digital communication, with its cool and unchanging letter forms, brings with it an ambiguity of meaning and tone. This has led to an explosion in the use of digital paralanguage – ASCII characters on a single line for non-verbal communication – to prevent misunderstandings. These are also known as emoticons (from "emotion" and "console," not "icon"), and should not to be confused with ASCII art, which occupies multiple lines. The most familiar examples are the question and exclamation marks, ? and ! More recent is the use of x, o, and :-) to denote a kiss, a hug, and a smiley. (The first documented use of the smiley was on September 19, 1982, by Scott Fahlman.) Emoticons fall into several classes, each containing variations on a theme. Examples, which are easily extended, are shown below.

Smileys are the most popular in the United States and are read sideways.

:-)	smiley	:-D	big smile	:-P	tongue out
;-)	winking	:-]	polite smile	:-Q	smoking
:-#	with braces	:-(	frown	:-*	kissing
8-)	with glasses	:'-(	crying	:-v	lying

Head and hands, read vertically, show the head, o, and one or both arms.

\o/	joy	o\	scratching head	\o_/ _o/	fencing
/o\	despair	<o>	covering ears	\o/	drowning
o/	waving	o7	saluting	>-<o	jumping off

Kaomoji (face characters) originated in Japan, and are also read vertically.

(ˆ ˆ)	smiley	m( )m	bowing	@ˆˆ@	blushing
(ˆ)	winking	(* *)	dazed	(ˆˆ;	sweating

ARTS AND SCIENCES

A riddle • Traveling down a road, you come to a fork. One path leads to paradise, the other to death, but you do not know which path to take. At the start of each path stands a guard. One guard always tells the truth, the other always lies, and again you do not know which is which. You can ask one guard a single question about which path to choose. What would it be? (See Colophon, p 229, for answer.)

Ernest Hemingway • There is nothing to writing. All you do is sit down at a typewriter and bleed.

Albert Einstein • Reading, after a certain age, diverts the mind too much from its creative pursuits. Any man who reads too much and uses his own brain too little falls into lazy habits of thinking.

Richard Feynman • People who wish to analyze nature without using mathematics must settle for a reduced understanding.

Samuel Johnson • Knowledge is of two kinds. We know a subject ourselves, or we know where we can find information upon it. (Boswell, *Life of Johnson*, 1791)

Lord Chesterfield • Wear your learning, like your watch, in a private pocket; and do not pull it out and strike it merely to show that you have one (*Lord Chesterfield's Letters*, 1776)

Anonymous • What is mind? No matter. What is matter? Never mind.

Joseph Long • When I was your age we didn't have integration. We had to add up differential units by hand. (Conversation, Caltech, 1993)

Benjamin Franklin • Would you persuade, speak of interest, not of reason. • There are lazy minds as well as lazy bodies. • Read much, but not too many books. • He's a fool that cannot conceal his wisdom. (*Poor Richard's Almanack*, 1732–1757)

❦76 USEFUL FACTS

Sometimes the best way to remember something is to reduce it to a list before committing it to memory. Below is a list of well-known lists, ordered by length, from the ancient world and the modern.

76.1 THREE

Parts of man	*Graces*	*Fates*	*Magi*
Mind	Aglaia	Clotho	Melchior
Body	Thalia	Lachesis	Gaspar
Spirit	Euphrosyne	Atropos	Balthazar

Enemies of man	*Christian graces*	*Eminent good works*	*Primary colors*
The world	Faith	Prayer	Red
The flesh	Hope	Fasting	Yellow
The devil	Charity	Almsgiving	Blue

76.2 FOUR

Cardinal virtues	*Elements*	*Loves*	*Last things*
Prudence	Earth	Affection	Death
Justice	Air	Friendship	Judgment
Fortitude	Fire	Eros	Heaven
Temperance	Water	Charity	Hell

Fundamental forces	*Estates*	*Freedoms*	*Gospels*
Gravitational	Nobility	Of speech	Matthew
Electromagnetic	Clergy	Of worship	Mark
Strong	Commoners	From fear	Luke
Weak	Press	From want	John

76.3 FIVE

Pillars of Islam	*Orders of architecture*	*Platonic solids*	*Tastes*
Profession of faith	Doric	Tetrahedron	Salty
Prayer	Ionic	Cube	Sour
Charity	Corinthian	Octahedron	Sweet
Fasting	Tuscan	Dodecahedron	Bitter
Pilgrimage	Composite	Icosahedron	Savory

76.4 SIX

Ages of the world	*Orders of Mishnah*	*Rugby nations*	*Quarks*
Adam to	Zeraim	England	Up
Noah to	Moed	France	Down
Abraham to	Nashim	Ireland	Strange
King David to	Nezikin	Italy	Charm
Babylonian exile to	Kodashim	Scotland	Bottom
Advent of Christ to now	Tohorot	Wales	Top

76.5 SEVEN

Wonders of the world	*Sacraments*	*Liberal arts*	*Ages of man*
Colossus of Rhodes	Baptism	Grammar	Infancy
Gardens at Babylon	Eucharist	Logic	Childhood
Pharos of Alexandria	Penance	Rhetoric	Lover
Pyramids of Egypt	Confirmation	Arithmetic	Soldier
Statue of Zeus	Holy Orders	Music	Justice
Temple of Diana	Matrimony	Geometry	Old age
Tomb of Mausolus	Last Rights	Astronomy	Dementia

Blunders of the world	*Champions of Christendom*	*Deadly sins*	*Opposing virtues*
Wealth w/o work	St. George	Lust	Chastity
Pleasure w/o conscience	St. Andrew	Gluttony	Temperance
Knowledge w/o character	St. Patrick	Greed	Liberality
Commerce w/o morality	St. David	Sloth	Diligence
Science w/o humanity	St. Denis	Wrath	Meekness
Worship w/o sacrifice	St. James	Envy	Kindness
Politics w/o principle	St. Anthony	Pride	Humility

76.6 EIGHT

Beatitudes		
Blessed are the...	for...	*Planets*
poor	theirs is the kingdom of heaven	Mercury
mourners	they shall be comforted	Venus
meek	they shall inherit the earth	Earth
hungry	they shall be filled	Mars
merciful	they shall obtain mercy	Jupiter
pure	they shall see God	Saturn
peacemakers	they shall be called children of God	Uranus
persecuted	theirs is the kingdom of heaven	Neptune

76.7 NINE

Muses and their attributes		*Worthies*	*Choirs of angels*
Calliope	Epic poetry	Hector	Seraphim
Clio	History	Alexander the Great	Cherubim
Euterpe	Lyric song	Julius Caesar	Thrones
Thalia	Comedy	Joshua	Dominions
Melpomene	Tragedy	David	Virtues
Terpsichore	Dance	Judas Maccabaeus	Powers
Erato	Love song	King Arthur	Principalities
Polyhymnia	Sacred song	Charlemagne	Archangels
Urania	Astronomy	Godfrey of Bouillon	Angels

76.8 TEN

Scout essentials (p 96)	*Essential exercises (p 22)*	*SMS input*	
Canteen or water bottle	Curls	0	_
Extra clothing	Triceps extensions	1	.,-?!'@:;/1
First-aid kit	Wrist curls	2	abc2
Map and compass	Bench press	3	def3
Matches and fire starter	Military press	4	ghi4
Pocketknife	Calf raises	5	jkl5
Rain gear	Squats	6	mno6
Sun protection	Leg curls	7	pqrs7
Flashlight	Sit-ups	8	tuv8
Trail food	Chin-ups	9	wxyz9

76.9 TWELVE

	Birthstones		*Apostles*	*Olympians*
Jan	garnet	dark red	Peter	Zeus
Feb	amethyst	purple	Andrew	Hera
Mar	aquamarine	pale blue	James	Poseidon
Apr	diamond	clear	John	Hermes
May	emerald	green	Philip	Hestia
Jun	pearl	white	Bartholomew	Demeter
Jul	ruby	red	Thomas	Aphrodite
Aug	peridot	pale green	Matthew	Athena
Sep	sapphire	blue	James, son of Alphaeus	Apollo
Oct	opal	variegated	Jude	Artemis
Nov	topaz	yellow	Simon	Ares
Dec	turquoise	sky blue	Judas Iscariot	Hephaestus

❦77 USEFUL FIGURES

77.1 ROMAN NUMERALS

There are seven symbols used to construct roman numerals: I, V, X, L, C, D, and M. Putting a line over a symbol is equivalent to multiplying it by 1,000.

I	1	VII	7	XL	40	C	100	DCC	700
II	2	VIII	8	L	50	CC	200	DCCC	800
III	3	IX	9	LX	60	CCC	300	CM	900
IV	4	X	10	LXX	70	CD	400	M	1,000
V	5	XX	20	LXXX	80	D	500	MM	2,000
VI	6	XXX	30	XC	90	DC	600	MMIX	2,009

77.2 BIG AND SMALL NUMBERS

The prefixes to the left can be combined with SI units. Some conventional larger numbers are googol (10^{100}), centillion (10^{303}), and googolplex ($10^{10^{100}}$).

deca	da	$\times 10$	ten	deci	d	$\times 10^{-1}$	tenth
hecto	h	$\times 10^2$	hundred	centi	c	$\times 10^{-2}$	hundredth
kilo	k	$\times 10^3$	thousand	milli	m	$\times 10^{-3}$	thousandth
mega	M	$\times 10^6$	million	micro		$\times 10^{-6}$	millionth
giga	G	$\times 10^9$	billion	nano	n	$\times 10^{-9}$	billionth
tera	T	$\times 10^{12}$	trillion	pico	p	$\times 10^{-12}$	trillionth
peta	P	$\times 10^{15}$	quadrillion	femto	f	$\times 10^{-15}$	quadrillionth
exa	E	$\times 10^{18}$	pentillion	atto	a	$\times 10^{-18}$	pentillionth
zetta	Z	$\times 10^{21}$	sextillion	zepto	z	$\times 10^{-21}$	sextillionth
yotta	Y	$\times 10^{24}$	septillion	yocto	y	$\times 10^{-24}$	septillionth

77.3 SI UNITS

The Système International d'Unités, or SI units, is a coherent system of base 10 (metric) units, all of which can be combined with the 20 prefixes above. SI units are the customary system of units throughout most of the world.

Base units		mole (mol)	amount of substance
meter (m)	length	candela (cd)	luminous intensity
kilogram (kg)	mass	*Associated units*	
second (s)	time	are (a) = 100 m²	unit of area
ampere (A)	electric current	liter (l) = <u>0.001</u> m³	unit of volume
kelvin (K)	temperature	Note: 1 l of water weighs 1 kg	

77.4 IMPERIAL UNITS

Imperial units are the traditional British units of measurement. Despite attempts to adopt SI units, they are popular in the United Kingdom, much of the British Commonwealth, and, with some differences, the United States.

Apothecaries' capacity

20 minims	scruple
3 scruples	drachm
8 drachms	fluid ounce
20 fluid ounces	pint

Apothecaries' weight

20 grains	scruple
3 scruples	dram
8 drams	ounce
12 ounces	pound

Area

144 square inches	square foot
9 square feet	square yard
1,210 square yards	rood
4 roods	acre
640 acres	square mile

Avoirdupois (common) weight

16 drams	ounce (oz)
16 ounces	pound (lb)
14 pounds	stone
2 stones	quarter
4 quarters	hundredweight
20 hundredweight	ton

Capacity (US)

4 fluid ounces	gill
4 gills	pint
2 pints	quart
4 quarts	gallon
2 gallons	peck
4 pecks	bushel

Length

3 barleycorns	inch (in)
12 inches	foot (ft)
3 feet	yard (yd)
1,760 yards	mile
3 miles	league

Surveyors' length

0.66 feet	link
25 links	rod
4 rods	chain
10 chains	furlong
8 furlongs	mile

Troy weight (precious metal)

24 grains	pennyweight
20 pennyweights	ounce
12 ounces	pound

77.5 CONVERSION BETWEEN UNITS

inch	2.54 centimeters	pound	0.4536 kilograms
foot	0.3048 meters	fluid ounce (US)	29.57 ml
mile	1.609344 kilometers	quart	1.136 liters
acre	0.4047 hectares	temp (°C)	temp (K) − 273.15
ounce (avoirdupois)	28.35 grams	temp (°C)	(5/9 × (temp (°F) − 32)
ounce (apoth. & troy)	31.10 grams	temp (°F)	(9/5 × temp (°C)) + 32

KEY   All integers and underlined decimal numbers are exact.

77.6 OTHER UNITS

Alcoholic strength	see p 103		*8 exercises*	workout

Angular measure

60 seconds	minute	*Microscopic length*	
60 minutes	degree	angstrom (Å)	10^{-10} m
360 degrees	circle	micron (μ)	10^{-6} m
circle	2π radians		

Astronomical distance

Nautical measures

		6 feet	fathom
astronomical unit	1.50×10^8 km	100 fathoms	cable
light year	9.46×10^{12} km	1,852 m	nautical mile (intl)
parsec	3.08×10^{13} km	3 nautical miles	league (at sea)
		knot	1 nautical mile/hour

Beauty (p 38)

Paper sheets

25.6 Helenas	Helen	25 sheets	quire
10 Helenas	beauty to die for	20 quires	ream
		10 reams	bale

Cigars	see p 136	

Paper size

Computer memory

8 bits	byte (B)	letter	8.5 × 11 in
2^{10} = 1,024 bytes	kilobyte (kB)	legal	8.5 × 14 in
2^{10} kilobytes	megabyte (MB)	A4	210 × 297 mm
2^{10} megabytes	gigabyte (GB)	A0	841 × 1,189 mm
2^{10} gigabytes	terabyte (TB)	B0	1,000 × 1,414 mm
		C0	917 × 1,297 mm

A0 = 2 A1 = 4 A2 = 8 A3, etc.
Same for B0 and C0.

Cooking & drinks	see pp 146, 103	

Gem weight

Shoe size   see p 52

100 points	carat	
5 carats	gram	*Typography*

Typography

12 points	pica
6 picas	0.9961 inches

Gym (typical)

10 repetitions	set		
3 sets	exercise	*Wine bottle sizes*	see p 114

77.7 MATHEMATICAL CONSTANTS

γ	Euler constant	0.57722		√3	Square root of three	1.73205
√2	Square root of two	1.41421		*e*	Base of natural log	2.71828
φ	Golden ratio	1.61803		π	Pi	3.14159

❦78 BOOKS

Below is a collection of classic books for men. In general the earliest date of publication is listed. Some of the books have remained continuously in print, others have been reissued after a dormant period. Those that are out of print or out of copyright can often be found second-hand or free online:

Out of print
www.abebooks.co.uk
www.bibliofind.com

Out of copyright
www.gutenberg.org
www.digital.library.upenn.edu/books

This list attempts to strike a balance between old classics and more recent publications where the dust has not settled between trendy and trusted.

78.1 50 MOST ESSENTIAL BOOKS FOR MEN

★ *The Imitation of Christ*	Thomas à Kempis	*c.* 1470
The Book of the Courtier	Baldassare Castiglione	1528
The Compleat Angler	Izaak Walton	1653
Lord Chesterfield's Letters	Philip Stanhope	1776
Pelham; or	Edward Bulwer-Lytton	1828
the Adventures of a Gentleman		
A Hero of Our Time	Mikhail Lermontov	1840
Manners for Men	Mrs. Humphry	1897
★ *Scouting for Boys*	Robert Baden-Powell	1908
The Stag Cook Book	C. Mac Sheridan	1922
The Pipe Book	Alfred Dunhill	1924
★ *The Ashley Book of Knots*	Clifford Ashley	1944
Brideshead Revisited	Evelyn Waugh	1945
★ *The Fine Art of Mixing Drinks*	David A. Embury	1948
★ *Esquire's Handbook for Hosts*	Esquire	1949
★ *Scarne on Cards*	John Scarne	1949
With or Without Beans	Joe Cooper	1952
Dandies	James Laver	1968
★ *Esquire's Encyclopedia of*	O. Schoeffler & W. Gale	1973
20th Century Men's Fashions		
★ *Arnold: The Education of a Bodybuilder*	Arnold Schwarzenegger	1977
Spirits and Liqueurs	Peter Hallgarten	1979
★ *The Gentlemen's Clubs of London*	Anthony Lejeune	1979
★ *The James Bond Bedside Companion*	Raymond Benson	1984
★ *The Ultimate Pipe Book*	Richard Carlton Hacker	1984
★ *The SAS Survival Handbook*	John Wiseman	1986

The Theory of Poker	David Sklansky	1987
The Tie	Sarah Gibbings	1990
★ *The Elements of Typographic Style*	Robert Bringhurst	1992
A History of Men's Fashion	Farid Chenoune	1993
★ *Beer Companion*	Michael Jackson	1993
The Englishman's Suit	Hardy Amies	1994
Sex and Suits	Anne Hollander	1995
A James Bond Omnibus	Ian Fleming	1997
Tree Houses You Can Actually Build	D. Stiles & J. Trusty Stiles	1998
Gentleman	Bernhard Roetzel	1999
★ *Malt Whisky Companion*	Michael Jackson	1999
The 85 Ways to Tie a Tie	Thomas Fink & Yong Mao	1999
London Man	Francis Chichester	2000
The Boutonnière	Umberto Angeloni	2000
The Faber Book of Smoking	James Walton	2000
The Chap Manifesto	G. Temple & V. Darkwood	2001
★ *Dressing the Man*	Alan Flusser	2002
The Modern Gentleman	P. Mollod & J. Tesauro	2002
US Army Survival Manual 3-05.70	Department of Defense	2002
Who's a Dandy?	George Walden	2002
Mr. Boston Official Bartender's and Party Guide	Chris Morris (ed.)	2005
★ *Hugh Johnson's Pocket Wine Book*	Hugh Johnson	2006
Manliness	Harvey Mansfield	2006
★ *The Dangerous Book for Boys*	Conn & Hal Iggulden	2006
★ *Diffords Guide to Cocktails 7*	Simon Difford	2008
Quantum of Solace (collected stories)	Ian Fleming	2008

KEY   ★ means that the book is the definitive work in its field

78.2 SELECTED NOTES

The Imitation of Christ · This book of spiritual devotion is widely believed to be the most printed book after the Holy Bible. Saint Thomas More prized it above all others and General Gordon kept it with him in the battlefield.

The Compleat Angler · Walton's guide to catching and eating fish is the most printed book in English after the Bible and *Pilgrim's Progress*. It describes the spirit of fishing as well as the mechanics, much of which has little changed.

A Hero of Our Time · A collection of short stories about the Byronic hero Pechorin and his romantic conquests. The story "Princess Mary" provides a telling insight into the mind of a woman falling in love against her wishes.

Scouting for Boys • This is the original Scouting handbook by the founder of the Scouts, Robert Baden-Powell. Edited by Elleke Boehmer, it was reissued by Oxford University Press in 2005. Readers will notice that modern-day Scouting has drifted far from what Baden-Powell originally set up, which focused on boys, God, adventure, common sense, and manly pursuits.

The Ashley Book of Knots • Universally regarded as the most comprehensive and entertaining book on knots, this handsome treatise contains nearly 4,000 knots and over 7,000 drawings. It is still in print. "It is a prodigy," writes *The Observer*. "Knots, in the world of books, have thus been tied forever."

The Fine Art of Mixing Drinks • This is, simply put, the most influential treatise on cocktails ever written, "the Escoffier of cocktail books." It focuses as much on the theory behind cocktail construction as on the recipes themselves. In 2008 this classic was retypeset and reissued by Mud Puddle books.

Esquire's Handbook for Hosts • Republished in its original form in 1999 by Black Dog & Leventhal, this splendid guide remains surprisingly insightful. It is divided into three parts: Eat: the world's best chefs wear pants; Drink: liquor is quicker; And Be Merry: how to be happy though host.

With or Without Beans • The subtitle explains what the book is about: "Being a compendium to perpetuate the internationally famous bowl of chili (Texas style) which occupies such an important place in modern civilization."

Esquire's Encyclopedia of 20th Century Men's Fashions • A detailed, comprehensive overview of the trends in men's dress up to the early 70s. Copies are considered prize possessions, and second-hand copies are expensive.

Arnold: The Education of a Bodybuilder • Written early on in Schwarzenegger's career, this slim volume remains the best book on lifting available. The first half is autobiographical, telling Arnold's tale of extraordinary mental discipline, and the second describes his back-to-basics lifting routines.

The SAS Survival Handbook • For 26 years the author served with the SAS (Special Air Forces), generally regarded as the most elite special force in the world. His book is the definitive survival manual, a grown-up's *Scouting for Boys*. If you could have one thing on a desert island, this would be it.

The Elements of Typographic Style • Not an obvious choice but a welcome lesson in, and example of, beautiful design, proportion, and layout. "I wish to see this book become the Typographers' Bible," writes Hermann Zapf.

Beer Companion • Many men have only experienced the tip of the beer iceberg, usually in the form of pale lager. Written by the world's preeminent beer expert (until his death in 2007), this award-winning book contains beer history and classification and notes on beers from around the world.

The Englishman's Suit • This slim volume is, word for word, the best book on men's dress. It is witty, authoritative, and outspoken. Hardy Amies was founder of the eponymous Savile Row tailor and dressmaker to the Queen.

A James Bond Omnibus • Many men are not aware that Ian Fleming's original Bond novels are more entertaining and consistent than their film adaptations. This is a single-volume collection of the Fleming novels *From Russia With Love*, *Dr. No*, and *Goldfinger*, often considered the three best Bond novels. There are 14 Bond books by Fleming in all, a list of which is on p 180.

The 85 Ways to Tie a Tie • The story of the knotted neckcloth and the modern necktie and how to tie both, with forays into history, mathematics, and men's dress along the way. The book was inspired by two mathematics papers by the authors in which they prove that there are exactly 85 necktie knots and explain how to tie them. The papers are for experts; the book is for laymen.

The Chap Manifesto • "A rallying point for the classic bloke beleaguered in postmodern confusion, a *cri de coeur* from the manly bosom, a hail-well-met to gentlemen of all pinstripes." Written along the lines of *The Chap* magazine, it precedes *The Chap Almanac* (2002) and *The Best of The Chap* (2005).

Dressing the Man • One of the most comprehensive and best illustrated books on men's dress. Also notable are Flusser's *Clothes and the Man* (1985), a shorter, less glossy, but equally authoritative volume, and *Style and the Man* (1996), a guide to the best men's clothes shops around the world.

Who's a Dandy? • This slim volume is in two parts. The first is an exploration of modern dandyism; the second, a new translation of the French dandy Jules Barbey d'Aurevilly's 19th-century essay on George Brummel (a.k.a. Beau Brummel).

Manliness • Harvard government professor Mansfield makes a spirited defense of the importance of manliness and the cultural differences between the sexes. What is common sense to some is scandalous to others, and this eminently sensible volume has sharply divided readers and critics alike.

Diffords Guide to Cocktails 7 • The best guide to cocktails in print. Also noteworthy is Difford's *Sauce Guide to Drink & Drinking* (2002). Difford's *Guide* series are extensively researched, beautifully designed, and clearly written.

❦79 FILMS

Films seem to divide the sexes more than any other form of art: women like chick flicks and men like guy films. How many men have watched *The Devil Wears Prada*? How many were under duress when they did? In fact, one test for determining if a movie is a guy film is whether or not a girl would rent it on her own. A woman is about as likely to rent a copy of *Scarface* or *Goodfellas* as a man is likely to rent *Thelma & Louise* or *Love Actually*.

79.1 WHAT IS A GUY FILM?

What makes a film a guy film? As you examine the list below, some themes emerge: men prefer entertaining over improving; action over drama; friendship over romance; war over peace; admiration over identification; gadgets over relationships; male actors over female ones. Of the 50 men's films below, only three were classified as "romance" by the Internet Movie Database: *Spartacus*, *On Her Majesty's Secret Service*, and *Rocky*. Not exactly chick flicks. Contrary to the popular view that sex sells, when it comes to films, men are much less concerned with pretty actresses than heroic actors. A guy film needn't have any women in it at all, and many of the films below have almost entirely male casts.

79.2 50 ESSENTIAL FILMS FOR MEN

Here are 50 films that every man should see at least once. How were the films chosen? Some are so iconic that they instantly qualify, such as *The Godfather* and *Unforgiven*; others are less well known but have become cult classics, like *Deliverance* and *Pumping Iron*. All could easily be watched twice.

	Film	*Starring*	*Year*
1	*The Maltese Falcon*	Humphrey Bogart	1941
2	*Hamlet*	Laurence Olivier	1948
3	*The Seven Samurai*	Takashi Shimura	1954
4	*North by Northwest*	Cary Grant	1959
5	*Spartacus*	Kirk Douglas, Laurence Olivier	1960
6	*Lawrence of Arabia*	Peter O'Toole, Alec Guinness	1962
7	*The Great Escape*	Steve McQueen	1963
8	*The Good, the Bad and the Ugly*	Clint Eastwood	1966
9	*The Dirty Dozen*	Charles Bronson, Telly Savalas	1967
10	*On Her Majesty's Secret Service*	George Lazenby	1969
11	*Dirty Harry*	Clint Eastwood	1971
12	*Deliverance*	Burt Reynolds	1972

79.3 SOME STATISTICS

Some actors turn up in the top 50 men's films more often than others. The following star in the largest number of films: Robert De Niro (7 films), Al Pacino (4), Clint Eastwood (3), and Arnold Schwarzenegger (3).

Each film is assigned to one or more genres according to the Internet Movie Database. Below are the number (No.) of guy films in each genre and the expected number (Exp.) if the 50 films were chosen randomly. The ratio of these numbers (Amp.) is the amplification of that genre in guy films: high numbers mean it is more important to guy films (war, thriller, history, biography, adventure); low numbers, less important (comedy, fantasy, romance).

Genre	No.	Exp.	Amp.	Genre	No.	Exp.	Amp.
Action	22	3.2	6.9	History	5	0.5	10.0
Adventure	15	2.0	7.5	Horror	4	1.7	2.4
Biography	5	0.6	8.3	Mystery	4	1.1	3.6
Comedy	3	12.1	0.2	Romance	3	3.2	0.9
Crime	13	2.2	5.9	Sci-fi	5	1.0	5.0
Documentary	1	1.0	1.0	Sport	4	0.7	5.7
Drama	35	16.1	2.2	Thriller	25	2.4	10.4
Fantasy	1	1.2	0.8	War	11	0.8	13.8
				Western	2	1.4	1.4

50 ESSENTIAL FILMS FOR MEN (CONTINUED)

Below is more information about the films listed opposite, including the number of Academy Awards and membership in each of the 17 genres (•).

#	Director	Academy Awards	Nominations	Action	Adventure	Biography	Comedy	Crime	Documentary	Drama	Fantasy	History	Horror	Mystery	Romance	Sci-fi	Sport	Thriller	War	Western
1	John Huston	0	3				•							•						
2	Laurence Olivier	4	7							•										
3	Akira Kurosawa	0	2	•	•					•										
4	Alfred Hitchcock	0	3		•								•		•			•		
5	Stanley Kubrick	0	1	•	•	•				•				•		•		•		
6	David Lean	7	10		•	•				•									•	
7	John Sturges	0	1	•	•					•								•	•	
8	Sergio Leone	0	0	•	•					•										•
9	Robert Aldrich	1	4	•			•			•								•		
10	Peter Hunt	0	0	•	•											•		•		
11	Don Siegel	0	0	•				•		•						•		•		
12	John Boorman	0	3		•			•		•								•		

	Film	Starring	Year
13	*The Godfather*	Al Pacino, Marlon Brando	1972
14	*The Exorcist*	Jason Miller	1973
15	*Enter the Dragon*	Bruce Lee	1973
16	*The Godfather: Part II*	Al Pacino, Robert De Niro	1974
17	*Jaws*	Robert Shaw, Roy Scheider	1975
18	*Rocky*	Sylvester Stallone	1976
19	*Taxi Driver*	Robert De Niro	1976
20	*Pumping Iron*	Arnold Schwarzenegger	1977
21	*The Deer Hunter*	Robert De Niro	1978
22	*Alien*	Sigourney Weaver	1979
23	*Apocalypse Now*	Marlon Brando, Martin Sheen	1979
24	*Mad Max*	Mel Gibson	1979
25	*Raging Bull*	Robert De Niro	1980
26	*The Shining*	Jack Nicholson	1980
27	*Chariots of Fire*	Ian Charleson, Ben Cross	1981
28	*Scarface*	Al Pacino	1983
29	*The Terminator*	Arnold Schwarzenegger	1984
30	*Platoon*	Charlie Sheen	1986
31	*The Untouchables*	Kevin Costner, Sean Connery	1987
32	*Wall Street*	Charlie Sheen	1987
33	*Withnail & I*	Richard E. Grant, Paul McGann	1987
34	*Die Hard*	Bruce Willis	1988
35	*Goodfellas*	Robert De Niro, Joe Pesci	1990
36	*Terminator 2: Judgment Day*	Arnold Schwarzenegger	1991
37	*Unforgiven*	Clint Eastwood, Morgan Freeman	1992
38	*The Shawshank Redemption*	Tim Robbins, Morgan Freeman	1994
39	*Braveheart*	Mel Gibson	1995
40	*Casino*	Robert De Niro, Joe Pesci	1995
41	*Heat*	Al Pacino, Robert De Niro	1995
42	*Saving Private Ryan*	Tom Hanks	1998
43	*Fight Club*	Edward Norton, Brad Pitt	1999
44	*The Matrix*	Keanu Reeves	1999
45	*The Talented Mr. Ripley*	Matt Damon, Jude Law	1999
46	*Gladiator*	Russell Crowe, Richard Harris	2000
47	*Ocean's Eleven*	George Clooney	2001
48	*The Lord of the Rings (1–3)*	Elijah Wood, Ian McKellen	2001–2003
49	*The Bourne Ultimatum*	Matt Damon	2007
50	*There Will Be Blood*	Daniel Day-Lewis	2007

	Director	Academy Awards	Nominations	Action	Adventure	Biography	Comedy	Crime	Documentary	Drama	Fantasy	History	Horror	Mystery	Romance	Sci-fi	Sport	Thriller	War	Western
13	Francis Coppola	3	11							•									•	
14	William Friedkin	2	10							•			•							
15	Robert Clouse	0	0	•				•										•		
16	Francis Coppola	6	11							•									•	
17	Steven Spielberg	3	4		•							•						•		
18	John Avildsen	3	10							•					•		•	•		
19	Martin Scorsese	0	4				•			•										
20	G. Butler, R. Fiore	0	0						•											
21	Michael Cimino	5	9							•									•	
22	Ridley Scott	1	2									•				•		•		
23	Francis Coppola	2	8	•	•					•									•	
24	George Miller	0	0	•	•											•				
25	Martin Scorsese	2	8			•				•							•			
26	Stanley Kubrick	0	0										•	•						
27	Hugh Hudson	4	7			•				•		•					•			
28	Brian De Palma	0	0					•		•										
29	James Cameron	0	0	•												•				
30	Oliver Stone	4	8	•						•									•	
31	Brian De Palma	1	4					•		•			•	•						
32	Oliver Stone	1	1					•		•										
33	Bruce Robinson	0	0				•													
34	John McTiernan	0	4	•												•				
35	Martin Scorsese	1	6					•		•										
36	James Cameron	2	6	•						•								•		
37	Clint Eastwood	4	9							•										•
38	Frank Darabont	0	7					•		•										
39	Mel Gibson	5	10	•						•								•		
40	Martin Scorsese	0	1				•	•		•				•						
41	Michael Mann	0	0	•				•		•							•			
42	Steven Spielberg	5	11	•						•								•		
43	David Fincher	0	1	•						•						•				
44	A. & L. Wachowski	4	4	•	•											•				
45	Anthony Minghella	0	5					•		•					•					
46	Ridley Scott	5	12	•	•					•								•		
47	Steven Soderbergh	0	0				•	•								•				
48	Peter Jackson	17	30	•	•					•	•									
49	Paul Greengrass	3	3	•	•							•				•				
50	Paul Anderson	2	8							•						•				

❦80 WEBSITES

Unlike books (p 192), websites are free and never go out of print. They tend to be more current, usually updated daily or weekly. Here are some indispensable sites for men with a bias towards depth over breadth. The sites are organized in accordance with the chapters of this book, with general content sites listed first. All sites start "www" unless otherwise shown.

80.1 50 ESSENTIAL WEBSITES FOR MEN

General
www.askmen.com . . . . Essays and forums on all men's questions
www.ehow.com . . . . How to do just about everything
www.craveonline.com . . . . Everything that males crave on the Net
www.howstuffworks.com . . . . From crafts to home improvement
www.collegehumor.com . . . . Frat humor pictures, videos, and links
www.repairclinic.com. . . . . Directions and advice on fixing appliances

Health
www.webmd.com . . . . Health information and health management
www.baldrus.com . . . . In defense of men without hair
www.medlineplus.gov . . . . Trusted health information from the NIH
www.health.com . . . . Vital information with a human touch

Sports and Games
www.profootballtalk.com. . . . . Entertaining football news and rumors
www.baseball-reference.com . . . Major league baseball statistics and history
www.kongregate.com . . . . Free games that you can play online
espn.go.com . . . . The website of "the worldwide leader in sports"

Women
www.retro-housewife.com. . . . . Putting pride back into the housewife
www.carstuckgirls.com . . . Cars that get stuck and the girls that drive them
www.fathers.com . . . . Everything you need to know about fathering
marriage.rutgers.edu . . . . The sociology of marriage

Dress
men.style.com . . . . Men's blog, fashion, and forums
www.dandyism.net . . . . The most elitist and self-important review
hypebeast.com. . . . . . . One-stop news source for street fashion enthusiasts
asuitablewardrobe.dynend.com. . . . . . Thoughts on classic men's clothing

Outdoors

www.wildwoodsurvival.com . . . . . Wilderness survival , tracking , nature
www.scouting.org. . . . . Official website of the Boy Scouts of America
equipped.com/fm21-76.htm. . . Pdf of US Army Survival Manual FM 21-76
www.explorersweb.com . . . . . . Mountaineering, ocean sailing, polar treks

Drinking

www.ratebeer.com . . . . Beer reviews, forums, and information
www.wineanorak.com . . . . Online wine magazine and compendium
www.webtender.com . . . . 6,000 drinks recipes and bartender's handbook
www.moderndrunkardmagazine.com . . . How to get falling-down drunk

Smoking

www.cigreviews.com . . . . Cigarette reviews and forums
www.cigars-review.org . . . . Directory and reviews of cigars
www.snuffhouse.org. . . . . Dedicated to nasal snuff
www.forestonline.org . . . . A haven for smokers and freedom of choice

Cooking

www.seriouseats.com . . . Fresh, hot, delicious food content served up daily
www.cookingforengineers.com . . Have an analytical mind? Like to cook?
www.barbecuen.com . . . . Tutorials, tips, techniques, and recipes
www.chilicookoff.com. . . . . Website of the International Chili Society

Idling

www.imeem.com. . . . . The world's best social music community
www.spudtech.com. . . . . . . No. 1 site for making and buying potato guns
www.penny-arcade.com . . . . Popular online comic for techno-geeks
www.mi6.co.uk . . . . The world's most visited unofficial 007 website

Arts and Sciences

www.engadget.com . . . . Regularly updated technology weblog and review
wordie.org . . . . Lists of words, words you love, words you hate
www.gutenberg.org. . . . . . Over 25,000 free books available for download
www.mathworld.wolfram.com . . . . Most extensive mathematics resource

Almanac

www.almanac.com. . . . . *The Old Farmer's Almanac* online
wikisky.org . . . . A point-and-click map of the stars, galaxies, and nebulae
www.tondering.dk/claus/calendar.html . . . . FAQ about calendars
www.timeanddate.com . . . . . Time, sun, moon, and calendar for any date

❦81 RULES TO LIVE BY

Here are four famous guides to character selected from the last three centuries.

81.1 TWELVE GOOD RULES

Charles I, king of England from 1625 until his execution in 1649, is credited with composing these rules of conduct. At 41 words in length, these 12 maxims remain one of the most concise and elegant codes of behavior.

Urge no healths
Profane no divine ordinances
Touch no state matters
Reveal no secrets
Pick no quarrels
Make no comparisons

Maintain no ill opinions
Keep no bad company
Encourage no vice
Make no long meals
Repent no grievances
Lay no wagers

81.2 FRANKLIN'S VIRTUES

Benjamin Franklin, 18th-century American statesman, businessman, scientist, and author of *Poor Richard's Almanack*, composed this list of 13 virtues for private use in the 1720s. He later published them in his autobiography.

Temperance • Eat not to dullness. Drink not to elevation.

Silence • Speak not but what may benefit others or yourself. Avoid trifling conversation.

Order • Let all your things have their places. Let each part of your business have its time.

Resolution • Resolve to perform what you ought. Perform without fail what you resolve.

Frugality • Make no expense but to do good to others or yourself: i.e., waste nothing.

Industry • Lose no time. Be always employed in something useful. Cut off all unnecessary actions.

Sincerity • Use no hurtful deceit. Think innocently and justly; and if you speak, speak accordingly.

Justice • Wrong none, by doing injuries or omitting the benefits that are your duty.

Moderation • Avoid extremes. Forbear resenting injuries so much as you think they deserve.

Cleanliness • Tolerate no uncleanliness in body, clothes, or habitation.

Tranquility • Be not disturbed at trifles, or at accidents common or unavoidable.

Chastity • Rarely use venery but for health or offspring; never to dullness, weakness, or the injury of your own or another's peace or reputation.

Humility • Imitate Jesus and Socrates.

81.3 RULES OF CIVILITY

George Washington transcribed the *Rules of Civility and Decent Behavior* in the 1740s, and ever since, Americans have revisited them as an aid to self-improvement. The *Rules* are largely derived from a 16th-century French Jesuit etiquette guide. Many go into arcane detail; the 26 most concise are here.

When in company, put not your hands to any part of the body not usually discovered.

Put not off your clothes in the presence of others, nor go out of your chamber half dressed.

When you sit down, keep your feet firm and even, without putting one on the other or crossing them.

Shift not yourself in the sight of others, nor gnaw your nails.

Let your countenance be pleasant but in serious matters somewhat grave.

Show not yourself glad at the misfortune of another though he were your enemy.

Let your discourse with men of business be short and comprehensive.

Strive not with your superior in argument, but always submit your judgment to others with modesty.

Undertake not to teach your equal in the art himself professes; it savors of arrogancy.

When a man does all he can, though it succeed not well, blame not him that did it.

Wherein you reprove another be unblameable yourself, for example is more prevalent than precepts.

Use no reproachful language against any one; neither curse nor revile.

Eat not in the streets, nor in the house, out of season.

Detract not from others, neither be excessive in commanding.

Reprehend not the imperfections of others, for that belongs to parents, masters, and superiors.

Treat with men at fit times about business and whisper not in the company of others.

Be not tedious in discourse or in reading unless you find the company pleased therewith.

Be not curious to know the affairs of others, neither approach those that speak in private.

Undertake not what you cannot perform but be careful to keep your promise.

Be not tedious in discourse, make not many digressions, nor repeat often the same manner of discourse.

Speak not evil of the absent, for it is unjust.

Take no salt or cut bread with your knife greasy.

Drink not nor talk with your mouth full; neither gaze about you while you are drinking.

If others talk at table be attentive, but talk not with meat in your mouth.

Let your recreations be manful not sinful.

Labour to keep alive in your breast that little spark of celestial fire called conscience.

81.4 IDEA OF A GENTLEMAN

In *The Idea of a University* (1854), Cardinal John Henry Newman wrote one of the most eloquent pieces of prose on the modern ideal of manliness.

Hence it is that it is almost a definition of a gentleman to say he is one who never inflicts pain. This description is both refined and, as far as it goes, accurate. He is mainly occupied in merely removing the obstacles which hinder the free and unembarrassed action of those about him; and he concurs with their movements rather than takes the initiative himself… The true gentleman in like manner carefully avoids whatever may cause a jar or a jolt in the minds of those with whom he is cast – all clashing of opinion, or collision of feeling, all restraint, or suspicion, or gloom or resentment; his great concern being to make every one at his ease and at home. He has his eyes on all his company; he is tender towards the bashful, gentle towards the distant and merciful towards the absurd; he can recollect to whom he is speaking; he guards against unseasonable allusions or topics which may irritate; he is seldom prominent in conversation and never wearisome. He makes light of favours while he does them, and seems to be receiving when he is conferring... He never speaks of himself except when compelled, never defends himself by a mere retort; he has no ears for slander or gossip, is scrupulous in imputing motives to those who interfere with him, and interprets everything for the best… From a long-sighted prudence, he observes the maxim of the ancient sage, that we should ever conduct ourselves towards our enemy as if he were one day to be our friend. He has too much good sense to be affronted at insults, he is too well employed to remember injuries and too indolent to bear malice. He is patient, forbearing and resigned, on philosophical principles; he submits to pain, because it is inevitable, to bereavement, because it is irreparable, and to death, because it is his destiny.

If he engages in controversy of any kind, his disciplined intellect preserves him from the blundering discourtesy of better, perhaps, but less educated minds, who, like blunt weapons, tear and hack instead of cutting clean, who mistake the point in argument…and leave the question more involved than they find it. He may be right or wrong in his opinion, but he is too clear-headed to be unjust; he is as simple as he is forcible, and as brief as he is decisive. Nowhere shall we find greater candour, consideration, indulgence: he throws himself into the minds of his opponents, he accounts for their mistakes. He knows the weakness of human reason as well as its strength, its province and its limits.

If he be an unbeliever, he will be too profound and large-minded to ridicule religion or to act against it; he is too wise to be a dogmatist or fanatic in his infidelity. He respects piety and devotion; he even supports institutions as venerable, beautiful or useful, to which he does not assent; he honours the ministers of religion, and it contents him to decline its mysteries without assailing or denouncing them. He is a friend of religious toleration, and that, not only because his philosophy has taught him to look on all forms of faith with an impartial eye, but also from the gentleness and effeminacy of feeling, which is the attendant on civilization.

ALMANAC

The fyrste moneth is Januarye, the childe is without might tyll hee bee 6 yeere olde, he can not helpe him selfe.

The 6 yeere that is the first time of the springinge of all flowres, and so the childe till 12 yeere groweth in knowledge and learning, and to doo as he is taught.

Marche is the buddinge time, and in that 6 yeere of Marche the Childe waxeth bygge and apte to doo seruice, and learne scyence from 12 to 18, such as is shewed hym.

Aprill is the springing tyme of flowres, and in that 6 yeere he groweth to mans state in heyght and bredthe, and waxeth wise and bolde, but then beware of sensualitie, for he is 24.

Maye is the season that flowers byn spreade, and bee then in theyr vertue with sweet odours. In these 6 yeeres he is in his most strength, but then let him geather good maners betyme, for if his tary past that age it is an hap if euer he take them, for then he is 30 yeare.

In June he beginneth to close his mynde, and then hee waxeth rype, for then he is 36 yeere.

In July he is 42, and he begynneth a lyttle to declyne, and feeleth hym not so prosperous as he was.

In August he is by that 6 yeere 48 yeere and then he goeth not so lustely as he dyd, but studieth howe to geather to fynde him in his olde age to liue more easely.

In September he is 54 yeere he then purueyethe against the winter to cherish himselfe withall and keepe neere together the goods y^t he gat in his youth.

Then is a man in October 60 yeere full, if he haue ought he gladdeth, and if haue nought he weepeth.

Then is man 66 in Nouember, he stoupeth and goeth softly, and leeseth all his beauty and fayrnesse.

In December he is 72 yeeres, then had he leuer haue a warme fire then a fayre lady, and after this age he goeth into decrepitie to waxe a childe again, and can not welde him selfe, and then young folkes be wery of his company but if they haue much good they beene full lytell taken heede of.

Kalendar of Sheepehards, 16th c., in *Oxford Companion to the Year*.

❦82 ASTRONOMICAL EVENTS

82.1 SOLSTICES AND EQUINOXES

The solstices mark the points in the Earth's orbit where its axis is maximally tilted towards the sun; the equinoxes, where its axis is perpendicular to the sun. Because the Earth's orbit is slightly elliptical, its distance from the sun varies throughout the year, although this has only a nominal effect on the seasons. All times below are in Greenwich Mean Time (GMT), also called Universal Time (UT). The US time zones are between 5 and 8 hours earlier.

	Earliest (2000–2020)		*Latest (2000–2020)*	
Vernal equinox	03:49	Mar 20	01:00	Mar 21
Summer solstice	21:43	Jun 20	19:10	Jun 21
Autumnal equinox	13:30	Sep 22	10:47	Sep 23
Winter solstice	10:02	Dec 21	07:04	Dec 22

82.2 SEASONS

Although ancient, the division of the year into four parts, or seasons, is not universal. At the equator, the association of seasons with hot and cold breaks down, and the length of the day is 12 hours all year round. Here two seasons, rainy and dry, provide a more useful division. Subtropical regions sometimes assume three: hot, rainy, and cool. Even today there is no broad agreement about when one season ends and another begins. The most common starting points – and those used by Americans – are the equinoxes and solstices. Thus winter, for example, begins on the shortest day of the year (the winter solstice) and continues until the days and nights are of equal length. More sensible is the Elder Pliny's division, with winter approximately centered on the winter solstice, and so on. The Irish calendar and British meteorological conventions associate seasons with months, winter beginning with November 1 and December 1, respectively.

	US & astronomical	*Elder Pliny*	*Irish calendar*	*UK Met. office*
Spring begins	Vernal equinox	Feb 8	Feb 1	Mar 1
Summer begins	Summer solstice	May 10	May 1	Jun 1
Autumn begins	Autumnal equinox	Aug 11	Aug 1	Sep 1
Winter begins	Winter solstice	Nov 11	Nov 1	Dec 1

Part of the confusion rests with the fact that the shortest and longest days do not correspond with the coldest and hottest. Because it takes weeks for the Earth's surface to warm and cool in response to more or less sunshine, the temperature lags behind the period of greatest sunshine by about 40 days.

82.3 ZODIAC

The zodiac is the imaginary band in the heavens marked out by the path of the sun and 8 degrees to either side. It is broken into 12 segments, each of which is associated with a star sign (*zodia*, which means "little beasts"). These have by convention taken on fixed periods within the year, below.

Sign	Association	Symbol	Man of signs	Duration
Aries	ram	♈	head	Mar 21 – Apr 20
Taurus	bull	♉	neck, throat	Apr 21 – May 20
Gemini	twins	♊	arms, shoulders	May 21 – Jun 20
Cancer	crab	♋	chest	Jun 21 – Jul 22
Leo	lion	♌	heart, upper back	Jul 23 – Aug 22
Virgo	virgin	♍	belly	Aug 23 – Sep 22
Libra	scales	♎	lumbar region	Sep 23 – Oct 22
Scorpio	scorpion	♏	genitals	Oct 23 – Nov 22
Sagittarius	archer	♐	thighs	Nov 23 – Dec 21
Capricorn	sea-goat	♑	knees	Dec 22 – Jan 19
Aquarius	water bearer	♒	legs, ankles	Jan 20 – Feb 19
Pisces	fish	♓	feet	Feb 20 – Mar 20

82.4 METEOR SHOWERS

Because meteor showers result from the Earth's passage through trails of dust left by comets, they tend to be annual events. The major annual showers can vary in intensity from year to year, depending on how recently the parent comet passed. The showers last several days, sometimes weeks. The peak days of major showers, which can vary by a day or two, are given below.

Name	Meteors/hr	Parent comet	Peak days
Quadrantids	30–50	minor planet 2003 EH$_1$	Jan 3–4
Lyrids	10–20	Thatcher	Apr 21–22
Eta Aquarids	10–20	Halley	May 4–6
Delta Aquarids	20–30		Jul 28–29
Alpha Capricornids	0–10		Jul 29–30
Perseids	50–100	Swift-Tuttle	Aug 12–13
Draconids	0–10	Giacobini-Zinner	Oct 8–9
Orionids	10–20	Halley	Oct 21–22
Taurids	0–10	Encke	Nov 1–10
Leonids	20–30	Temple-Tuttle	Nov 17–18
Geminids	50–100	3200 Phaethon	Dec 13–14
Ursids	10–20	Tuttle	Dec 19–22

❦83 HOLY DAYS AND FASTS

The two principal days of Christian significance are Christmas, set by the solar cycle, and Easter, set by the lunar cycle. From the date of Easter all movable holy days and fasts are fixed by their separation in number of days, apart from Advent Sunday (the first day of Advent) and Christ the King.

83.1 HOLY DAYS

Epiphany	Jan 6
Presentation of the Lord	Feb 2
Ash Wednesday	7th Wed before Easter
Annunciation (Lady Day)	Mar 25
Palm Sunday	Sun before Easter
Holy (Maundy) Thursday	Thu before Easter
Good Friday	Fri before Easter
Easter	see below
Rogation Sunday	5th Sun after Easter
Ascension Day	6th Thu after Easter
Whit Sunday (Pentecost)	7th Sun after Easter
Trinity Sunday	8th Sun after Easter
Corpus Christi	9th Thu after Easter
All Saints' Day	Nov 1
All Souls' Day	Nov 2
Christ the King	Sun before Advent Sunday
Advent Sunday	Sun nearest to Nov 30
Christmas Day	Dec 25

83.2 EASTER DAY

Easter is the first Sunday after the first full ecclesiastical moon falling on or after the vernal equinox; if the full moon falls on a Sunday, Easter is the following Sunday. The ecclesiastical moon is not the astronomical moon but a tabulated theoretical moon which closely approximates it, deemed full on its 14th day. The equinox is defined to be March 21. The earliest and latest dates of Easter are March 22 and April 25; the most likely date, April 19.

The Book of Common Prayer (1662) gives a prescription for determining the date of Easter. The problem is somewhat complicated, and the instructions fill three pages. Devising an elegant and concise prescription has attracted the attention of amateur and professional mathematicians alike. The following algorithm (P. Kenneth Seidelmann, ed., *Explanatory Supplement to the Astronomical Almanac*) is a refined version of Oudin's 1940 algorithm. It gives the month and day of Easter for any Gregorian calendar year.

83.3 AN ALGORITHM FOR EASTER DAY

Let "year" be the Christian year AD, "month" the number 3 (March) or 4 (April) and "day" a number between 1 and 31. In all divisions the integer is kept and the remainder discarded. The operation "mod" is the opposite: the remainder is kept and the integer discarded. For example, $23/5 = 4$ and $23 \bmod 5 = 3$. In the case of year = 2009, we find from below that $A = 20$, $B = 14$, $C = 20$, $D = 20$, and $E = 5$. This gives month = 4 and day = 12, that is, April 12th. The algorithm is guaranteed to repeat only after 5,700,000 years.

$$A = \frac{\text{year}}{100} \qquad B = \text{year} \bmod 19 \qquad C = \left(A - \frac{A}{4} - \frac{8A+13}{25} + 19B + 15 \right) \bmod 30$$

$$D = C - \frac{C}{28}\left(1 - \frac{29}{C+1} \frac{21-B}{11} \right) \qquad E = \left(\text{year} + \frac{\text{year}}{4} + D + 2 - A + \frac{A}{4} \right) \bmod 7$$

$$\text{month} = 3 + \frac{D-E+40}{44} \qquad \text{day} = D - E + 28 - 31 \times \frac{\text{month}}{4}$$

83.4 FASTS

In order to correspond in length to the 40 days that it commemorates, it is customary to omit from the Lenten fast the six Sundays preceding Easter, Sundays always being feast days. Fasting, which originally meant avoiding all food, is today taken to mean that only one meal should be had. Fasting should not be confused with abstinence, which means avoiding only meat.

Lent . . . . Ash Wednesday to Sat before Easter, inclusive
Advent . . . . Advent Sunday to Dec 24, inclusive

Wednesday, Friday, and Saturday on or after
Spring Embertide (Ember days) . . . . 1st Sunday of Lent
Summer Embertide . . . . Whit Sunday (Pentecost)
Autumn Embertide . . . . Triumph of the Cross (Sep 14)
Winter Embertide . . . . St. Lucy's Day (Dec 13)

Monday, Tuesday, and Wednesday after
Rogation Days . . . . Rogation Sunday

The two principal periods of abstinence or fasting, Advent and Lent, are customarily preceded by celebrations and feasts. The days before Lent are called Shrovetide, which culminates on Shrove Tuesday, also known as *Mardi Gras* (Fat Tuesday). On the Sunday before Advent Sunday, popularly known as Stir-up Sunday, wives are encouraged to begin preparations for Christmas. The day's collect from *The Book of Common Prayer*, which reads "Stir up, we beseech thee, O Lord, the wills of thy faithful people," is commonly taken to be an indication to begin making the Christmas desserts.

❦84 SAINTS' DAYS

The association of certain days with saints and martyrs, sometimes called the calendar of saints, has been customary since the early Church. In medieval times, at least one saint was associated with almost every day. These observances offered cause for more frequent and significant celebration than the federal holidays which have in effect replaced them. Alongside days marking the events of Christ's life, the saints' days are formalized as follows.

84.1 ROMAN CATHOLIC CHURCH

The most longstanding and detailed calendar of saints is codified by the Catholic Church. According to the General Roman Calendar, saints' days are divided into three kinds: Solemnities, Feasts, and Memorials. Memorials, some of which are optional, are the least significant and are not listed here.

Solemnities

All Sundays in the year		Sacred Heart	10th Sat after Easter
Solemnity of Mary	Jan 1	Birth of St. John the Baptist	Jun 24
Epiphany	Jan 6	SS Peter & Paul	Jun 29
St. Joseph	Mar 19	Assumption	Aug 15
Annunciation	Mar 25	All Saints	Nov 1
Ascension	6th Thu after Easter	Christ the King	
Holy Trinity	8th Sun after Easter		Sun nearest to Nov 23
Corpus Christi		Immaculate Conception	Dec 8
	9th Thu after Easter	Nativity of Our Lord	Dec 25

Feasts

Baptism of the Lord	Sun after Jan 6	Triumph of the Cross	Sep 14
Conversion of St. Paul	Jan 25	St. Matthew	Sep 21
Presentation of the Lord	Feb 2	SS Michael, Gabriel	
Chair of St. Peter	Feb 22	& Raphael	Sep 29
St. Mark	Apr 25	St. Luke	Oct 18
SS Philip & James	May 3	SS Simon & Jude	Oct 28
St. Matthias	May 14	Dedication of Lateran	
Visitation of the BVM	May 31	Basilica	Nov 9
St. Thomas	Jul 3	St. Andrew	Nov 30
St. James	Jul 25	St. Stephen	Dec 26
Transfiguration of the Lord	Aug 6	St. John	Dec 27
St. Lawrence	Aug 10	Holy Innocents	Dec 28
St. Bartholomew	Aug 24	Holy Family	Sun after Dec 25
Birthday of the BVM	Sep 8	and before Jan 1; if none, Dec 30	

84.2 EPISCOPAL CHURCH

The Episcopal Church and the Church of England observe the feast days set out in *The Book of Common Prayer* (1662); the former has since added others.

All Sundays in the year		St. John the Baptist	Jun 24
Circumcision of Our Lord	Jan 1	St. Peter	Jun 29
Epiphany	Jan 6	St. James	Jul 25
Conversion of St. Paul	Jan 25	St. Bartholomew	Aug 24
Purification of the BVM	Feb 2	St. Matthew	Sep 21
St. Matthias	Feb 24	St. Michael & All Angels	Sep 29
Annunciation of the BVM	Mar 25	St. Luke	Oct 18
Monday after Easter	Apr 9	SS Simon & Jude	Oct 28
Tuesday after Easter	Apr 10	All Saints	Nov 1
St. Mark	Apr 25	St. Andrew	Nov 30
SS Philip & James	May 1	St. Thomas	Dec 21
Ascension	6th Thu after Easter	Nativity of Our Lord	Dec 25
Monday after Whit Sunday		St. Stephen	Dec 26
Tuesday after Whit Sunday		St. John the Evangelist	Dec 27
St. Barnabas	Jun 11	Holy Innocents	Dec 28

84.3 PATRON SAINTS OF MEN

Many professions have associated with them patron saints, whom are believed to intercede for us in prayer. Some of the more popular are as follows (feast days are given in accordance with *Butler's Lives of the Saints,* 1956):

Profession	Saint	Feast Day
Athletes	St. Sebastian	Jan 20
Bankers	St. Matthew	Sep 21
Barbers	St. Martin de Porres	Nov 3
Brewers	St. Augustine of Hippo	Aug 28
Builders	St. Vincent Ferrer	Apr 5
Criminals	St. Dismas	Mar 25
Doctors	St. Luke	Oct 18
Farmers	St. Isidore the Farmer	May 15
Lawyers	St. Thomas More	Jun 22
Merchants	St. Francis of Assisi	Oct 4
Pawnbrokers	St. Nicholas	Dec 6
Scientists	St. Albert the Great	Nov 15
Soldiers	St. Martin of Tours	Nov 11
Taxi drivers	St. Fiacre	Sep 1

❦85 HOLIDAYS

Holiday, while derived from, and once synonymous with, "holy day," now refers to any day of national festivity, which may or may not have religious significance. America has particularly few, as one New Yorker notes:

> Our Protestant Faith affords no religious holiday & processions like the Catholics. From the period of the Jews & Heathens down thro the Greeks & Romans, the Celts, Druids, even our Indians all had & have their religious Festivals. England retains numerous red letter days as they are called which afford intervals of rest, together with the Christmas, Easter & Whitsun holidays, for all the public offices Banks &c., but with us, we have only Independence, Christmas & New Year, 3 solitary days, not enough & which causes so much breach of the Sabbath in this city...   John Pintard, 1823

Unlike many countries, the US does not technically have any national holidays. Instead, it observes one quadrennial and ten annual days. These are called federal holidays, during which government employees do not normally work. Some Canadian holidays are also observed in parts of America.

85.1 MOVABLE NATIONAL HOLIDAYS

★ Inauguration Day* .... Jan 20, but if Sun, Jan 21
★ Martin Luther King's Birthday .... 3rd Mon in Jan
  Mardi Gras.................................. 7th Tue before Easter
★ Washington's Birthday (a.k.a. Presidents' Day)........ 3rd Mon in Feb
  Easter .... see p 209
  Arbor Day.. last Fri in Apr
  Mother's Day .... 2nd Sun in May
● Victoria Day (Canada) .... Mon on or before May 24
★ Memorial Day .... last Mon in May
  Father's Day .... 3rd Sun in Jun
★ Labor Day .... 1st Mon in Sep
★ Columbus Day .... 2nd Mon in Oct
● Thanksgiving (Canada).......................... 2nd Mon in Oct
  Election Day .... Tue after 1st Mon in Nov
  Sadie Hawkins Day .... Sat closest to Nov 9
★ Thanksgiving..................................... 4th Thu in Nov

KEY ★ US Federal holidays
     ● Canadian statutory holidays (this is a partial listing)
     * Only in years following a presidential election (quadrennial).

85.2 FIXED NATIONAL HOLIDAYS

★ New Year's Day	Jan 1	★ Independence Day	Jul 4
Groundhog Day	Feb 2	Patriot Day	Sep 11
St. Valentine's Day	Feb 14	Halloween	Oct 31
St. Patrick's Day	Mar 17	All Saints' Day	Nov 1
April Fools' Day	Apr 1	All Souls' Day	Nov 2
Cinco de Mayo (Mexico)	May 5	★ Veterans Day	Nov 11
Flag Day	Jun 14	★ Christmas	Dec 25
• Canada Day	Jul 1	• Boxing Day (Canada)	Dec 26

85.3 STATES' DAYS

The 50 states' analogue to the national days of countries are their days of admission into the United States, which are their principal days of celebration.

State	Date of admission		West Virginia	Jun	20	1863
Georgia	Jan	2	1788	New Hampshire	Jun	21	1788
Alaska	Jan	3	1959	Virginia	Jun	25	1788
Utah	Jan	4	1896	Idaho	Jul	3	1890
New Mexico	Jan	6	1912	Wyoming	Jul	10	1890
Connecticut	Jan	9	1788	New York	Jul	26	1788
Michigan	Jan	26	1837	Colorado	Aug	1	1876
Kansas	Jan	29	1861	Missouri	Aug	10	1821
Massachusetts	Feb	6	1788	Hawaii	Aug	21	1959
Oregon	Feb	14	1859	California	Sep	9	1850
Arizona	Feb	14	1912	Nevada	Oct	31	1864
Ohio	Mar	1	1803	North Dakota	Nov	2	1889
Nebraska	Mar	1	1867	South Dakota	Nov	2	1889
Florida	Mar	3	1845	Montana	Nov	8	1889
Vermont	Mar	4	1791	Washington	Nov	11	1889
Maine	Mar	15	1820	Oklahoma	Nov	16	1907
Maryland	Apr	28	1788	North Carolina	Nov	21	1789
Louisiana	Apr	30	1812	Illinois	Dec	3	1818
Minnesota	May	11	1858	Delaware	Dec	7	1787
South Carolina	May	23	1788	Mississippi	Dec	10	1817
Rhode Island	May	29	1790	Indiana	Dec	11	1816
Wisconsin	May	29	1848	Pennsylvania	Dec	12	1787
Kentucky	Jun	1	1792	Alabama	Dec	14	1819
Tennessee	Jun	1	1796	New Jersey	Dec	18	1787
Arkansas	Jun	15	1836	Iowa	Dec	28	1846
				Texas	Dec	29	1845

☙86 INTERNATIONAL DAYS

In medieval times, nearly every day marked some feast, fast, or observation, some of major and some of minor significance. Today, in addition to America's federal and customary holidays, there are 66 international United Nations days. The UN officially recognizes the days (and weeks, marked ★) below, to be observed internationally throughout all its member countries. Why pass up such sources of celebration as Book, Food, and Television days? Notably, there are days for Children, Youth, and Women, but not for men. Perhaps a sensible proposal for Men's Day is January 6, the sixth day of the year, corresponding to the sixth day of creation when God made man, there being a dearth of UN days in January.

The United Nations comprises 191 member states, the only notable exception being the city-state Vatican City, which has not sought membership but is an observer state. Palestine is also a permanent observer.

86.1 66 UNITED NATIONS DAYS AND WEEKS

❦87 INAUSPICIOUS DAYS

87.1 DISMAL DAYS

From medieval times certain days, collectively called *dies mali*, or "evil days," were held to be unwise for starting any enterprise. Thus the word dismal was originally a noun referring to these unlucky days, only later taking on its descriptive sense of causing gloom. The most common accounts list two days per month, one in the first half and one in the second:

January	1 25	May	3 25	September	3 21
February	4 26	June	10 16	October	3 22
March	1 28	July	13 22	November	5 28
April	10 20	August	1 30	December	7 22

87.2 MONDAYS

While all Mondays are associated with bad tempers and questionable fortune (cf., "Manic Monday," Bangles), the first Monday in April and August and the last in December were once held to be particularly inauspicious:

> Anyone who lets blood of man or beast on them will not last the week, anyone who accepts a drink, or eats goose, will die within the fortnight, and any child, male or female, born on them will come to a bad end.
> B. Blackburn and L. Holford-Strevens, *Oxford Companion to the Year*

87.3 DOG DAYS

Dog days, generally accepted to last from July 3 to August 11, correspond to the hottest days of the year (though not the longest, see p 206). In ancient times they were thought to result from the coincidence of the rising and setting of the sun and the star Sirius, the major star of the constellation Canis Major (Big Dog). Sirius is the brightest of the stars in the night sky, and the combined heat of it and the sun was thought to be the cause of this sweltering period. It is traditional to avoid bloodletting and medical treatment and also to abstain from women. Not everyone agrees with the latter:

> Husband give me my due, the woman saies;
> The man replies, 'Tis naught Wife these Dog daies;
> But she rejoins, Let women have their rights,
> Though there be Dog daies, there are no Dog nights.
> *Poor Robin's Almanack* (1675)

87.4 LEAP DAY

February 29, when it occurs, is called a leap day, and on it women may by tradition propose to men. There are two other prescribed days of feminine initiative. In France, on the feast day of St. Catherine of Alexandria (November 25), women may ask men to marry. In the US, on Sadie Hawkins Day (Saturday closest to November 9), women are meant to invite men out, a refreshing variation but in direct conflict with *The Rules'* first prescription (First Date, p 42): don't talk to a man first (and don't ask him to dance).

Leap days are necessary because of an astronomical discrepancy. Because the length of the year is 365.2422 days, to keep the seasons and the months aligned it is necessary from time to time to insert an extra day in the year. Years which have 365 days are called common years, and those with 366 days are called leap years. The extra day is always added to the end of February, and this day – February 29 – is called a leap day. The rule for determining leap years is as follows: years divisible by 4 are leap years, but those divisible by 100 are not, but those divisible by 400 are after all. This approximates the year by $365\,{}^{97}\!/_{400} = 365.2425$ days, exceeding the tropical year by only 27 seconds. No plan has been put forward to address this discrepancy, which will have accumulated to one day by the year 4800.

87.5 FRIDAY THE 13TH

Friday the 13th is the coincidence of two events in themselves associated with ill fortune. Friday, the day on which Adam fell and Christ was crucified, is thought to be the least lucky of the weekdays: "Sneeze on a Friday, sneeze for sorrow"; "Cut your nails on a Friday, cut them for woe." The number 13 is prime, and is the number of men who sat at the Last Supper. In Dan Brown's novel *The Da Vinci Code*, the decimation of the Knights Templar under King Philip IV of France occurred on Friday, October 13, 1307.

Friday the 13ths occur on average once every 213 days, but they are not evenly distributed; some years have one, some two, and some three. The table below repeats every 28 years from 1901 to 2099. Curiously, the 13th is (marginally) more likely to be a Friday than it is any other day of the week.

Years				Fri 13th in			Years			Fri 13th in		
2001	2007	2018		Apr	Jul		2009	2015	2026	Feb	Mar	Nov
2002	2013	2019	2024	Sep	Dec		2010	2021	2027	Aug		
2003	2008	2014	2025	Jun			2012			Jan	Apr	Jul
2004				Feb	Aug		2020			Mar	Nov	
2005	2011	2016	2022	May			2028			Oct		
2006	2017	2023		Jan	Oct							

INDEX

COLOPHON

AUTHOR

Thomas Fink grew up in New York and Texas. He is a physicist and writer and lives in London. He designed *The Man's Book* himself. He is a man.

DESIGN

This book was designed and typeset by the author in QuarkXPress 7.0 on a Macintosh computer. Figures were drawn by www.maadesigns.co.uk.

LOCATION

This book was written and researched in New York and Texas, where the author grew up, and in the British Library and Cambridge University Library.

LAYOUT

The page layout for this book can be constructed with a straightedge and compass (below). The proportion of the text block is ϕ:1, where the Golden ratio $\phi = (\sqrt{5} + 1)/2 = 1.618$. ϕ can be derived from the regular pentagon and it can be approximated by the ratio of two consecutive Fibonacci numbers (1, 2, 3, 5, 8, 13, 21, 34 55,...); the ratio approaches ϕ as the series continues.

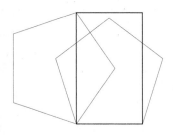
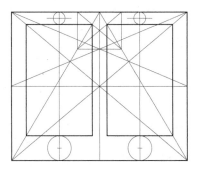

FONT

The text was set in Palatino, a font designed by Hermann Zapf in 1948. Based on the fonts of the Italian Renaissance, it is one of the most popular and admired of the serifed typefaces and is thought to be highly legible.

❦ (SECTION SYMBOL)

Section names are preceded by a hedera (❦), a typographical ornament or dingbat in the shape of an ivy leaf. Decorative hederae can be found in ancient inscriptions and medieval manuscripts. Here it is also used as a flag.

ANSWER TO RIDDLE ON P 185

"Which path would the other guard tell me to take?"

WEBPAGES

Author's homepage:	www.tcm.phy.cam.ac.uk/~tmf20
Publisher's homepage:	www.hachettebookgroup.com
Wikipedia entry:	en.wikipedia.org/wiki/The_Man's_Book

TYPOGRAPHICAL SUMMARY

Note: This book was printed at 101% magnification of the typesetting below.

Page height	8.25 in	Number of chapters	11
Page width	5.5 in	Number of sections	87
Text block proportion	1.618:1	Number of subsections	316
Text block height	6.37 in	Number of pages	240
Text block width	3.94 in	Number of words (approx)	77,000
Ideal margin ratio (inside:		Number of figures	64
top:outside:bottom)	2:3:4:6	Number of index entries	847
Typeface	Palatino	Chapter head block height	14 lines
Text size, principal	8.78 pt	Chapter head size (caps)	14.14 pt
Text size, displayed	7.9 pt	Section head size (caps)	8.9 pt
Lines per page	42	Subsection head size	
Characters per line	73	(small caps)	8.78 pt
Leading	11 pt	Chapter head tracking	70
Vertical spacer	1 line	Section head tracking	50
Indent	0.2 in	Subsection head tracking	30
Gutter width	0.2 in	Paper weight	45 lb

3 1170 00810 4386